Conscience, Virtue, and Worship

Theological Perspectives

Thomas Ryan

Copyright © 2023 Thomas Ryan
Copyright © 2023 Generis Publishing

All rights reserved. This book or any portion thereof may not be reproduced or used in any manner whatsoever without the written permission of the publisher except for the use of brief quotations in a book review.

Title: **Conscience, Virtue, and Worship**

Theological Perspectives

ISBN: 979-8-88676-411-6

Author: Thomas Ryan

Cover image: www.pixabay.com

Publisher: Generis Publishing
Online orders: www.generis-publishing.com
Contact email: info@generis-publishing.com

Dedicated to

James F Keenan, SJ
Priest, Theologian, Mentor, Agent of Change

Table of Contents

ACKNOWLEDGEMENTS 8

Introduction 11
Overview of the Book 13

THE FACES OF CONSCIENCE 17

1. Conscience as Primordial Moral Awareness: 18
Theological Considerations 18
2. A Case Study in Conscience: Religious Freedom 40
3. Conscience, Culture and Sin: A Church in Disgrace 58

VIRTUE AT WORK 75

4. Jesus – 'Our Wisest and Dearest Friend': Aquinas and Moral Transformation
.... 76
5. Wisdom as Loving Knowledge in Dag Hammarskjöld's *Markings* 95
6. Witness, The Pedagogy of Grace and Moral Development 114
7. Joseph in Matthew's Gospel: Conscience and Moral Integrity 130

WORSHIP AND MORAL FORMATION 145

8. Evelyn Underhill: Spirituality, Liturgy and Moral Responsibility 146
9. Moral Conversion and Worship 165

RETROSPECTIVE 183

10. The Changing Landscape of Catholic Theological Ethics 184

ACKNOWLEDGEMENTS

The chapters of this book were originally articles written in the past decade or so. The journals in which they were published are acknowledged at the start of each chapter. Reproduced material is used with the permission of the following publishers:

Australian Ejournal of Theology (chapter one);
The Australasian Catholic Record (chapters six, seven and eight);
Australian Journal of Liturgy (chapter nine);
Compass: A Review of Topical Theology (chapters three, ten);
Solidarity: The Journal of Catholic Social Thought and Secular Ethics (chapter two);
New Blackfriars (chapter four);
Spiritus: A Journal of Christian Spirituality (chapter five).

I would also like to acknowledge the co-author of chapter six, namely, Daniel J Fleming.

Minor amendments have been made to the original texts, for example, the revision of references; a modifying of the layout of the material. The final (and retrospective) chapter involved more substantial revisions to offer an updated discussion of the topic.

In the process of revision, I noticed, at times, repetition of an issue, idea or source found in an earlier chapter. Given the nature of the book, this is, to some extent, inevitable. I have tried to minimize any such duplications while maintaining the integrity of the text. In all this, I can only hope for some forbearance on the part of any reader.

My thanks to Dr. Gerald Arbuckle, SM for reading the text and for his comments and helpful suggestions; to Rev. Anthony Corcoran, SM, Provincial of the Marist Fathers Australian Province, for his encouragement in the ministry of writing; finally, to Anna Rothman and the editorial staff of Generis Publishing. Their interest, creative energy, and professionalism make them a pleasure to work with.

The final text and any inadequacies are, ultimately, mine.

Introduction

Returning to articles written some years earlier can prompt a range of reactions for their author: sometimes of the familiar, sometimes of the seemingly inadequate, sometimes of surprise, sometimes, even, of discovery.

Whatever the case, as I worked with the original materials, I detected a dominant thread in the various discussions that brings a level of cohesion to the collection. That unifying aspect is evident in the book's title. It reflects a concern discussed recently, namely, that conscience needs the setting of the virtues and, importantly, the redeeming and healing influence of Christ and the Holy Spirit.[1]

But there is also a need for a community of faith, of the Church, its worship, and its heritage. Hence, what also comes into view from this material is the role of a living tradition—as in the person of Thomas Aquinas. This is part of my background as a theologian working within the Roman Catholic context. In the past three decades, there has been a virtual industry in studies on the man and his legacy, namely, Thomism.

Any school or method (whether theology or any field of enquiry) is subject to the limitations of time and place. So too with Aquinas and Thomism.

But, as with others, it has its strengths. One was his openness to dialogue—within the Catholic heritage but also beyond it with philosophers from the Greek and Arabic traditions. This continues in other forms today with interchanges between Aquinas' thought and more modern approaches, as in the human sciences.

The other positive aspect is that Aquinas' approach to the moral life was anchored in an ethics of virtue, from a Christian perspective. The hub around which the various elements of his moral theory revolve is the person of Jesus Christ, described as 'our wisest and dearest friend' (a phrase that occurs later in this book).

Aquinas' approach finds common cause with recent studies in virtue ethics and moral development. Such interest can be traced back to the mid-twentieth century with the influence of philosophers such as Elizabeth Anscombe, Iris Murdoch, Mary Midgley and Philippa Foot.[2] For them, taking a cue from Wittgenstein, shared practices of life are not simply an individual enterprise; their context is a

---

[1] See Matthew Levering, *The Abuse of Conscience: A Century of Catholic Moral Theology* (Grand Rapids, MI: Eerdmans, 2021), 207.

[2] See Clare Mac Cumhaill, Rachael Wiseman, *Metaphysical Animals: How Four Women Brought Philosophy Back to Life* (UK: Chatto & Windus, 2022).

community and of values that enhance social and political life. It continues today in writers such as Harvard University's Michael Sandel.[3]

And so, to the book.

---
[3] Michael J Sandel, *The Tyranny of Merit: What's Become of the Common Good?* (Penguin Press, 2021).

Overview of the Book

The book unfolds in three parts—**The Faces of Conscience, Virtue at Work, Worship and Moral Formation**—with nine chapters and a final retrospective chapter.

The Faces of Conscience

Chapter 1: 'Conscience as Primordial Moral Awareness: Theological Considerations' investigates how, in two Catholic Church documents, foundational conscience is understood as affective knowing, namely, an appreciative grasp of basic moral values. For an interpretative window, the investigation uses 'participation' together with Aquinas and the model of triune consciousness developed by philosopher Andrew Tallon. What emerges is that four epistemological processes mediate the human person-in-relationship's intuitive and affective appreciation of value—recognition, responsiveness, participation and participative knowing in the form of affective connaturality.

Chapter 2: 'A Case Study in Conscience: Religious Freedom' deals with conscience in the context of the *Declaration on Religious Freedom* from the Second Vatican Council and as an instance of the development of doctrine. After explaining the key ideas in two foundational articles in the Declaration on the relationship of truth and freedom, the discussion puts the spotlight on, respectively, the human person, human rights and, finally, practical reason in relation to doctrinal development and the Declaration.

Chapter 3: 'Conscience, Culture and Sin: A Church in Disgrace'. In the light of the sexual abuse crisis facing the Catholic Church, this chapter suggests an appropriate ethical model in response. It outlines the general and specific characteristics of 'Covenant', noting the place of justice, of victims together with the role of relationship, gift, inclusive scope, and identity. Five signposts are suggested: covenant identity as gift; recognition of, and solidarity with victims; listening to learn; the transpersonal power of evil as demonic; the functional analogy with the destruction of the Temple.

Virtue at Work

Chapter 4: 'Jesus– 'Our Wisest and Dearest Friend': Aquinas and Moral Transformation' explores the place of Christ in the moral theology of Aquinas. It examines the role of the Word as embodied Wisdom, the soteriological emphasis on Jesus as exemplar, the redemptive love of his Passion and his formative influence as teacher. Such aspects help to illuminate Aquinas' sapiential approach to moral transformation, particularly, through the gifts of the Holy Spirit and, specifically, that of wisdom with its mode of operation as a form of joint attention in a second person relationship.

Chapter 5: 'Wisdom as Loving Knowledge in Dag Hammarskjöld's *Markings*' is anchored in the journal entries of Dag Hammarskjöld. After outlining the various forms of love found in his reflections, there is an investigation of one text in *Markings* (from the Gospel of St John) on the process of knowing and loving God. The chapter then analyzes key passages in *Markings* concerning wisdom as a virtue. Finally, the gift of wisdom is examined in the light of the theology of the gifts of the Holy Spirit and contemporary approaches based on the second person perspective and joint attention.

Chapter 6: 'Witness, the Pedagogy of Grace and Moral Development' (with Daniel J Fleming) is grounded in a reflection on philosopher Raimond Gaita's personal encounter with a religious sister and its implications for moral theory. This chapter offers a study of the meaning of such encounters and the corresponding implications for our theology of grace and our approach to the moral life. The discussion considers four aspects: witness in relation to moral understanding and intersubjectivity; intersubjectivity and conscience; a pedagogy of grace and the action of the Holy Spirit; finally, a pedagogy of grace in relation to moral development.

Chapter 7: 'Joseph in Matthew's Gospel: Conscience and Moral Integrity' is a discussion that examines St Joseph as a just man wrestling with a moral quandary. It suggests some lessons about conscience that we can learn from Joseph but also insights that can be gained from Joseph's precarious (and violent) historical context and its impact on him. The discussion considers Joseph as a man of integrity within the overall Jewish story and, finally, offers a brief correlation between Joseph as a model of wisdom and past and present perspectives.

Worship and Moral Formation

Chapter 8: 'Evelyn Underhill: Spirituality, Liturgy and Moral Responsibility' begins by clarifying four key aspects underpinning Evelyn Underhill's theological development—its nature, goal, scope, and transcendent source. It then considers the intersecting themes in her spiritual project: the Spirit's animating presence and centrifugal impulse; the ternary pattern of adoration/communion/ cooperation; finally, the fruits of that process. There are some reflections on Underhill's spirituality in relation to spiritual 'seekers' beyond the

	institutional Church and a final evaluation of her work in its original context and in today's world.
Chapter 9:	'Moral Conversion and Worship' begins by clarifying the notion of conversion with specific reference to two modes of moral conversion, namely, the personal, and the social/political. On that basis, it examines the dynamics of the Eucharistic liturgy in relation to moral formation with reference to our perceptions, dispositions, and identity. From there, the chapter gives specific attention to the Eucharistic Prayer for Reconciliation II in terms of its theme, tone, *tempo* and, importantly, as a template of the human person in responsive relationships.

Retrospective

Chapter 10:	'The Changing Landscape of Catholic Theological Ethics' presents a survey of major developments in Christian ethics in the Catholic tradition since the second Vatican Council. The first area of focus is the greater emphasis on the moral life as centered on the human person, relationships, love, and the role of virtue and the emotions. The discussion then turns to Catholic theological ethics as a discipline over the past two decades. Areas highlighted are: the self-understanding of the moral theologian; moral consciousness and the field of moral theology itself as increasingly global; the role of suffering as a source of moral insight; the increasing presence of Catholic social teaching on the agenda of Catholic theological ethics; finally, some brief comments on the synodal mentality of Pope Francis and the impact of the global pandemic with its accompanying loss and grief together with an increased awareness of shared vulnerability and mutual dependence.

THE FACES OF CONSCIENCE

1
Conscience as Primordial Moral Awareness: Theological Considerations

Think of some everyday phrases.

'What I said was hurtful. I apologize'.

'I felt really bad about that'.

'You're having a really hard time. Can I help in any way?'

We've heard such words. We've almost certainly said them.

They are the language of conscience.[1]

As Klaus Demmer points out: 'the experience of being summoned by a moral claim is common to everyone' and it emerges from 'prescientific insight and experience'.[2] In simple terms, he is referring to the awareness (real, even if, diffuse) of right and wrong, of being personally responsible in some way or another, of having a conscience. It is part of our common humanity.

On that basis, but also in relation to Christian faith, conscience is pivotal in the Catholic tradition. This is reflected in official documents of the Catholic Church, the first from a Church Council (*Gaudium et Spes*); the second from a Pope, namely, John Paul II (*Veritatis Splendor*), acknowledging the differences in contexts and concerns.[3] Theological discussion on conscience has tended to focus predominantly on its relationship to the truth and specifically as moral judgment in a particular situation.

In this chapter, I aim to investigate conscience in its more foundational sense—as primordial moral awareness without which we could not be moral (and even human) beings. In probing the nature of this 'prescientific insight and experience',

---

[1] This chapter (slightly amended) was originally published as 'Conscience as Primordial Moral Awareness in Gaudium et Spes and Veritatis Splendor', *Australian Ejournal of Theology* 18.1 (2011): 83-96.

[2] Klaus Demmer, MSC, *Shaping the Moral Life: An Approach to Moral Theology* (Washington DC: Georgetown University Press, 2000), 2. See also Patricia Lamoureux and Paul Wadell, *Christian Moral Life: faithful discipleship for a global society* (Maryknoll, NY: Orbis, 2010), 146.

[3] *Gaudium et Spes* in *The Documents of Vatican II*, ed. Walter M Abbott, SJ (Boston, America Press, 1965); Pope St John Paul II, *Veritatis Splendor* (Homebush, NSW: St. Pauls, 1993).

the investigation will be guided by this question:

> what is the role of evaluative knowing and human affectivity in basic moral consciousness in *Gaudium et Spes* and *Veritatis Splendor*?

I approach the task in these steps.

After clarifying language, I argue that, in these two documents, conscience understood as primordial moral awareness is presented in the setting of four epistemological processes which mediate the intuitive and affective appreciation of value, namely, through a) participatory responsiveness within relationship, b) participation as recognition, c) participation as collaboration and, finally, d) through a specific form of participative knowing, namely, affective connaturality.[4] Recourse to Thomas Aquinas' understanding of evaluative knowing and affective connaturality will help clarify content of the relevant passages and the sources that underpin them. Some critical evaluation and final comments will close the chapter.

Clarifying Language

First, we need to clarify some terminology used in Catholic moral theology.

'Practical reason' describes knowledge of something judged to be true precisely from the aspect of truth as good, of truth as a bearer of value, and, hence, to be pursued, promoted, and performed. This is a more general description based on a distinction found in moral theology between two modes of knowledge.

'Speculative' knowledge denotes information or understanding that considered, in itself, does not carry a deeply felt significance (although it may do so for a particular individual). For instance, New York is in the United States or two plus two equals four.

Alternatively, 'evaluative' knowledge involves an estimation or appreciation of something true as involving some value which a person appropriates as being personally significant. It is this judgment or appraisal that guides our decision and

---

[4] For Jan Jans, the image of God in *Veritats Splendor* is captured in the two themes of participation and subordination which helps explain the document's unresolved tensions. See Jan Jans, 'Participation-Subordination (The Image of God) in *Veritatis Splendor*' in Joseph A Selling & Jan Jans, *The Splendor of Accuracy: An Examination of the Assertions made by Veritatis Splendor* (Grand Rapids MI: Eerdmans, 1994), 152-168. The term 'affective connaturality' will be explained later in this chapter.

actions.⁵ For instance, 'I'm mortified at the very thought of acting like that'.

Brian Lewis notes two levels of conscience found in the Bible and later in, for instance, the work of Aquinas.⁶ Conscience, in its proper sense, is 'situational' in that it denotes the judgment about the morality of a particular act (*syneidesis*). Conscience understood as 'foundational' (*synderesis*) is 'the habitual and ineradicable grasp of fundamental moral principles' (love and do good, shun evil, seek truth) that is natural and innate and which judgment needs as a benchmark and a guide.⁷ Lewis says that foundational conscience is 'somewhat akin to the sense of moral value'⁸ without further comment. Foundational conscience seems to be, for Lewis, as for Aquinas, the developed, habituated form of this sense of moral value or of what we refer to above as 'primordial moral awareness'.⁹

Church Teaching

We turn now to Church teaching as reflected in *Gaudium at Spes* pars. 14 -17 and *Veritatis Splendor* (Ch.2, Section 2 *Conscience and Truth*).[10]

Gaudium et Spes

The starting point is the lapidary statement of the dignity of moral conscience found in *Gaudium et Spes* par.16 (its first paragraph is repeated in *Veritatis*

---

[5] See Timothy E O'Connell, *Making Disciples: A Handbook of Christian Moral Formation* (New York: Crossroad, 1998), 29, 70. Also, Richard M Gula, SSS, *Reason Informed by Faith: Foundations of Catholic Morality* (New York/Mahwah: Paulist, 1989), 85-7.

[6] Brian Lewis, 'The Primacy of Conscience in the Roman Catholic Tradition', *Pacifica* 13 (October, 2000): 299-306. Also, Dennis J Billy, C.Ss.R., 'Christ's Redemptive Journey and the Moral Dimension of Prayer', *Studia Moralia* 37 (1999): 127-152, at 146.

[7] Lewis, 'The Primacy', 300.

[8] Ibid, 300.

[9] The distinction within conscience noted by Lewis has various modulations in the theological tradition. For instance, it is threefold for O'Connell comprising *synderesis*, moral science and particular judgment (*syneidesis*). See Timothy E O'Connell (Revised Ed.), *Principles for a Catholic Morality* (HarperSanfrancisco, 1990), 109-113. O'Neil and Black more recently speak of the four 'moments' of conscience. The foundational level is 'conscience as desiring and knowing the good'. This moment is followed by conscience as discerning the particular good, then as a judgment for right action, and finally as self-evaluating. See Kevin O'Neil, C.Ss. R and Peter Black, C.Ss. R., *The Essential Moral Handbook: A Guide to Catholic* Living (Liguori, Missouri: Liguori Publications, 2003), 58-83, at 60.

[10] Some brief correlation will be made with the *Catechism of the Catholic Church* (Homebush, NSW: St. Pauls, 1994).

Splendor par. 54).[11] After a brief comment on its context, I will examine its epistemological setting and intentionality followed by the extent to which foundational conscience is a form of evaluative or appreciative knowing. The text of the document reads:

> In the depths of his conscience, man (sic) detects a law which he does not impose upon himself, but which holds him to obedience. Always summoning him to love good and avoid evil, the voice of conscience can when necessary speak to his heart more specifically: do this, shun that. For man has in his heart a law written by God. To obey it is the very dignity of man; according to it he will be judged [Rom. 2:15-16].
>
> Conscience is the most secret core and sanctuary of a man. There he is alone with God, whose voice echoes in his depths. In a wonderful manner conscience reveals that law which is fulfilled by love of God and neighbor. In fidelity to conscience, Christians are joined with the rest of men in the search for the truth…[12]

This statement's significance can only be appreciated in its broader context, namely, the first chapter of *Gaudium et Spes,* namely, 'The Dignity of the Human Person'. Human dignity is manifest first in 'authentic freedom' which is 'an exceptional sign of the divine image'. Moeller points out that this approach, rather than one based on natural law, was preferred by the Council Fathers for biblical and ecumenical reasons.[13]

Second, human dignity reflecting the divine image is specified further: it is the divine will that the human person is left 'in the hand of his own counsel' to know and choose what is true and good *freely*.[14] The foundation of this is further elaborated in the Declaration on Religious Freedom (*Dignitatis Humanae*) which, as Klaus Demmer notes, is classically referred to as a 'turning point' or, in epistemological terms, a 'paradigm shift' in the Catholic tradition.[15]

---

[11] In the *Catechism of the Catholic Church*, No. 1776, this paragraph is found under the heading 'Moral Conscience' without any comment.

[12] The correlation of the wording of some of this section with Aquinas' *Summa Theologiae* cannot be a coincidence. The question of the relevant article is 'Can the Law of Nature be abolished from the Heart of Man' (sic) and cites Romans 2:14 in the first sentence. See Thomas de Aquino, Summa Theologiae, I^a-IIae q. 94, a.6 (corpusthomisticum.org), accessed 10 May 2022 (henceforth, *ST*).

[13] Charles Moeller, 'History of the Constitution' in Herbert Vorgrimler, *Commentary on the Documents of Vatican II* (New York: Herder & Herder; London: Burns and Oates, 1969), 65.

[14] *Gaudium et Spes,* par. 17; my emphasis.

[15] Demmer, *Shaping the Moral Life*, 4-5. This decree will be discussed in the next chapter of this book.

We come to the first process that mediates the appreciation of value.

Primordial Moral Awareness through Participative Responsiveness in Relationship

For Gaffney and Ratzinger, the thought and language of this text cited above (par. 16) draw on John Henry Newman.[16] Traces of Aquinas and the scholastic tradition are evident but within a framework of interiority.

A reading of the passage indicates that foundational moral consciousness appears to emerge not primarily by way of interaction with the outer world; rather it is by attentiveness to the inner world through self-reflexivity. Earlier in the Church document, modern insights into interiority ('interior qualities' or *interioritas*) are acknowledged.[17] This form of unique self-awareness, couched in affective language, in fact, connotes the deepest core of the reflexive self, endowed with a capacity to be moved to respond to a call. *Interioritas* is the 'distinctively human capacity' enabling the human person to outstrip 'the whole sum of mere things'.[18]

Joseph Ratzinger comments that paragraph 14 of *Gaudium et Spes* is influenced by two aspects. It reflects an Augustinian synthesis of a more historically-oriented biblical anthropology with a modified metaphysical conception.[19] How is this the case?

First, the distinction between 'homo interior' and 'exterior' (rather than body/soul) sees the person in historical and dynamic terms. At the same time, it 'introduces a greater element of personal responsibility and decision regarding the direction of life'. Second, for Augustine, the biblical understanding of the heart 'expresses the unity of interior life and corporeality'.[20]

In his discussion of par. 16 of *Gaudium et Spes*, Lewis notes a further aspect; in the freedom and interiority of the person where one is a distinctive yet mysterious reality, there is a 'vital and dynamic overture towards God, the

---

[16] James Gaffney, *Matters of Faith and Morals* (St. Louis: Sheed & Ward, 1987), 130. Also, Joseph Ratzinger, 'Introductory Article and Chapter I: The Dignity of the Human Person' in Vorgrimler, *Commentary on the Documents of Vatican II*, 134-5.

[17] *Gaudium et Spes*, par. 14.

[18] *Gaudium et Spes*, par. 31, 212.

[19] 'Anthropology' here is used not in a cultural or sociological sense but as a faith-informed understanding of the human person, as in 'theological anthropology'.

[20] Ratzinger, 'Introductory Article and Chapter I,', 128. The biblical understanding of the 'heart' will be clarified later in this chapter.

Supreme Good and Ultimate End of all human striving'.[21] This is equivalent to O'Neil and Black's view of conscience as 'desiring and knowing the good' noted earlier.[22]

Further, considered in the light of Bernard Lonergan's model of intentional consciousness, the desire to search for, know and appropriate what is true and good is driven by affectivity, or as one author expresses it, is 'grounded in the pure *desire* to know'.[23] This desire highlights one dimension of affectivity in fundamental or primordial conscience.

Lewis suggests this personalist view is at the heart of paragraph 16 of *Gaudium et Spes*. He also notes that the human person's capacity to outstrip 'the whole sum of mere things' points to the capacity for self-transcendence, Again, on entering the heart, one finds God waiting to draw us into a meeting and a dialogue between persons.[24] This intimate exchange develops in the 'experience of the moral "tug", the sense of obligation', not just to law, or to this or that action, but to be a certain kind of person, namely, 'a loving, relating person'.[25] This underscores the second aspect of affectivity in primordial conscience—an orientation towards loving actions and relationships.

What more can be said of the setting of the discussion, namely, about creation in relation to revelation?

Creation and Revelation

Interestingly, the wording of this passage concerning law as 'detected' or 'revealed' seems to concern the human being within creation. 'Revelation' is not presented in terms of the Word of God embodied in Jesus Christ. Rather, it is the divine wisdom present in the created order (as providence) that is mediated through conscience.

---

[21] Lewis, *The Primacy*, 301.

[22] See n. 9 above.

[23] Cynthia S W Crysdale, 'Heritage and Discovery: A Framework for Moral Theology', *Theological Studies:* 63:3 (2002): 559-578, at 568 n. 23; emphasis in original. Underlying this is Lonergan's 'intentionality analysis', which places an emphasis on self-appropriation in accord with four transcendental imperatives, namely, be attentive, be intelligent, be reasonable, be responsible. As we shall soon see, the imperative to be loving will come into play in our considerations here.

[24] Lewis, 'The Primacy', 301. See the comment that conscience is a dialogue of man with himself and also a dialogue of man with God 'the author of the law, the primordial image and final end of man', *Veritatis Splendor*, par. 58

[25] Lewis, *The Primacy*, 302.

The primary focus, then, appears to be more theistic than specifically Christian. Hence, the Council text notes that the 'law revealed by conscience' finds its *fulfilment* in the call to love God and neighbor, and cites Mt 22: 37-40 and Gal 5:14. Or, as Ratzinger sums it up, 'natural law is identified with the Golden Rule and thereby equated with the kernel of the Gospel'.[26]

This theistic emphasis appears to be confirmed in the final sentence where Christians are called to 'join' with the rest of humanity in searching for truth 'in fidelity to conscience'. Conscience is presented as the experience of the primordial moral awareness of our common humanity.[27] Only at the end of Ch.1 of *Gaudium et Spes,* as a type of climax, does the Council speak of the fullness of humanity revealed and realized in 'the mystery of the incarnate Word' and of the paschal mystery at work in an 'unseen way' in the hearts of 'all men (sic) of good will'.[28]

Again, a richer appreciation of *Gaudium et Spes* par. 16 ('Dignity of Moral Conscience') is possible by viewing it in relation to the preceding section namely 'Dignity of the Mind'. Here, the search for truth, as Ratzinger notes, is influenced by Augustine and his metaphysics of light (later picked up in *Veritatis Splendor*).

The Council, then, appeals to the dynamism of desire, in the gentle attraction of *wisdom* in the quest and love of what is true and good. It takes us beyond scientific knowledge, to a grasp of reality 'beyond the visible' and into contact with realities that are 'unseen'. This process finds its fulfillment in the gift of the Holy Spirit in faith that brings an 'appreciation of the divine plan'. The search for wisdom provides the broader epistemological setting within which conscience exercises its dignity. This anticipates the discussion of participative knowledge later in this chapter.

So far, then, *Gaudium et Spes* par. 6, reveals the epistemological character of primordial moral awareness as a form of wisdom under the impulse of desire. At the same time, this foundational moral consciousness with its capacity to be moved to respond to a call, is a dialogical relationship with God mediated through conscience, whose intentionality (its trajectory and object) is directed towards the transcendent and is embodied in love. Foundational moral awareness has its roots in a participative responsiveness in relationship.

---

[26] Ratzinger, 'Introductory Article and Chapter I,' 135.

[27] 'Conscience is presented as the meeting point and common ground of Christians and non-Christians and consequently as the real hinge on which dialogue turns', Ratzinger, 'Introductory Article and Chapter I', 136.

[28] *Gaudium et Spes,* par. 22.

This brings us to the second document in this discussion and the second epistemological process.

Veritatis Splendor

In the section 'Conscience and Truth' of this encyclical, Pope St John Paul II, as expected, sees conscience as *practical reason* since it concerns what is truly good to be done. Generally, the Pope's language is not couched in terms of *synderesis* (foundational moral awareness of right and wrong). For all that, equivalent phrases indicate its presence in his thought and his dependence on sources from within the theological tradition. What does emerge is the second aspect of foundational moral knowledge—our next concern.

Primordial Moral Awareness: Participation as Recognition

Pope St John Paul notes that a moral judgment is made in terms of a criterion, which is:

> ... the rational conviction that one must love and do good and avoid evil. This first principle of practical reason is part of the natural law; indeed, it constitutes the very foundation of the natural law, inasmuch as it expresses the primordial insight about good and evil, that reflection of God's creative wisdom which, like an imperishable spark (*scintilla animae*), shines in the heart of every man.[29]

When this passage is related with *Veritatis Splendor* par. 54[30] and other concepts in the encyclical, it is possible to detect the four epistemological strands that have influenced its development.

The first strand, in common with *Gaudium et Spes* par.16 seen above, involves a recovery from Augustine and the Franciscan school where conscience is the center of a person. Here, we find the locus of a *participatory relationship* taking the form of a loving *dialogue* between God and the human being (the spark or 'peak' of the soul). It is more than reason, will or feeling but is 'the depth of human existence, the innermost core of the person in his directedness towards God and in his ultimate sustenance by him'.[31]

However, significant here is John Paul II's complementary view of foundational moral awareness as grounded in the experience of *horizontal relationships* and of *embodiment*. The dignity of the person is revealed in 'the primordial requirement of loving and respecting the person as an end and never

---

[29] *Veritatis Splendor*, par. 59.

[30] Which cites the passage of *Gaudium et Spes,* par. 16 discussed earlier.

[31] A Auer cited by Karl H Peschke, *Christian Ethics: Moral Theology in the Light of Vatican II*, Vol 1, (Warwickshire, UK: Goodliffe Neale, 1986), 205.

as a mere means'.³²

Again, as the values that cluster around self-transcendence are those towards which 'the person is naturally inclined', practical reason (assisted by virtue) can 'discover in the body the anticipatory signs, the expression and the promise of the gift of the self, in conformity with the wise plan of the Creator'.³³ *Participation* is as much an expression of embodiment and responsiveness in interpersonal relationships as it is of the divine-human relationship.

Second, there is discernible later in the document (par. 59), two strands suggested by Ratzinger in his discussion on conscience. There is not only a Stoic background but especially the Platonic notion of *anamnesis* (with its biblical overtones) that entails a moment of *recognition* of the truest self. This is a key influence on the word *synderesis* (and its connotations). Ratzinger explains that the Platonic (and biblical) notion of *anamnesis* is captured in the:

> spark of love...that something like an original memory of the good and the true (both are identical) has been implanted in us...(which)... is not a conceptually articulated knowing, a store of retrievable contents. It is so to speak an inner sense, a capacity to recall, so that the one who it addresses, if he is not turned in on himself, hears its echo from within. He sees: that's it! That is what my nature points to and seeks.³⁴

Ratzinger refers to this as the 'ontological level of the phenomenon of conscience' which the human person at the level of ones being 'resonates with some things and clashes with others' or, for Aquinas, is an 'inner repugnance to evil and an attraction to the good'. ³⁵

This brings us to the next aspect of the epistemological process.

Primordial Moral Awareness: Participative Collaboration

The third form of participation emerges by probing Ratzinger's comment about the 'Stoic background'. The reference is to the Stoic notion of the microcosm participating in the *Logos*. An ordered *cosmos* expresses the wisdom of its creator. Humans, as the microcosmic expression of this macrocosmic order, find their purpose and harmony by accepting and observing the intrinsic laws that inhabit nature through the universal reason (*logos*). Moral obligation arises from the

---

³² *Veritatis Splendor,* par. 48.

³³ *Veritatis Splendor,* par. 48.

³⁴ See Joseph Cardinal Ratzinger, *Conscience and Truth* (United States Bishops Workshop, Knights of Columbus, 1991), 1-22, at 14.

³⁵ Ratzinger, *Conscience and Truth*, 14, 17.

purpose-directed reason inhabiting nature.

This finds later expression in Aquinas where law is an ordering of reason for the common good. All law participates in the divine law in so far as it is oriented to what is good. The emphasis is not voluntaristic such as in Divine Command theory of ethics. It is rather on reason as intelligibility in which truth is the bearer of value.

Natural Law, then, is from God the creator for achieving the good, for realizing the purpose of the created order and thus expresses God's governance and providence over all things. Pope St John Paul II writes of humanity's call to 'share in God's dominion' and to its responsible exercise 'over the world'. [36]

This view is in continuity with that of Aquinas. Humankind is called to share actively in divine providence through the virtue of prudence.[37] This is another way of speaking of the 'spark', the 'reflection' of divine 'creative wisdom' shining the human heart—the basic orientation to what is true and good. From Ratzinger's knowing through *recognition,* we move to an epistemology of *participation leading to collaboration.*

In all this, Pope St John Paul II is tapping into the sapiential tradition. For Aquinas, creation is the work of the divine craftsman, who gives intelligible form to his art in which humankind shares in divine wisdom and is called to be perfected in wisdom (its proper perfection) by participating in the Word of God.[38] A contemporary approach brings two angles to this process. Divine Wisdom in the Scriptures as 'the self-communication of God in and through creation' and, for Roland Murphy, as 'the divine summons in and through creation, sounding through the vast realm of the created world, and heard on the level of human

---

[36] *Veritatis Splendor,* par. 38.

[37] '... participates in providence, providing for himself and for others'. See *ST* 1.2.91.2 and 1.103.6 and 8. Matthew Levering comments that 'God gives our intellect and will the power to act and their natural inclinations to truth and goodness. God gives the forms by which our intellect understands, and God is the source of the goodness that moves our will. Second, we cognitively participate in the eternal law by knowing and agreeing with the divine ratio for ordering us to our ultimate end'. Matthew Levering's review of John Rziha, *Perfecting Human Actions: St. Thomas Aquinas on Human Participation in Eternal Law* (Washington: Catholic University of America, 2009) in *Theological Studies* 71: 4 (2010): 297-8.

[38] *ST* 3. 23. 3. *Veritatis Splendor*, par. 45 notes that all law and 'the different ways God acting in history cares for the world...have their origin and goal in the eternal, wise and loving counsel whereby God predestines men and women "to be conformed to the image of his Son" (Rom. 8:19)'.

experience'.[39]

We come now to the fourth participative epistemological process that is suggested as mediating primordial moral awareness. This becomes evident when the Pope St John Paul II advances from the 'heart' as the locus of primary moral consciousness ('knowledge of God's law in general') which is necessary but not sufficient. There is also needed the 'heart' converted to the Lord, to love of 'what is good and is really the source of *true* judgments of conscience'. Citing Aquinas, this is expressed as a 'sort of *connaturality between man and the true good*' by following 'the way' of Jesus and participating in his virtues.[40]

Given the significance of this shift in emphasis and the role of Aquinas in its development, a separate section will be devoted to the topic.

Primordial Moral Awareness: Participation, Affective Connaturality and Aquinas.

In approaching this topic, the first task is the issue of language.

Clarifying Language

'Connaturality' (*connaturalitas*) is part of the vocabulary of the Thomistic tradition. It denotes a) of like nature; b) a natural relation or agreement with something; c) a natural inclination or attraction to something.[41] In contemporary terms, it signifies 'an intimate attunement of human consciousness to the realm of aesthetic and moral values', hence, it is similar to what is currently referred to as 'emotional intelligence'.[42]

A full treatment of connaturality is beyond the scope of this discussion.[43] For

---

[39] Denis Edwards, *Jesus the Wisdom of God: An Ecological Theology* (Homebush, NSW: St. Pauls, 1995), 70, citing Roland E Murphy, *The Tree of Life: An Exploration of Biblical Wisdom Literature* (NY: Doubleday, 1990), 135, 138.

[40] *Veritatis Splendor,* par. 64 citing *ST* 2.2.45.2; italics in original.

[41] Roy J Defarrari, *A Lexicon of Saint Thomas Aquinas* (Fitzwilliam, NH: Loreto Publications, 1949), 209.

[42] Anthony J Kelly review of RJ Snell, *The Perspective of Love: Natural Law in a New Mode* (Eugene, OR: Pickwick, 2014) in *Studies in Christian Ethics* 29:4 (2016): 506-508, at 507. Helpful here is the original definition of emotional intelligence: 'the ability to monitor one's own and others' feelings and emotions, to discriminate among them and to use this information to guide one's thinking and actions'. See PJ Salovey & JD Mayer, 'Emotional intelligence' in *Imagination, Cognition and Personality*, 9: 185–21, at 189. The moral implications of emotional intelligence are the subject of recent studies in moral development and moral philosophy.

[43] See Thomas Ryan, 'Revisiting Affective Knowing and Connaturality in Aquinas,' *Theological Studies* 66:1, (March) 2005: 49-68.

our purposes, what is more helpful is to approach it through the model based on intentionality analysis by the contemporary philosopher Andrew Tallon.

Forms of Connaturality

Tallon suggests that Aquinas' approach is built on three dimensions of connaturality—the ontological, the habitual and, bridging the two, the epistemological.

What was true for Aquinas is true today; living beings are drawn to respond to the world around us. It is connaturality that makes our 'faculties' operate with spontaneity, responsive to what is akin to them, befitting them. Our eyes do not need to *know* that light, color, and harmonious form are good for them, but in the presence of the visible they naturally act and experience fulfillment (*complacentia*).[44] This is *ontological* connaturality.

Further, for sentient and animal creatures, this form of sympathy and responsiveness has an incipiently rational expression in emotions and instinct. With its fuller expression in humans (conceptual knowledge, desires, love, imagination, and choice etc.), the cognitive, affective, and volitional operations of rational consciousness *respond* to their proper objects (being as true and good) because of their 'cor-*respond*-ence with their proper objects'. This is the *epistemological* form of an experienced befittingness, belongingness, affinity, attunement.[45]

A helpful tool to investigate this is John Paul II's use of the term 'inclinations' in relation the realization of authentic humanity.[46] Underlying this is an Aristotelian/Thomistic teleology and ontology, specified here as 'every agent acts on account of an end and to be an end carries the meaning to be good'.[47] Reason can discern some universal moral goods which, if denied, would defy what it

---

[44] Andrew Tallon, *Head and Heart: Affection, Cognition and Volition as Triune Consciousness* (NY: Fordham University Press, 1997), 235.

[45] Tallon, *Head and Heart*, 235. For an extensive application of Tallon's phenomenological approach see Heidi Ann Russell, *The Heart of Rahner: The Theological Implications of Andrew Tallon's Theory of Triune Consciousness* (Milwaukee, WI: Marquette University Press, 2009).

[46] In *Veritatis Splendor,* he speaks of 'the moral value of certain goods to which the person is naturally inclined' (par.48). Further, natural inclinations take on moral relevance 'only in so far as they refer to the human person and his authentic fulfillment, a fulfillment which for that matter can take place always and only in human nature' (par.50).

[47] *ST* 1.2.94.2.

means to be a rational agent.⁴⁸

Keith Ward asks whether there are states at which all rational agents would aim. He suggests 'it seems plausible to say that pleasure would be chosen over pain, knowledge over ignorance, beauty over ugliness, and freedom over slavery'. Our common humanity brings us a general awareness of acts as right or wrong in so far as they lead to states that are 'universally desirable or undesirable'.⁴⁹

Ward, with Ratzinger, notes that these moral principles take the compressed form of, for instance, the Golden rule. Again, this is connaturality expressed in its epistemological form. As a task of moral reason, it is directed to the *habitual* aspect, after specifying content, to bring these inclinations to perfection, which points us to the question of virtues—our next task.

Connaturality, Practical Reason and Wisdom

The reference to Aquinas and to true judgments of conscience having their source in a 'sort of *connaturality between man and the true good*' not only has parallels with emotional intelligence, noted earlier. It also taps into a rich vein in the tradition, specifically concerning the gift of wisdom (which we will examine in more detail later).⁵⁰

For our present purposes, connaturality, as a virtue, is described as a 'taste' for what is truly good and is a kind of 'discerning' love.⁵¹ It is variously described as experiential or appreciative knowing and characterized by congeniality or attunement.⁵² It is a participative knowledge arising from a felt attraction to, a love for, an appreciation of what is good that is personally appropriated.

Significant here (and implied in the Pope's statement above), is that this form of appreciative knowledge is not confined to 'second nature', namely, the activation and habituation of our 'first nature' (its inclinations) through virtue. For Aquinas, connaturality, properly speaking, connotes 'first nature' whereby a person has a natural affinity between powers and their proper objects.

---

⁴⁸ For Aquinas, the distinguishing 'inclinations' for humankind are survival, procreation, life in community, to seek and find the truth and to know God.

⁴⁹ Keith Ward, *Veritatis Splendor* Section 4, http://www.gresham.ac.uk/uploads/JPII-ward.1.doc.accessed Dec. 15, 2010.

⁵⁰ In chapter four of this book.

⁵¹ 'Love is said to discern because it moves the reason to discern' ST 2.2.47.1 ad 1. Also 2.2.45.2.

⁵² Aquinas calls connatural knowledge 'judgment by inclination' (*per modum inclinationis, ST* I.1.6 ad 3); 'affective cognition' (*cognitio affectiva*, ST 1.64. 1; 2.2.162.3 ad 1) and 'experiential cognition' (*cognitio experimentalis*, ST 2.2.97.2).

As has been noted with Tallon's approach, in contrast with habitual connaturality (second nature), there is, to adapt Ratzinger's phrase used earlier, an 'ontological' connaturality appropriate to rationality, namely, a receptiveness and aptness for right judgment to be actualized.

This brings us to how this receptiveness in the rational human being takes the form of an epistemological connaturality. Alternatively, how does Aquinas approach the foundational moral experience, the first principle of practical reason, 'the rational conviction that one must love and do good and avoid evil'?[53] Aquinas' terminology is interesting here. For practical reason, he normally uses the phrase *ratio practica*. However, Maguire notes that, twice in the treatise *De Malo*, Aquinas, in the one context, uses the phrase 'practical or affective reason'.[54] In other words, it is a form of affective knowing.

Practical Reason and Natural Law

For Aquinas, one is not capable of moral virtue without an awareness of primary moral principles. In his treatment of this, while he uses the metaphor of the 'heart' as the site of this knowledge, there is no explicit use of the phrase 'connatural knowledge' or its equivalents noted above.[55] This awareness is not one of *ratio* or discursive, reasoned knowing but of *intellectus*, which is both non-discursive insight 'from within' and an initial form of loving knowledge with the immediacy that accompanies contemplation.[56] This takes habitual form (foundational conscience) but its initial expression as primordial moral awareness (or Lewis' 'basic sense of moral value') is innate and universal. it is from this foundation that virtue emerges. It is traceable to understanding or immediate, intuitive insight (*intellectus*) that is embedded 'within the very structure of human moral cognition (i.e., synderesis or anamnesis)'.[57]

Intuitive insight, then, is a form of cognition that involves an immediate grasp of what is true which, in its habitual form (epitomized in the gift of understanding) denotes 'a certain excellence of knowledge that penetrates into the heart of

---

[53] *Veritatis Splendor,* par. 59.

[54] Daniel Maguire, *The Moral Revolution: A Christian Humanist Vision* (San Francisco: Harper and Row, 1986*)*, 258 citing *de Malo,* Q. 16, a 6 ad 13 and ad 8 for the phrase *'cognitio practica seu affectiva'*. For a more extensive treatment of the role of affections and emotions in the virtues and the moral life, see Diana Fritz Cates, *Aquinas on the Emotions: A Religious-Ethical Inquiry* (Washington, DC: Georgetown University Press, 2009).

[55] *ST* 1.2.94.6.

[56] *De Veritate*, q. 16, a. 1, resp.; q.1, a.2.c; also, *ST* 2.2.180.4 and 7.

[57] Billy, 'Christ's Redemptive Journey', 146. Also, *ST* 1.2.94.1 ad 2 and *sed contra* where Aquinas speaks of insight or understanding as *synderesis* or 'lex intellectus'.

things'.[58] Here, it is an intuitive appreciation of the truth precisely as a good that is fitting and congenial to being authentically human. It is the epistemological expression of ontological connaturality.

In saying that this knowledge is innate and universal, Aquinas points to the capacity in every human person for this form of awareness, a condition of possibility for human existence. It is another way of speaking of the natural 'fittingness' for the good, or *connaturality*. Aquinas is continually qualifying his position here. On one hand, he holds that this habit of basic moral awareness arises naturally in the mind so spontaneously that no person 'can be entirely bereft of it' but it needs to be cultivated if it is to develop appropriately.[59]

Elsewhere, Aquinas denies that the habit of foundational conscience is given with our nature at birth.[60] The capacity for moral awareness and accountability is activated through experience. Intuitive insight requires other operations of knowing: some prior reflection on data from the senses (if only minimal as in 'the whole is greater than the part') so that certain judgments arise naturally, easily, without deliberation.[61]

Further, this capacity needs to be complemented by conceptual analysis, by inductive reasoning and especially the consolidation by habits without which affective knowing or intuitive insight 'would remain feeble in its penetration and clarity'.[62] Thus, it is subject to development, to varying degrees and to limits and qualification.[63] Basic principles may be only partially known, inadequately appreciated and even distorted or obstructed by culture or upbringing (factors whose implications are not really developed by Aquinas).

Our concern remains about the way in which the basic elements of morality first come into human consciousness. Jacques Maritain develops Aquinas'

---

[58] ST 2.2 8.1 ad 3.

[59] Gregory M Reichberg, 'The Intellectual Virtues (Ia IIae, qq. 57-58)' in *The Ethics of Aquinas*, ed. Stephen J Pope (Washington, DC: Georgetown University Press, 2002), 131-150, at 137.

[60] ST 1.2.51.1.

[61] Reichberg, 'The Intellectual Virtues', 146 n. 34 commenting on ST.1.2.51.1.

[62] Reichberg, 'The Intellectual Virtues', 137.

[63] See ST 1.2. 94.1 ad 3; ST 1.2. 94.4; ST 1.2. 94. 6. What is striking about Aquinas' approach is that, while he sees all law as participating in the Eternal Law, this is muted in Q. 94 on Natural Law. He treats conscience (and here foundational conscience) as a natural or secular reality rather than, as in Newman, a religious one. This is reflected in the contrast between the simple, direct vocabulary of Aquinas and the religious, even mystical language of Newman.

position by arguing that these basic insights come into awareness through a form of affective or connatural intuition. He sees this in terms of the proper way things should be used and takes the example of a stringed instrument. Anything in nature has within it its own 'natural law', the 'normality of its function', in how it should act 'to achieve fullness of being in its growth and in its behavior'.[64] This knowledge of natural law (basic moral sense) has increased slowly as the moral conscience of humanity developed. The knowledge is not 'clear' through concepts and conceptual judgments. Maritain continues

> ...it is obscure, unsystematic, vital knowledge by connaturality or congeniality, in which the intellect, in order to bear judgment, consults and listens to the inner melody that the vibrating strings of abiding tendencies make present in the subject.[65]

Primordial moral awareness rests on the sense of certain perceived realities as good, as 'in tune with' the deepest self, if only in a groping and non-thematic way. To capture awareness of a resonance at the level of one's being, perhaps 'affective connaturality' is a better phrase than 'evaluative knowledge'. The awareness from *connaturality* converges with the notion of *anamnesis* and ontological conscience described earlier by Ratzinger. It is openness to the ground of one's being. Snell suggests that for *connaturality*, since it is in the realm of affection, we could borrow from Heiddeger and use the equivalent *Befindlichkeit* or *Stimmung* which denotes mood or attunement to Being itself and, in the context of faith, is understood as attunement toward the Divine.[66]

Neither Aquinas (nor Maritain), considers that this foundational moral sense is a cluster of innate ideas, a form of Augustinian illuminationism. With Aristotle, all knowledge ultimately comes through the senses. Just as 'being' is found only in individual 'things' presented by sense experience, the same is true of what is 'good' or valuable. The formula 'do good and avoid evil' distills in general terms what has its roots in individual instances of what is perceived as 'good' or 'evil.' One can ask whether this is sufficient to the human person as an embodied and relational being? This brings us to some considerations about the 'heart'—noted earlier in the context of Aquinas' discussion of natural law.

---

[64] Jacques Maritain, 'Natural Law in Aquinas' in Charles E Curran and Richard A McCormick, SJ, eds. *Readings in Moral Theology*, No. 7 (Mahwah, NJ: 1991), 114-123, at 115.

[65] Ibid., 119.

[66] RJ Snell, 'Connaturality in Aquinas: The Ground of Wisdom', *Quodlibet* 5:4 (October 2003): 1-8, at 3. Available on-line at http://www.Quodlibet.net and accessed 15, 10, 2003. Ibid. 3. Snell argues that connaturality or attunement to Being is the transcendental condition of the dynamism of the structure of the operations of intentional consciousness. While consistent with what is said here, that precise aspect is not our concern in this chapter.

Evaluative Knowledge and the Heart

From the discussion so far, basic moral awareness is associated with four affective aspects: with the human desire to know, with the epistemological intentionality of what is known ('love and do good and avoid evil'), with the existential intentionality of loving God and neighbor and, most importantly, with an incipient form of 'loving knowledge' that is a four-dimensional participation in divine wisdom. Nevertheless, these Church texts must be carefully understood when they refer to the cognition involved in foundational conscience as knowledge of the 'heart'.

It would appear, *prima facie*, from *Gaudium et Spes* par. 16, that the building blocks of this 'foundational' awareness (conscience) are affective (law written by God in the heart). This is confirmed when Pope St John Paul II writes that the 'relationship of man's freedom and God's law' is not only grounded in the 'heart' but 'is most deeply lived out in the "heart" of the person, in his moral conscience'.[67]

We must beware of interpreting the use of 'heart' as indicating a contemporary understanding of the word, namely as the center of a person's affective life. In *Gaudium et Spes* par. 16 (as cited above) the reference to a law written in the human heart by God 'by which he shall be judged' carries as a note Rom 2:15-16. In *Gaudium et Spes* par.14 where it says 'God, who probes the heart...' there is a footnote reference to I Kg 16:6 and Jer 17:10. Two points can be made concerning 'law' and the 'heart'.

First, as noted earlier, Ratzinger argues that *anamnesis* (rather than *synderesis* with its Stoic resonances) captures precisely the meaning of Rom 2:14f.[68] Paul here speaks of Gentiles who do not have the Law (from a revealed source) yet do by nature or reason (instinctively observe) what the Law prescribes. They have *physis* (nature or 'the regular material order or of things') as a guide for their conduct, one that is beyond the relative and psychological and is absolute and objective.[69] Ratzinger sees it as a moment of recognition, of disclosure where '[Someone] sees: that's it! That is what my nature points to and seeks'.[70]

---

[67] *Veritatis Splendor,* par. 54.

[68] Ratzinger, *Conscience and Truth*, 14. See n. 34 above.

[69] Joseph A Fitzmyer, SJ., 'The Letter to the Romans,' in Raymond E Brown, SS, Joseph A Ftizmyer, SJ and Roland E Murphy, O. Carm., eds. *The New Jerome Biblical Commentary* (Geoffrey Chapman, 1990), 830-868, at 837.

[70] n. 34. Fitzmyer shares Ratzinger's hesitations about foundational conscience viewed as *synderesis* when he remarks about Paul '[A]nd so it is difficult to be certain about his view of the "natural law," an idea more at home in Gk. Philosophy. Perhaps the most that should be

Second, to see this type of primordial or foundational awareness as affective in character (in the modern sense of the term) because of the use the 'heart' language in *Gaudium et Spes* pars. 14 & 16 and *Veritatis Splendor* par. 54 would distort the meaning of the texts. It does have affective connotations insofar as it is appreciative and because of its association with other aspects of the person. The usage here approximates to the 'heart' as a symbol of the whole person found in the Hebrew and Christian Scriptures in that it connotes the 'inside' of a person and 'embraces feelings, memories, ideas, plans, decisions'.[71] In the inclusive and concrete anthropology of the Bible, the heart is the principle of morality, the center of one's freedom, of decisive choices and the place where one enters to be in dialogue with oneself and where one opens oneself or closes oneself to God.[72]

Overall, these Church texts with the repeated link between 'moral conscience' and the metaphor of the heart, do suggest a mode of knowing of good and evil that is intuitive and evaluative, arising from insight in the immediacy of self-awareness and within a relationship. However, without some critical assessment, there is a risk of falling into Ratzinger's 'epistemological optimism'—which brings us to the final task.

Assessment and Reflections

In his commentary on *Gaudium et Spes* par.16, Ratzinger makes the point that, in this conciliar text, '[C]onscience is made the principle of objectivity, in the conviction that careful attention to its claim discloses the fundamental common values of human existence'.[73] He notes the 'epistemological optimism' underling this view, even though qualified, in that conscience can be dulled and practically blinded by 'negligence in the search for the values of truth and goodness and the habit of sin'.[74]

---

admitted is that the idea should be regarded as the sensus plenior of Paul's teaching (in view of the patristic tradition about it.)'. In Joseph A Fitzmyer, SJ., 'Pauline Theology' in Raymond E Brown, SS, Joseph A. Ftizmyer, SJ & Roland E Murphy, O. Carm., eds. *The New Jerome Biblical Commentary* (London: Geoffrey Chapman, 1990) 1382-1416, at 1414.

[71] X Léon-Dufour, 'Heart' in *Dictionary of Biblical Theology* (London: Geoffrey Chapman, 1988), 228.

[72] Ibid., 228. This is reflected in the Catechism's wording of Prayer as Covenant. 'According to the Scripture it is the heart that prays…the heart is our hidden centre…the heart is the place of decision, deeper than our psychic drives. It is the place of truth…it is the place of encounter because as image of God we live in relation: it is the place of covenant'. *Catechism of the Catholic Church*, n. 2563.

[73] Ratzinger, 'Introductory Article and Chapter I,' 135.

[74] Ratzinger, 'Introductory Article and Chapter I,' 135.

While a guarded optimism characterizes Christian anthropology within the Catholic tradition, in reality, moral awareness is subject to obscurity, distortions, and fragmentation. Aquinas is conscious of this in a general way. *Veritatis Splendor* appears to exhibit a more critical approach to contemporary culture and currents of thought compared with *Gaudium et Spes* from thirty years earlier.

Generally, we cannot ignore the impact of prejudice, bias, evil, cultural distortions and destructive tendencies in the human heart and behavior (whether personal or communal) and how these can be transmitted across generations. Conscience, particularly as *evaluative* and personally involved knowledge (compared with the speculative or factual) is inherently linked with emotions and the affective dimensions of the person. Hence, it is particularly susceptible to conditions and variables (cultural, anthropological, social) that influence the unconscious, deeper biases, and motivations.[75]

Again, we cannot ignore insights from the human sciences on moral development, personal responsibility, and evaluative knowledge.[76] Nor can we overlook factors at the psychological level such as low self-esteem and deficit of affect (e.g., defective empathetic response). It is through such influences that perceptions and appreciations of what is truly good or evil can be distorted, even nullified, even though, at times, moral responsibility might be diminished. The limit case of this is the sociopath. Such realities should be acknowledged but are beyond the scope of this chapter.

Finally, there is a greater awareness within the theological tradition and Church teaching of the impact of social and structural evil on personal attitudes, dispositions, and behavior—highlighted, in recent times, by the crisis (and profound damage) of sexual abuse within the Catholic Church (to be discussed in chapter three of this book).

From these considerations, we are reminded that the shared content of

---

[75] Selling reminds us that insights of contemporary psychology and sociology give us a better appreciation that, for many people, 'natural inclinations' are 'nothing more than learned reflexes supported by a social-political-economic structure that has little to do with nature and a great deal to do with cultural history'. He offers examples such as accumulating possessions beyond ones needs; to destroy or at least neutralize one's enemies; allow market forces to control our lives; seeing some racial groups as superior to others. See Joseph A Selling, 'Context and Arguments' in Selling and Jans, eds. *The Splendor of Accuracy,* 68.

[76] See Darcia Narvaez, 'Human flourishing and moral development: Cognitive and neurobiological perspectives of virtue development' in *Handbook of Moral and Character Education,* edited by LP Nucci & D Narvaez (Hoboken: Routledge, 2008), 310–327. She explores the relationship between deliberative reasoning, emotions, dispositions, and imagination (communal and personal) in the role of moral appraisal and decision-making. Also, Michael Segon and Chris Booth, 'Virtue: The Missing Ethics Element in Emotional Intelligence', *Journal of Business Ethics,* 128 (2015): 789–802.

primordial moral consciousness is very foundational and minimal. Further, any philosophical framework used to undergird it or cultural settings in which it is experienced need to be addressed critically. Ultimately, the benchmark is the integral human person and 'authentic' humanity. Selling reminds us of those within and outside the Church who, from a sense of our shared humanity, seek other routes for establishing the basic criteria of right and wrong. There are efforts to ground a natural law ethic on the Universal Declaration of Human Rights or, as Robert Gascoigne attempts, to use such a resource to explore an 'ontology of the human'.[77]

Ultimately, primordial moral awareness is never found in a pure state. We may get occasional glimpses of it, for instance, when there is a spontaneous sense of public outrage at an action that is abhorrent and degrading. Moral sensitivities are repelled by evil done to other human beings, even though, at times, it may be difficult to explain or justify our instinctive response. Or it may be revealed in the courage and dignity with which an individual confronts evil and suffering that prompts a moment of self-transcendence—for the person and for the observer. We admire and are inspired. This is a shared experience of moral beauty that points to our common bonds in responding to those in whom authentic humanity is revealed at its very best.[78]

Conclusion

Our investigation has shown that, in *Gaudium et Spes* and *Veritatis Splendor*, primordial moral awareness (conscience) is understood as affective knowing or an appreciative grasp of basic moral values. The theme of 'participation' has been a helpful hermeneutical lens and investigative tool in this process and Aquinas a valuable resource together with the model of triune consciousness developed by philosopher Andrew Tallon. The discussion highlighted four epistemological processes which mediate the intuitive and affective appreciation of value, namely, through first, participatory responsiveness within relationship; second, participation as recognition; third, participation as collaboration; finally, through a specific form of participative knowing, namely, affective connaturality (and its relation to natural law).

These two documents discussed reflect the general confidence within the Catholic theological and magisterial tradition of a basic unity in humankind's moral consciousness underpinning the capacity for moral judgment. Nevertheless, we must not forget the broader context of the Christian moral life epitomized in

---

[77] Robert Gascoigne, *The Church and Secularity: Two Stories of a Liberal Society* (Washington DC: Georgetown University Press, 2009).

[78] See Thomas Ryan, *The Eyes and Ears of Conscience: Lessons of Encouragement* (Strathfield, NSW: St Pauls, 2022), chapter six.

the controlling metaphor of *Veritatis Splendor*, namely, the call of the young man to respond in love to a personal call from Jesus. Basic moral awareness is fully realized in following 'The Way' by an increasing *participation* in the virtues of Jesus (to be discussed further in chapter four of this book).

Some limits and difficulties have been noted. In reality, we see mirrored in these texts the 'typology of positions' of Vatican II and its subsequent reception—the Augustinian and Thomist—that did arrive at a 'common agreed vision of the Church'.[79] However, one is left with the question of how successful is the effort to integrate, within the theme of participation, a metaphysical conception (from Stoic, Neo-Platonic, Thomistic sources) with one more personal, interior and historically conscious (from Augustine and Newman).[80] While the intentionality of the epistemological process is clearly relational, its personal expression, particularly in *Gaudium et Spes,* is couched mainly in terms of the individual person and God or of the self's interiority. Again, conscience's mediating role is presented in mainly individualistic terms.

The language used to describe the object of foundational conscience tends to be expressed in universal and abstract statements, e.g., do good and avoid evil, respect life, seek truth. Are these the immediate object of the primordial moral sense? Or are these formulations induced from more concrete experiences in human life?

The reality is that we are embodied, historical beings whose existence begins and ends in the setting of relationships (both vertical and horizontal). Conscience and the divine call to moral responsibility are deeply personal. However, they can also be mediated in the pattern of interactive responsiveness that constitutes human life at the familial, social, environmental, and cultural levels.

We have seen how this approach, centered on the worth of the person, is anticipated by Pope St John Paul II in *Veritatis Splendor*. What has emerged is the need to explore further how primordial moral awareness is anchored in, and shaped by, the experience of an affectively receptive embodiment that enables *participation* in horizontal (and vertical) forms of relationality.

---

[79] See Ormond Rush, *Still Interpreting Vatican II: Some Hermeneutical Principles* (New York: Mahwah, NJ: Paulist, 2004), 61 and 17.

[80] The hermeneutical question as addressed by Rush is beyond the scope of this article. Suffice it to note that the use of 'participation' in this investigation appears, generally speaking, to be congruent with Rush's concern to incorporate the best of these two 'positions' through a theological anthropology that rests on God's loving self-communication in Christ. Rush argues that our *participation* in the life of the Trinity entails an active and creative share in the work of divine providence through the guidance of the Spirit so that we 'understand, interpret and apply the Gospel anew in a thousand new situations'. *Still Interpreting Vatican II:* 77.

Such a consideration sets the scene for the following chapter. Authentic freedom and the dignity of the person demand that human beings know and choose what is true and good *freely*. This underlies the question of religious freedom (and its relationship to conscience)—our next concern.

2
A Case Study in Conscience: Religious Freedom

Early in the previous chapter it was noted how 'authentic freedom' is an 'exceptional sign of the image of God' in the human person. This was further specified: human dignity and associated rights demand that what is true and good must be pursued, known, and claimed *freely,* bringing a person to conviction by 'its own power'.

Such an issue is relevant in both personal and social life, particularly in the more pluralistic and secular societies of the modern world.[1] In the 1960s it was a topic of significant concern for the Catholic Church at the Second Vatican Council resulting in the Declaration on Religious Freedom, namely, *Dignitatis Humanae* (DH)—the basis of this chapter.[2]

Recent studies have been a timely reminder of the contribution made by the American Jesuit, Fr. John Courtney Murray in the writing of this declaration. When the final tally was announced (2,308 in favor, 70 against), the bishops responded with applause. The next day, the *London Times* referred to the vote as 'a great event in the history of Catholicism and in the history of freedom'.[3]

In any discussion of DH, the relationship to ideas developed by Murray himself is a needed ingredient. Having acknowledged that, my principal concern here is within the ambit of DH as an instance of the development of doctrine. I argue that there are three controlling concepts (one anthropological, the other two, moral) in DH that, themselves, can be seen in a developmental framework. I begin by exposing key ideas in two foundational articles of DH on the relationship of truth and freedom. On that basis, the discussion will focus on, respectively, the human person, rights and, finally, practical reason in relation to DH and doctrinal development.

---

[1] This chapter was originally published as 'Declaration on Religious Freedom: Three Developmental Aspects', *Solidarity: The Journal of Catholic Social Thought and Secular Ethics* 8:2 (2018): 1-13, online journal.

[2] See Nicholas J Healy, 'Dignitatis Humanae' in Matthew L Lamb and Matthew Levering, *The Reception of Vatican II* (UK: Oxford University Press, 2017) 1-34 from www.oxfordscholarship.com Also, Ladislas Orsy, SJ, 'The Divine Dignity of Human Persons in Dignitatis humanae', *Theological Studies* 75:1 (2014): 8-22.

[3] Barry Hudock, *Struggle, Condemnation, Vindication: John Courtney Murray's Journey toward Vatican II* (Collegeville, MN: Liturgical Press, 2015), 155. This is a gripping account of the development of Murray's thought, his personal struggle, the other 'combatants' (Joseph Clifford Fenton and Francis A Connell), his rejection and ultimate vindication by the promulgation of DH.

Foundational Article

As already noted, there are more extensive analyses and evaluations of *Dignitatis Humanae* (DH). For the purposes of this book, the most appropriate starting point is article 2 of DH. There we find three interwoven ideas: the dignity of the human person; the duty to seek the truth; the freedom (and rights) essential in appropriating truth through the mediation of conscience.

These three elements are succinctly distilled in art. 2. The right to religious freedom is grounded in 'the very dignity of the human person as known through the revealed Word of God and by reason itself'. The dignity of persons is understood as 'beings endowed with reason and free will' with the privilege of bearing 'personal responsibility—that all men (sic) should be at once impelled by nature and also bound by moral obligation to seek the truth, especially religious truth'. There is a consequent duty to 'adhere to the truth once it is known' and to 'order their whole lives' in accordance with its demands'.

These obligations, however, can only be discharged in a 'manner in keeping with (their) own nature' only if 'they enjoy immunity from external coercion as well as psychological freedom'. The right to religious freedom has its foundation 'not in the subjective disposition of the person, but in his every nature'. The exercise of this right should not be 'impeded', with due care taken to preserve public order. Importantly, 'the right to this immunity continues to exist even in those who do not live up to their obligation of seeking the truth and adhering to it'.[4]

In art. 3, the specific implications of art. 2 are spelt out. Every person's duty to seek the truth 'in matters religious', has a correlative right: the interplay of duty and right is needed so that a person may 'with prudence form for himself right and true judgments of conscience, with the use of all suitable means'. It is by such means the human person can 'participate' in the divine law and come to an increasing grasp of the truth 'under the gentle disposition of divine Providence'.[5]

The first wing of human dignity concerns the truth: the second wing balancing it is freedom. Seeking the truth is to be done in a 'manner proper to the dignity of the human person and his social nature'. Search for, and inquiry into, the truth must be free. It is carried out through instruction, communication, explanation, and dialogue. While it is a shared quest, 'as the truth is discovered, it is by personal assent that men are to adhere to it'.

---

[4] 'Declaration on Religious Freedom' (*Dignitatis Humanae*) in *The Documents of Vatican II*, ed. Walter M Abbott, SJ (New York: Guild Press, 1966), 672-700, art. 2, at 679-80 (henceforth DH). Murray did the translation, introduction, and annotations of the document in this publication. One reviewer suggested the possible use of an inclusive language rendition of the Vatican II documents. Unfortunately, I did not have access to that version.

[5] DH, art. 3, 680.

Central here is the role of conscience: the human person 'perceives and acknowledges the imperatives of the divine law through the mediation of conscience'. In everything we do, we are bound to follow our conscience faithfully in order to come to God, for whom we were created'. It follows that no one is to be forced to act 'contrary to his conscience' nor be restrained from acting in accord with conscience, 'especially in matters religious'.[6] This is the foundation of religious freedom in the public and legislative sphere. It embraces the private and public domains, whether 'alone or in association with others, within due limits'.[7]

Mgr. Pietro Pavan, one of the theologians who collaborated with Fr. Murray in the draft and defense of the Declaration, states in his commentary: 'Article 2 is undoubtedly the most important article of the Declaration'.[8] He goes on to say that:

> the right to religious freedom must be regarded as *a fundamental right of the human person or as a natural right, that is one grounded in the very nature of man*, as the Declaration itself repeats several times.[9]

Our discussion can be guided by Pavan's comment.

Personhood

We noted above that religious freedom is grounded in 'the very dignity of the human person as known through the revealed Word of God and by reason itself'. Ladislas Orsy opens his article on the 'divine' dignity of the person in *Dignitatis Humanae* by citing French Benedictine Ghislain Lafont: 'the history of the Christian churches is perhaps the history of their struggle to believe finally in man' (sic). [10] He goes on to observe that Christ died because he 'believed' in the human person.[11] Lafont's observation suggests further considerations.

We are guided by the phrase 'the very dignity of the human person' (art. 2). Elsewhere, the Council Fathers say that human dignity is grounded in the God-

---

[6] DH, art. 3, 680-81.

[7] DH, art. 2, 679.

[8] H Vorgrimler, ed. *Commentary on the Documents of Vatican II* (New York: Herder and Herder, 1968), 4: 64.

[9] Ibid., 65; emphasis in original.

[10] Orsy, 'The Divine Dignity', 8, citing Ghislain Lafont's original French: 'L'histoire des Églises est peut-être celle d'un combat pour finalement croire en homme', in *L'Église en travail de réforme*, Imaginer l'Église catholique (Paris: Cerf, 2011), 23.

[11] So too, Pope St John Paul II sees 'this' (each individual) man is the primary and fundamental way of the Church' *Redemptor Hominis* (Boston, MA: St Paul, 1979), no. 14.

like nature of the human person as created 'to God's image' referring to Gen 1:26.[12] This is not simply a semblance or 'mirror image', as Orsy explains, but a 'replica' of God, as a child is a replica or 'reproduction' of its parents.[13] Yet, in the theological tradition, 'image' has a stronger sense; it is a mode of participation in God that that comes to full realization ('in the likeness') through dominion over our eternal destiny in sharing in the life of the Son.[14] Hence, as Orsy notes, 'the divine dignity of persons' in Vatican II continues the patristic tradition of 'divinisation'. [15]

Helpful here are insights from Bernard McGinn. He points out that Christian thought has contained three main understandings of the nature of humanity as an image of God. The intellectual approach founds the image essentially in the human being's gift of reason and intelligence as a sharing in divine knowing such that it sets humanity apart from other creatures. The volitional tradition, while not denying the cognitive aspect, places more emphasis on the human ability to act freely where, to be *imago dei*, is to share in God's freedom. The third approach accentuates interpersonal relationships. Here, created in God's image and likeness means being called to share in the self-transcending love of the Trinity and to communicate this love to others.[16]

McGinn sums up the *imago dei* anthropology as involving a) the dignity given to all human beings 'in their capacity as God's image' and b) the dignity as the duty to engage in the goal-oriented free exercise of freedom flowing from the gift of that image.[17] Orsy reflects those aspects from another angle. While human dignity emerges from 'the God-like nature of a human person (hence, it is universal), the authenticity of a human person is grounded in her or his integrity

---

[12] '…in our own image, in the likeness of ourselves'. The biblical text proceeds to say that the image is exercised in having stewardship over creation and in the capacity for relationships.

[13] Orsy, 'The Divine Dignity', 15.

[14] *Summa Theologica* 1.35. 2 (henceforth ST). For translations of the Summa, the author has consulted the *Summa Theologica* of St. Thomas Aquinas, 2nd rev. ed. 1920, translated by Fathers of the English Dominican Province in the on-line version www.newadvent.org/summa/ and the new translation by Alfred J Freddoso, on-line version at http://www.nd.edu/~afreddos/summa-translation/TOC.htm accessed 20/12/2017. Unless indicated, translations are from the Freddoso version. Summaries or paraphrases are the author's.

[15] Orsy, 'The Divine Dignity', 15, n. 15.

[16] Bernard McGinn, 'Humans as *Imago* Dei: Mystical Anthropology Then and Now', in Edward Howells and Peter Tyler, *Sources of Transformation: Revitalising Christian Spirituality* (London, UK: Continuum, 2010), 19-40, at 23-4.

[17] McGinn, 'Humans as Imago Dei', 33.

(hence, it is personal)'.[18] Orsy notes that while 'integrity' is not used in DH, the concern for the sincere search for truth and goodness (and choices made to that end) is a central aspect of the document. In other words, its focus is on the volitional aspect of *imago dei*—our next concern.

We have noted earlier that, central to the argument in this Declaration (and in Murray's thought), is the understanding of the human person.[19] As noted above, in the document, the dignity of persons has a precise focus, namely, as beings endowed with reason, free will and capable of personal responsibility. The Declaration is not offering a comprehensive treatment of the dignity of the human person. Its context is provided by the opening lines of the Declaration, namely, that the 'dignity of the human person has been impressing itself more and more deeply on the consciousness of contemporary man' (sic). There is an increasing demand that human beings should act 'on their own judgment', make use of 'responsible freedom, driven, not be 'coercion' but 'motivated by a sense of duty'.[20]

In the Catholic tradition, much discussion on the human subject, for some centuries, had been couched in terms of the substance/accident distinction of Aristotle. A person or '*suppositum*' (supposit) is a being that subsists by itself. Hence, we find in Aquinas, the traditional definition of Boethius: a suppositum (person) is 'an individual substance of a rational nature'.[21] The underlying assumption was that a 'person' was so constituted as a) rational (intellect and will) and b) as a specific instantiation of what is held in common, namely, a human nature.

But, as is implied in the various aspects of *imago dei* explained by McGinn, there is needed an account of the human subject that incorporates what is unique. Each human being is not just one example of something held in common—a human nature. Each human being is rational, certainly, but also distinctive, irreplaceable and, importantly, relational, in other words, a *person*. This final quality, muted in the Boethius definition, is more developed in Aquinas through his treatment of the Trinity and of the human being as *imago dei*—to which we now turn.

Qualities of Personal Existence

Elements of the Aristotelian/Thomistic tradition are clearly detectable in articles 2-8 of DH and its theological anthropology. Aquinas, too, engaged in the

---

[18] Orsy, 'The Divine Dignity', 15.

[19] Murray's more philosophical rationale is reflected in Ch 2 and the influence of European theologians (with a more biblical and patristic approach) in Ch. 3. See Hudock, *Struggle, Condemnation, Vindication*, 131.

[20] DH, introduction, 673.

[21] *ST* 1.29. 1.

'struggle' to 'believe in man'. At the very beginning of his discussion on the persons of the Trinity, Aquinas speaks of the human person (viz., that which subsists in a rational nature) as 'that which is the most perfect in all of nature'.[22] While he does not appear to pursue this thought in further detail, elsewhere there are clues that Aquinas sought and anticipated a dynamic and existentially grounded approach to the human person congruent with this observation.

In his discussion of precisely this point, Norris Clarke is our guide. For Aquinas, an individual rational nature needs more, namely, that it be 'a complete, actually existing being with its own act of existence which renders it the ultimate, autonomous source of its own actions'. In other words, this is a rational being who is *self-possessing*, encapsulated in the phrase 'master of itself' (*dominus sui*), who is self-aware, self-directing and morally responsible, even if these are exercised as part of a journey to wholeness 'ever imperfect and incomplete'. [23]

Personal existence involves not only self-presence but also presence to others, hence, is relational and social. Human self-presence must be awakened by being open to the world of others, to be 'awakened by their action on it and their own active response', hence, in mutual relations with others. The person is *self-communicative*.

Third, the self must have an intentionality toward another than oneself. All 'knowing and loving is a 'transcending of one's own self limits' (whether horizontally or vertically). A person, then, is *self-transcending.* [24]

Such an understanding of the person illuminates the Vatican Council's statement that 'authentic freedom' as 'an exceptional sign of the divine image within man', namely, 'that he acts according to a knowing and a free choice'.[25] We find antecedents for such a statement in the patristic authors (as McGinn explained) and in Aquinas, as we have discussed above. Aquinas introduces his extensive treatise on the moral life with a summary of this earlier discussion and a pointer to his next stage (drawing on St John Damascene): having spoken of the exemplar (God), it is time to speak of the divine image, namely, the human person as an intellectual and free being but, importantly, as self-directing (*per se potestativus*).[26]

---

[22] *ST* 1.29. 3. The quoted phrase applies to rational creatures and super-eminently to God.

[23] See T Norris Clarke. 'To be is to be self-communicative: St. Thomas' view of personal being', *Theology Digest* 33:4 (Winter) 1986: 441-452, at 444-5.

[24] Clarke. 'To be is to be self-communicative', 446-450.

[25] *Gaudium et Spes* in *The Documents of Vatican II*, ed. Walter M Abbott, SJ, (New York: Guild Press, 1966), 183-316, no.17, at 214.

[26] *ST*. 1.2. prol.

It must be remembered that, as Aquinas notes, 'exemplar' is a more 'proper' description of the Trinity in whose 'image' humans are made. Whereas the Son is the 'perfect image of the Father', so humans are made 'in the divine image' in having a certain tendency to perfection, namely, realizing the image by sharing the life of the Son. This is realized through knowing and loving God such that we share in God's own life.[27] By implication, the self-directing capacity is, as we have seen, also self-communicative and self-transcending. This process entails a three- stage movement of the human being: as 'image' by nature; growing towards 'likeness' in grace (virtue); and, finally, in glory.[28]

Personhood, then, for Aquinas, is both a state and a task, one characterized by the drive to reach out beyond the self—in seeking truth, goodness and, crucially, through love: 'to lose oneself in order to find oneself'. The gifts of rationality, self-direction in freedom and conscience are at the service of the person through the thrust towards self-transcendence, especially in its moral expression in relationships, specifically through love and justice (the highest of the cardinal virtues).[29] It is precisely in the possession and exercise of these rational and relational gifts that the human person is made in the divine image and grows into the divine likeness. To this end, also, as implied in Pavan's comment above, there is an integral role for rights—our next consideration.

Rights

What is the foundation of human dignity according to DH article 2? It is a person's relationship with God, especially, its religious dimension in that one is created to 'come to God', to share in the divine law, through the faithful following of conscience. There is an associated duty to seek the truth (especially the truth about God) to achieve that goal and pursued through adherence and assent that is free— in terms of psychological freedom and external coercion.

The right to religious freedom, then, is integral to the responsibility to seek the truth and to how it is appropriated, namely, with immunity from coercion. The right is natural, is absolute and inalienable, cannot be removed or surrendered— because it has a transcendent foundation and purpose, namely, the personal relationship with God. To obey the law written in the human heart by God 'is the very dignity of man; according to it he will be judged'.[30]

Religious freedom can be seen in terms of a balance of the duty and the 'right' to seek the truth. In so doing, there is the complementarity of the objective and

---

[27] *ST* 1.35.1 and 1 35. 2.

[28] *ST* 1.93.4 and 135.2 and 3.

[29] *ST* 1.2.58.12.

[30] *Gaudium et Spes* in Abbott, *The Documents*, 213.

the subjective, the two poles within which freedom of conscience must be understood.[31] In considering 'rights', we have recourse to the ideas of J C Murray that informed the text of DH—the next consideration.

John Courtney Murray and the Subject of Rights

DH exemplifies a conviction of Murray; rights could not be attributed to abstract terms such as error or truth, as in 'error has no rights' and, conversely, 'the exclusive rights of truth'. Rights could be 'predicated only of persons (or of institutions').[32] Such a distinction does not appear, *prima facie,* to be particularly innovative.

For the contemporary reader such language may seem rather puzzling. Its significance, in this context, is better appreciated in the light of an underlying issue. If the Church believes that it is the unique bearer of divine revelation in the name of Jesus Christ, it has a claim (right) to be the medium of the truth. What is the Church's relationship to other cultural and religious traditions? How can it articulate its relationship to society and the governmental authority if the state is confessional (Catholic), or, alternatively, non-confessional (a Church in the minority)? What or who is the subject of rights in that context?

In earlier writings, Murray grappled with this Church/State question by returning to its fifth century Gelasian foundations about what is permanent teaching and what is historically conditioned on this matter.[33] Concerning Church and State, there was an 'in-house' Catholic terminology, namely, 'thesis/hypothesis' that can be traced back to Boethius (c. CE 475-526).[34]

---

[31] As theologians, and later Popes, Paul VI, John Paul II, and Benedict XVI participated in the conciliar debates on the question of religious freedom. Each emphasized the fundamental importance of the right to religious freedom and sought to implement and develop DH's teaching. Contemporary discussion has probed further the relationship between freedom and truth and its ontological foundations. Some (e.g., Philippe André-Vincent and David L Schindler) consider the relationship between truth and freedom and the person's relation to truth as foundational for human dignity and as 'informing religious freedom'. Others such as Murray, Pavan and Martin Rhonheimer hold that religious freedom is a formally 'juridical concept' and does not concern 'the person's relationship to truth'. See Healy, 'Dignitatis Humanae', 4, 8,16-25.

[32] Hudock, *Struggle, Condemnation, Vindication,* 35, 133. See full discussion in John Courtney Murray, 'The Problem of Religious Freedom', *Theological Studies* 25:4 (December), 1964: 503-573, at 508-510 et passim.

[33] In 494 CE, Pope Gelasius I wrote a letter *Famuli vestrae pietatis* which laid the basis for the relationship between priestly spiritual authority and secular temporal authority for a millennium. The letter is often referred to in shorthand as 'Duo Sunt' and by Murray as 'Two There Are'.

[34] The words *thesis* and *hypothesis* were used by Boethius to describe two forms of communication. The first, Dialectic concerns what is universally true, regardless of the circumstances. Logic and syllogistic argument are used to make the truth clear, even to those

In the accepted view, the 'thesis' (or ideal) was the 'confessional state' where governments recognized Catholicism's unique status yet could place restrictions on other denominations. With the 'hypothesis' (or the exception, namely, a particular historical situation, where the Church was in a minority, for example in the USA), freedom of religion was a needed accommodation. Importantly, Murray viewed the thesis/hypothesis approach not as firm doctrine but as 'received opinion' (a matter we will pursue later).[35] As noted earlier, he disagreed with its underlying assumptions, namely, that exclusive rights applied to truth whereas 'error has no rights'.[36]

The hot point of disagreement is captured in the phrase noted above: 'the right to this immunity (from external coercion) continues to exist even in those who do not live up to their obligation of seeking the truth and adhering to it' provided there is due care to 'preserve public order' (art.2). This epitomizes the standing of the right to religious freedom (whether personal or social) as 'natural', namely, bound up with the inherent dignity of the person.

It is further captured in the same status accorded those who are in a state of invincible error or ignorance regarding the truth—our next consideration.

A Person Honestly Mistaken?

As a document discussed in the previous chapter notes, it can happen that 'conscience frequently errs from invincible ignorance without losing its dignity'.[37] Later, Pope St John Paul II expands this by saying that conscience maintains its dignity because:

> even when it directs us to act in a way not in conformity with the objective moral order, it continues to speak in the name of that *truth about the good* which the subject is called *to seek sincerely*.[38]

Such a statement does not relieve a person of the consequences of their actions, as in the case of a person causing damage to another, albeit without blame or fault. At the heart of what Pope St John Paul II says is the ongoing correlation of the

---

'who do not wish to accept it'. Dialectic's realm is *thesis*. Conversely, *hypothesis* is the concern of Rhetoric which gives attention to the circumstances and surrounding context and uses 'approximations to persuade the listener'. See Hudock, *Struggle, Condemnation, Vindication,* 13 citing Richard McKeon, 'Rhetoric in the Middle Ages', *Speculum* 17:1 (January), 1942: 1-32, at 10-11.

[35] Hudock, *Struggle, Condemnation, Vindication,* 17.

[36] The 'thesis/hypothesis' model with its grounding in abstract terms such as 'truth' and 'error' as the subject of rights was a key dividing point between Murray and other theologians such as Joseph Clifford Fenton and Francis J Connell.

[37] *Gaudium et Spes* 16 cited in *Veritatis Splendor* (Homebush, NSW, 1993), 62 (Henceforth *VS)*.

[38] *VS,* 62; my emphasis.

duty to seek the truth and the right to appropriate it freely. The authentic nature of the search is preserved by the 'sincere' or genuine desire to seek 'the truth about the good'. In the last analysis, it is the direction of the will that guarantees the dignity of the person when they are honestly mistaken. In other words, such a person is in 'good faith'. This is a reminder that the inviolability of the person in the exercise of conscience applies to God too. God respects the freedom of the being 'made in his image and likeness'.

Aquinas' Views?

This position is in continuity with a long-standing tradition. Seven hundred years earlier, Thomas Aquinas acknowledged the limit case of someone who strives to know what is right yet arrives at a position in which their conscience is at odds with Church teaching. For Aquinas, contra Peter Lombard, such a person should die excommunicated rather than violate their conscience.[39] Again, it would be wrong for someone, he says, to believe in Jesus Christ when this is erroneously apprehended as a bad thing. By acting against conscience, according to St Thomas, and the tradition of the Church, one would commit sin.[40]

Aquinas' position on conscience, which is standard in Catholic moral theology today, broke with the tradition of his time (including his own teacher St Albert the Great) and marked a moment of development. Though his insistence on this approach to conscience, Thomas represented an awakening in medieval consciousness of interiority and personal consciousness and its repercussions in moral and psychological existence.[41] As Walker Bynum sums it up: it is the twelfth century that discovered, within in a relational rather than an individualistic anthropology, 'the self, the inner mystery, the inner man, the inner landscape'.[42]

Again, regarding the moral life, the judgment of conscience and divine respect for our freedom and the human condition, Aquinas foreshadows another future development. Aquinas anticipates Vatican II's teaching with his view that 'each human being who achieves a mature self-determination, in so doing either turns to God and enters into divine grace with the remission of original sin, or culpably

---

[39] *Scriptum super Libros Sententiarum,* IV, 38.2.4 q. a 3 (exposition). Also, *Quolibetales* 3.12.2; *de Veritate* 17,4; 4 and 5; *In Galatians* Ch 5:1. It is worth noting, as does Orsy, that DH does not address the issue of a believer who finds themselves, in good faith, unable assent to a certain matter of Church teaching. Orsy suggests that such situations must be dealt with on a one-to-one basis as guided by equity and prudence. See Orsy, 'The Divine Dignity', 18-19.

[40] *ST* 1.2. I9. 5.

[41] See M D Chenu, OP, *L'Éveil de la conscience dans la civilisation medi*évale (Paris: Vrin, 1969), p.54.

[42] Caroline Walker Bynum, 'Did the Twelfth Century Discover the Individual?' In *Jesus as Mother: Studies in the Spirituality of the High Middle Ages* (Berkeley: University of California Press,1982), 82-109, at 105-6.

turns from God by not doing 'what within him lies'.[43] In citing this text, John Thornhill is illustrating Aquinas' 'noteworthy' view about the Spirit's action beyond the boundaries of the Church. His position, remarkable for its time and not representative of prevailing views, is another instance of how Aquinas was part of the struggle 'to believe in man'—highlighted by Lafont as emerging in the 12th. century and after (noted earlier).

Still, that 'struggle' to believe in the human person is multifaceted—our next concern.

Steps Leading to Modernity

Returning to religious freedom in a social and political context, we must keep in mind that there is a variety of human rights' traditions (e.g., Western liberal, Marxist, developing world approaches).

In this diversity, looking back, we can detect a developmental trajectory. Kasper points out that explicit talk of 'human rights' is peculiar to the modern period but that the associated ideas are as old as Christianity. Rather than the 'image of God' confined to the king or ruler, it was now 'democratized' to include every person 'irrespective of race, people, sex, or culture'.[44] Rights can be traced back to the 'dignity' of the human being created in the image and likeness of God (Gen 1:26) and strengthened by the covenant between God and humankind. So understood, human dignity is inviolable and inalienable, no matter how much it may be violated by oneself or others.

Such an approach offered a starting point for a secular theory of human rights. The Jewish understanding of the Torah, deepened by the New Testament ethos, displays a 'basic openness to human rights thinking'. It is only in modern times that the legal and political implications of this were systematically elaborated. [45]

Again, it must be remembered that the notion of rights remains a contested issue, particularly when it concerns their foundation and, consequently, their scope and limits. In the liberal political tradition, as represented by Robert Nozick, the emphasis is on the individual and freedom, with rights protected by the state but with minimal interference in personal freedom.[46] Alternatively, a shared life in a community and the natural duties from such bonds underpin what seems to

---

[43] John Thornhill, 'A Wholesome Agnosticism and Christianity's Coming Dialogue with the World Religions', *Pacifica* 6 (1993): 265-277, at 267 citing *ST* 1.2. 89. 6, corp. & ad 1.

[44] Walter Kasper 'The Theological Foundation of Human Rights' in *Human Rights and the Church: Historical and Theological Reflections* (Pontifical Council for Justice and Peace, Vatican City, 1990), 47-71, at 49, 55.

[45] Thomas Hoppe, 'Human Rights' in Judith A Dwyer, ed. *The New Dictionary of Catholic Social Thought* (Collegeville, MN: Liturgical Press/Michael Glazier, 1994), 454-470, at 455-6.

[46] Robert Nozick, *Anarchy, State, and Utopia* (New York: Basic Books, 1974).

be a more communitarian approach, as found in Michael Sandel in his criticisms of social democratic liberals John Rawls and Ronald Dworkin.[47]

Contested Views of Rights

Different (and debated) approaches to rights (their foundation and scope) also apply to Catholic theological discourse since Vatican II, even within a Thomistic framework. Authors such as Alasdair MacIntyre (and Tracey Rowland) find the use of 'rights' language problematic. Any claim to, or discussion of, rights cannot be isolated from a particular tradition nor be immune from the formative impact of culture and historical context (a flaw with classical Thomism). 'Rights' language in the context of Liberalism puts the focus on 'right' in the subjective sense, 'my claim' against another. This contrasts with the more classical and Thomistic sense of the objective sense of *ius,* namely, *what is right* or *due* to a person.

Underlying the first (Liberal) is a view of personhood as essentially autonomous and self-creative. The second (natural law) view sees self-development as founded on a gift—a call from God to share divine life in a receptivity to divine and human interactions. MacIntyre and Rowland are concerned that reading the natural law tradition within the Liberal framework while adopting the language of modernity distorts, even marginalizes, the classical tradition and the Catholic narrative. This is particularly relevant to social responsibility and the common good.[48]

Church and Religious Freedom

Having acknowledged the debates around the origin, nature, and scope of human rights, we return to the religious freedom issue and DH. In the context of Church, State, and social life in the modern period, it is wholesome to note Murray's comment about religious freedom: 'In all honesty, it must be admitted that the Church is late in acknowledging the validity of the principle'.[49]

Naturally, the Church's resistance to the principle must be understood in its historical context and the movements inimical to the Church, particularly in the post-enlightenment period and in nineteenth century Europe. With the changing context of the new world (especially the United States) and of post-revolutionary Europe, 'freedom' and 'secular' took on less antagonistic meanings. As with the United States, for instance, it was possible to have a situation of religious pluralism that was not divisive or subversive of the common good and social cohesion. For all that, the historical record clearly indicates how the Church's

---

[47] Michael Sandel, *Liberalism and the Limits of Justice* (Cambridge, UK/ New York: Cambridge University Press. 1998).

[48] Tracey Rowland, *Culture and the Thomist Tradition after Vatican II* (London, UK: Routledge, 2003), 148-155.

[49] Introduction to *Dignitatis Humanae* in Abbott, *The Documents of Vatican II*, 673.

thinking on, and attitude to, human rights in a more secular context gradually evolved from rejection, to discernment, to dialogue and, finally, to proclamation.[50]

Underlying the debate and the Declaration (DN), then, was the Church's own self-understanding, particularly in its stance toward the modern world, shaped by the Enlightenment and post-revolutionary Europe. This applied, most especially, to human and political rights. Central for Murray (and others), was the need for the Church to engage with, and learn from, democratic institutions since, with their emergence, the civil order 'grew up'. It is through such institutions that people 'govern themselves'.[51] Such arrangements provide the context where the worth of persons together with the shared and conscientious pursuit of truth and the common good are best realized. This brings us to the next consideration.

Practical Reason and the Development of Doctrine

The opening sentence of art.1 sets the tone and direction of DH: 'a sense of the dignity of the human person has been impressing itself more and more deeply on the consciousness of contemporary man'.

Before addressing the main issue in this section of the chapter, some brief observations are triggered by the above quote. It reflects a pattern of the Council itself as 'characterized by a sense of history, an awareness of the concrete world of fact, and a disposition to see in historical facts certain "signs of the times"'.[52] It is, then, an expression of 'historical consciousness'. Murray himself drew on Bernard Lonergan's binary of 'historical' compared with 'classical' consciousness.[53] The Gelasian thesis/hypothesis framework of how the 'ideal' and the 'particular historical situation' are related was formulated from within a 'classical consciousness' and its strong sense of stability and permanence.[54] Murray offers persuasive evidence of historical consciousness at work in the developing pattern of thought from Leo XIII, through Pius XII into John XXIII

---

[50] See Sandie Cornish, *From Rejection to Proclamation,* ACSJC website www.socialjustice.catholic.org.au Her discussion draws on Monsignor Franco Biffi, 'Human Rights in the Magisterium of the Popes of the Twentieth Century', in *Human Rights a Christian Approach,* (International Federation of Catholic Universities Research Coordination Centre, Manilla, 1988).

[51] Hudock, *Struggle, Condemnation, Vindication,*45.

[52] n. 2 in DH, Abbott, *The Documents of Vatican II*, 675.

[53] Bernard F Lonergan, 'The Transition from a Classicist World-View to Historical Mindedness' in *A Second Collection,* eds. William F Ryan and Bernard Tyrrell (Philadelphia: Westminster, 1974), 1-9.

[54] Murray, 'The Problem'…560.

with specific reference to truth, justice, love, rights and, especially concerning religious freedom.[55]

DH is grounded in historical sensitivity to where Holy Spirit is at work in surrounding culture and in events—a *locus theologicus*—as, for instance, in the emergence of democratic institutions noted above. Such shifts and movements can provide the context of the 'new order of human relations' in the unfolding of God's plan ('inscrutable designs') proclaimed by John XXIII in opening Vatican II in 1962.

Again, it must be remembered that while, within the 'classical' consciousness period, the intellectual tools of 'historical consciousness' associated with the modern period had not yet emerged (e.g., the rise of the individual, prevailing pattern of change and development), the Spirit was still at work. It was also true that people, in religious and cultural traditions beyond the Church, were trying to live 'according to their lights' and searching for the truth 'in good faith'— something appreciated by Aquinas, as we have noted.

This brings us to the final issue—DH as an example of development of doctrine. This was at the heart of the 'struggle' and contestation that involved Murray, Fenton, Connell, and the bishops themselves at the Council debates. Divided opinions reign during and since the Council.[56] Is DH a development or is it reversal and, even, a contradiction of doctrine?

Murray, Doctrinal Development and Religious Freedom

On this matter, it might be helpful to examine the relationship between *prudence and divine providence* to see how much that has a bearing on the Declaration itself. As noted earlier, DH states that we come to share gradually in the divine law through the guidance of divine providence in the exercise of prudential judgment. This converges with Aquinas' view (noted in the previous chapter), that we are called to share actively in divine Providence through the virtue of prudence.[57] In other words, we are in the realm of practical reason—helpful, here, in approaching DH and how it can be understood in terms of the development (and not the reversal) of doctrine.

As explained above, the hypothesis/thesis model was offered as a framework to understand the ideal when the boundaries of church and empire were coextensive and under the Divine law and its various human expressions (natural, positive law). For Gelasius and John of Paris (1255-1306), a civil ruler has real

---

[55] Murray, 'The Problem ', 533-555. Also, Abbott, ed. DH, n. 21.

[56] See Healy, 'Dignitatis Humanae', 9-10.

[57] *ST* 1.2.91.2 where Aquinas says: 'Now among all creatures, the rational creature is subject to divine providence in a more excellent manner, because he himself participates in providence, providing for himself and for others'. See also *ST* 1.103. 6 and 8.

and distinct power (from God and not by delegation from the Pope) in areas of 'peace, justice and prosperity for the people'.[58] The concern was for what was 'due' to the spiritual and temporal realms in terms of the exercise of power and authority. At stake, then, were matters of justice; of equity, of fairness, and, hence, within the arena of practical reason.

The thesis/hypothesis approach, so understood, appeared to see itself as a matter of 'firm doctrine', namely, considered simply as a matter of certainty of faith through speculative reason. But could it also be viewed as a matter of moral certainty from practical reason? As such, any model (or judgment) can subsequently be revised in the light of changed circumstances and other variables.[59] This could be another way of expressing Murray's view of the thesis/hypothesis model as 'received opinion'.

The 'practical reason' methodology was suggested in 1964 by Murray himself in an extensive and detailed analysis of the approaches to the religious freedom issue.[60] He couches his discussion in terms of the 'First' or thesis/hypothesis approach with its associated view of the abstract terms 'error' and 'truth' claiming rights versus the 'Second' or person-based view of rights as adopted in DH.

A Needed Distinction?

In his discussion, Murray offers a helpful distinction related to the 'Second' view.[61] There is the 'conceptual' question: in the light of contemporary historical existence, what is religious freedom and its correlate, constitutional government? The task here is to clarify the nature of freedom, conscience (viz. of personal religious decisions; of its social nature) and the free exercise of religion. The latter embraces the distinction between sacred/secular; society/state; common good/public order and, finally, the freedom of all under the law (and, ultimately, divine law). This question of definition is concerned with meaning and truth—the level of certainty associated with speculative reason.

---

[58] Hudock, *Struggle, Condemnation, Vindication*, 39-40.

[59] See a parallel in Neil Ormerod's discussion of Jesus, salvation, and Church structures. Ormerod makes the point that Church structures 'are not an end in themselves but means to an end of salvation. Their 'truth' is not the truth of speculative intellect, which is 'Yes/No' but of practical reason which is 'good/better/worse'. In that sense they have a certain provisionality to them, even if we trace them back to the will of Jesus. This allows us to consider say the three-fold order of ministry or the papacy in terms of the good they are meant to achieve rather than as an arbitrary structure imposed by Jesus as the only way the Church can operate. This then can provide a standard or norm against which to measure their effectiveness in practice and so on'. See Neil Ormerod, 'The Knowledge and Authority of Jesus—a Response to Bishop Robinson', *The Australasian Catholic Record* 88:1 (2011): 88-97, at 96.

[60] Murray, 'The Problem', 503-573.

[61] Ibid., 516-531.

Relevant here are the distinctions just noted between state/society and public order/common good. For Murray, the state is only 'one order within society, the order of public law and political administration'.[62] The state's role is to be serve society, not just through ensuring public order, at times, through legitimate application of coercive powers, but in relation to promoting the common good. As Murray explains, 'the common good includes all the social goods, spiritual and moral as well as material, which man pursues here on earth in accord with the demands of his personal and social nature'.

The pursuit of the common good, then, is the responsibility of all its members and its institutions 'in accord with the principles of subsidiarity, legal justice, and distributive justice'.[63] Religious freedom, then, is not just a matter of a personal and natural right. It is also integral to the common good that personal conscience be immune from coercion in its internal religious decisions. 'Even the Church, which has authority to oblige conscience, has no power to coerce it'.[64]

Practical Reason at Work

Having considered the 'conceptual' perspective concerned with meaning and truth with the 'Second' view, we move on to the 'judgment' question which, argues Murray, affirms the validity of religious freedom in a social context, specifically as expressed in constitutional government. This question's concern is effectiveness and value. Here, to justify religious freedom is not make it an ideal—a claim never made in constitutional law.[65] It is a judgment exercised within the framework of law. Law, as Aristotle and Aquinas remind us, is an ordinance of reason for the common good. As 'reasonable' it is measured against the criterion of the purpose it is meant to achieve, namely, the good of the community. Another way of saying this is offered by Murray citing Aquinas (who

---

[62] Murray, 'The Problem', 520.

[63] Ibid., 520-1.

[64] Ibid., 523. The issues discussed in this paragraph are part of the more extensive treatment of Murray's *We Hold These Truths*. They are also found elaborated in Murray's annotations on DH (Abbott edition) especially nn. 4-20, at 684-686. They have an ongoing relevance in the contemporary world concerning the Church in relation to secular society. For instance, current events in the United States have highlighted the role of Catholic politicians who are involved in the administration of governmental laws that they may not personally agree with, for instance, abortion.

[65] 'Traditional philosophies of politics, law, and jurisprudence do not recognize any such thing as an ideal instance of constitutional law. By reason of the very nature of law, the issue of the ideal never arises. The function of law, as the Jurist said, is to be useful to men. Necessity or usefulness for the common good—these are the norms of law'. Murray, 'The Problem', 515.

draws on Isidore of Seville—the 'Jurist'): the function of law is to be *useful* to people. Later, in the same article, Aquinas makes the comment that, in assessing the nature of a law and its purpose as 'useful', consideration must be given to what is 'appropriate to the time and the place'.[66]

In other words, the criteria of judgment about religious freedom are not the ideal/the tolerable, thesis/hypothesis, principle/expedience (the First View). Rather, the overarching benchmark is the 'reasonable'—what is useful and practical in relation to the law's purpose. This locates the question in the realm of practical reason and of prudential judgment. Or as Murray says 'the good and the bad, the just and the unjust, the more or less just and the more or less unjust' (the Second View), hence, by implication, subject to review. Importantly, such an approach ensures 'there a single standard equally applicable to any order of constitutional law'.[67]

In the last analysis, then, the Church/State issue is one of justice in the relationship between two orders of competence, the sacred and the secular. These are within the overarching norm of 'divine law—eternal, objective, and universal, whereby God orders, directs, and governs the entire'—and which humans 'are called to participate through 'the gentle disposition of Divine Providence'.[68]

But, as explained above, the Church/State question also entails the relationship between religious freedom's meaning and its justified and effective application. Variables and relevant factors may lead to a different prudential judgment about action and legislative formulation in a particular historical situation.

This is the point at which the effectiveness and value of religious freedom have a bearing on shifts in understanding of its meaning and truth, hence, a correlation between practical and speculative reason. Perhaps, in the ongoing debate about doctrine—its development or reversal (as in DH and religious freedom)—such considerations may be helpful.

Conclusion

Our investigation of DH has been in relation to the developmental trajectory in three key issues: the human person, human rights, and practical reason. It has revealed that we can reach back into the theological tradition, as in Aquinas and the Hebrew Scriptures, and find an openness to thinking and appreciation of these issues adumbrated there. Some developments started to become more evident in

---

[66] *ST* 1.2.95.3.

[67] Murray, 'The Problem', 571.

[68] DH, Art 1, 680.

the medieval period, particular with the 12th century renaissance. This process of development continued in the second Vatican Council, in human society and continues to do so today, especially about human dignity and human rights. Lafont's allusion to the struggle to believe 'finally in man' encapsulates the trajectory of that quest.

By probing our heritage, we can situate DH (and Murray) more clearly in terms of the human person, society, the right to religious freedom and the nature of doctrinal development. At the same time, we can better appreciate the Council's desire, by searching sacred tradition and Church teaching, to 'bring forth new things' in harmony with the old, especially more recent papal teaching on the 'inviolable rights of the human person'.[69]

From the foundational nature of conscience and its expression in a specific issue, namely, religious freedom, the focus will again shift in the next chapter. The context within which conscience is at work is that of good and evil. The dark side to conscience is an everyday reality—personally, socially, globally and, as is very apparent now, at the ecclesial level. Our next concern will discuss conscience and sin as represented by the sexual abuse crisis confronting the Catholic Church.

---

[69] DH, art. 1.

3
Conscience, Culture and Sin: A Church in Disgrace

The first two chapters dealt with conscience as a gift and a call for every person to live as a moral being, anchored in the world of relationships. The dignity that undergirds that foundational moral claim on us finds a significant expression in the right to religious freedom, as we have seen.

However, there is a dark side to conscience, one that manifests the corrosive presence of evil in each of us, in society and, as we shall see, in institutions, even religious ones. The world has seen this at work in the Catholic Church in recent times with the sexual abuse crisis.

The profound damage done to the innocent by individuals has been exacerbated by gross moral failure on the part of many Church leaders. At the same time, what has emerged is how evil and sin can infiltrate a culture and shape attitudes and behaviors.

This global phenomenon found a lightning rod in Australia, with the government sponsored Royal Commission into Institutional Responses to Child Sexual Abuse (2013-2017). This event—its findings and outcomes—have generated much reaction and discussion, both within and beyond the Church.

This chapter is an amended version of an article originally published in response to the announcement of the Royal Commission in Australia—with subsequent discussions in the intervening years.[1] I argue that 'Covenant' can act as a 'core' metaphor for the Church's self- understanding and the ethical tasks confronting it with the sexual abuse crisis. I approach this in three stages: first, to outline the general and, second, the specific characteristics of 'Covenant' noting the place of justice and of victims; third, to examine how 'Covenant' can act as a hermeneutical lens concerning the sexual abuse crisis facing the Church, leading to final comments.

---

[1] 'Covenantal Ethics, the Church and the Royal Commission on Sexual Abuse', *Compass: A Review of Topical Theology* 47:1 (Autumn), 2013: 4-13 available at Compass_2013_1_text.indd (compassreview.org). See also my *Shame, Hope and the Church: A Journey with Mary* (Strathfield, NSW: St Pauls Publications, 2020) and my 'Institutional Moral Failure: Emotional Intelligence and Practical Reason Serving Justice', in Claude-Hélène Meyer & Elisabeth Vanderheiden, eds. *Mistakes, Errors and Failures across Cultures: Navigating Potentials* (Springer,2020), 315-328.

Asking a Question

When the Australian Royal Commission was announced in 2012, I found myself wondering: amongst the various approaches in Christian ethics, is there one best suited to help us understand and address the sexual abuse issue and its impact on victims and the Australian Church (and elsewhere)?

Broadly speaking, in our Judeo-Christian heritage, two approaches to theological ethics seem to dominate: the Sapiential with its Hellenistic roots and focus on the individual, rationality, wise judgment and virtue; alternatively, the Covenantal model from the Hebraic context and centered on the community, relationship, love and intimacy.[2] Jesus embodies both: the wise teacher and the loving, compassionate Victim, in solidarity with all victims.

The wisdom approach is consonant with recent emphases in Catholic ethics on the person, conscience, and the virtues. But could we retrieve something from our Jewish roots through 'Covenantal Ethics'? Perhaps, in our current circumstances, the Sapiential tradition is best filtered through the lens of a Covenant community striving, humbly and hesitatingly, to respond to God and others within the framework of right relationships.

I am suggesting, then, that 'Covenant' can act as a 'core' metaphor, employed as both a hermeneutic lens and investigative tool for the Church's self-understanding and the ethical tasks confronting it with the sexual abuse crisis.[3] The first task is to outline the main characteristics of 'Covenant'.

Covenantal Ethics: A General Framework

It is increasingly appreciated that the foundational moral experience is being confronted by the 'other' (whether God, the person or creation as centers of value) who calls us 'out of ourselves, and calls for recognition, respect and response'.[4] In the Christian experience, it is the initiative of God's love reaching out to us and inviting us to respond. This is embodied in the person of Jesus. To answer his

---

[2] I suggest these categories adapting the approach of John Lakers who contrasts the metaphor of intimacy (relationship) with that of power and judgment (rationality). See John J Lakers, OFM, *Christian Ethics: An Ethics of Intimacy* (Quincy, IL: Franciscan Press, 1996), 62-86.

[3] For the use of 'core metaphor' in this manner, see Ormond Rush, *The Eyes of Faith: The Sense of the Faithful and the Church's Reception of Revelation* (Washington DC: The Catholic University of America Press, 2009), 5-7.

[4] Patricia Lamoureux and Paul J Wadell, *Christian Moral Life: faithful disciple for a global society* (Maryknoll, NY: Orbis, 2010), 13. Also, Daniel J Fleming, A*ttentiveness to Vulnerability: A Dialogue Between Emmanuel Levinas, Jean Porter and the Virtue of Solidarity* (Eugene, OR: Wipf and Stock, 2019).

invitation is not a solitary task. It is to become part of a community of faithful disciples.

There are many metaphors used to describe Jesus and his moral quest. Relevant here is that of Jesus as the 'New Covenant'—in the Eucharist, the Church, as mediator between God and humanity. By looking back to the Hebrew view of Covenant, how can we enrich our understanding of our faith community's identity and its associated attitudes and dispositions to the world around us? We do so around four ideas: relationship, gift, inclusive scope, and identity.

Relationship

First, the biblical account of Genesis affirms the Scriptural view that creation and human beings are inherently *relational*. God's call is always one towards life and into relationship. God's desire to be involved in our world, close to us, for our well-being and happiness, is expressed in the call into a Covenant relationship. Its use drew on the cultural experience of the Ancient Near East. Covenants expressed the need to work together effectively in order to ensure peace. The union created by them generated outcomes that take on a richer significance in the Israelite covenant, namely, 'loyalty, service and solidarity'.[5]

Gift

Second, Israel's faith conviction was of union, through a Covenant, with the one true God as the object of God's special love. This was unique in two ways. Nowhere else in the ancient Near East is there found 'the concept of a covenant between divine and human partners'.[6] Further, this covenant's foundation is not an agreement but divine *gift*. This makes the moral universe of Israel radically different from other cultures. Morality is secondary and subsequent to God's founding initiative of a privileged intimate relationship between human beings and God. It is a free response to the Covenant—the revelation of God's purpose and of divine gift.

The Torah (Law), then, as integral to that gift, is not a juridical but a theological concept expressed as the way (*derek*), a journey entered to remain 'in state of covenant'.[7] This revealed moral path continues the primordial and defining experience for God's people in the Exodus, namely, the process of liberation (interior and exterior). This is fulfilled and personified in Jesus. He shows us the way to share in his Paschal mystery, foreshadowed by the Exodus of old Israel.

---

[5] Marilyn M Schaub, 'Covenant', in Carroll Stuhlmuller, ed. *The Collegeville Pastoral Dictionary of Biblical Theology* (Collegeville, MN: The Liturgical Press, 1996), 178-181, at 179.

[6] Pontifical Biblical Commission, *The Bible and Morality: Biblical Roots of Christian Conduct* (Libreria Editrice Vaticana, 2008), 30.

[7] *The Bible and Morality*, 31.

The journey of salvation and deliverance is progressive, involving constant conversion.[8]

Loving-kindness (*hesed*) distinguishes the call to the covenant relationship. It signifies God's faithfulness and the divine concern for the welfare of people, especially God's predilection for the poor and vulnerable. Importantly, its basic self-understanding, to which Israel must always return when this is forgotten, is of a people who are poor and needy and, hence, the object of God's special love.

Inclusive Scope

Third, while *hesed* cannot be understood outside a context of relationship, its *inclusive scope* extends beyond one's family, acquaintances, and community of faith. As the God whose peace is a gift in right relationships, entering the Covenant means a call to be just, especially by sharing in God's special concern for the oppressed, the poor and the most disadvantaged, represented in the orphan, widow, and stranger (Deut 14:28-9).

Social justice is Israel's 'response in faith to the gift of God'.[9] Consistently, the prophets do not see the poor as closer to God because of their poverty. Schaub notes that '[T]he prophets see the poor as victims. Their fellow Israelites victimized them by violating the most fundamental stipulations of the covenant'.[10] When the community's eyes were blinded or ears closed to social inequality and to those in need, the call of the Prophet was to bring people back to the Covenant. Hence, for the Israelite faithful, religion and ethics were inseparable. The sabbath was truly 'made for humankind and not humankind for the sabbath' (Mk 2:22, *NRSV* rendition).

Identity

Fourth, the Covenant (and its God-given demands) was the source of the community's self-understanding and *identity,* encapsulated in the words 'you shall be my people and I will be your God' (Jer 30:22).

Corporate identity brings us to the realm of culture. Don Browning defines a culture as a 'set of symbols, stories (myths) and norms for conduct that orient a society or group cognitively, affectively and behaviorally to the world in which it lives'.[11] Importantly, the *Qahal Yahweh* was not a community turned in on itself.

---

[8] *The Bible and Morality*, 33.

[9] *The Bible and Morality*, 51.

[10] Schaub, 'Covenant', 742.

[11] Don Browning, *The Moral Context of Pastoral Care* (Philadelphia: Westminster, 1983), 73. Anthropologist Gerald Arbuckle offers a working definition that converges with that of Browning in terms of a culture's patterns of meaning that guide 'feeling, thinking and behaving'. See Gerald A Arbuckle, *Culture, Inculturation, Theologians: A Postmodern Critique* (Collegeville, MN: Liturgical Press, 2010), xiii, 17.

Its faithfulness was measured against the criteria of mercy and justice (widow, orphan, and stranger). Further, the election of Israel was not a privilege to be 'different' but, rather, to be 'for the rest' (the others) as John Thornhill reminds us.[12]

The newness and developmental nature of Israel's Covenant (relative to other covenants) is captured in the prophecy of a 'new covenant' in Jeremiah (31: 31-4). That the teaching of Yahweh will be written 'on their hearts' meant that, in the deepest core of the self, 'all people will know God and be able to hear God's call'.[13] In this capacity for discernment we find the sapiential aspect emerging within the Covenantal framework. In the global and concrete anthropology of the Bible, the heart is the principle of morality, the center of one's freedom. It embraces the whole person (as explained earlier in chapter one).

The summons to be God's community present in and *for* the world was meant, then, to have cognitive, affective, and behavioral consequences. The identity of the community was to be one in which its members could perceive and appreciate with God's eyes. Their dispositions were to be those which could be affected by events and people, appreciate their moral significance and, then, move to responsible and accountable action.

So far, what has emerged is the central place of relationship in the biblical notion of Covenant that grounds it as an inherently ethical reality. Covenantal Ethics, then, is an apt description. Its more specific character is evident in three ways.

Covenantal Ethics: Three Specific Features

The specific nature of Covenantal Ethics (and its moral consciousness) is suggested, first, through forms of *language*.

Language

Verbs built on the five senses offer a more concrete manner of engaging with human experience and its ethical claims in terms of the Covenant. Being attentive and positively responsive is expressed when the poor soul cries and was '*heard*

---

[12] John Thornhill SM, *Sign and Promise: A Theology of the Church for a Changing World* (London: Collins, 1988), 36.

[13] Lamoureux & Wadell, *Christian Moral Life,* 6. The Pontifical Biblical Commission says of this Jeremiah text and of the new Covenant that it marks a radical innovation in the history of the covenant. 'Through the pardon of their iniquity and the gift of the Holy Spirit, the LORD now gives his people a natural disposition to live according to the Torah'. *The Bible and Morality,* 57.

by the LORD' (Ps 34:6); Jesus, stretching out his hand, *touched* the leper (Mk 1: 41).

Alternatively, a negative response as a moral indicator to the 'true' Covenant is captured by nouns: when mercy is preferred to the *odor* of sacrifice normally pleasing to the LORD (Lev 1:9). Similarly, salt losing its *taste* (Mt 5:13) is an image used of those whose moral discernment has failed to 'taste and see that the LORD is good' (Ps 34.8). Loss of taste characterizes those who are not faithful to the Torah and neglect the burdens of 'afflicted humanity'.[14]

Perhaps Covenantal ethics' most telling expression is the image of *seeing/not seeing* as in Mt 25: 31-46 and the Great Judgment. Seeing, being affected, and responding constellate around works of mercy. It is here we find both a criterion of judgment and a recovery of authentic Covenantal ethics, but in a fresh and original manner. By his identification with the disadvantaged of the world ('the least'), Jesus brings together the two commandments into the 'greatest commandment of the Torah' and gives it new depth in his person.[15]

This brings us to the second specific aspect of Covenantal Ethics.

The Person of Jesus

Second, in Jesus, the ethical claims of the Covenant and the prophetic hope for the 'new covenant' in Jeremiah 31 (noted above) find their realization in *one person* and in the realm of interiority. In his person, Jesus embodies the kingdom of God, Covenant, and the Law.[16] This specification also highlights the limitations of the Covenant as an ethical framework before the coming of Jesus. The core of morality now shifts from allegiance to a group gifted by God to one based on commitment to a person (God incarnate), albeit anchored in relationships.

Such considerations are linked with later post-Enlightenment appeals to general concepts of humanity (e.g., 'the brotherhood of man') as an ethical benchmark. Tillar notes that such criteria can be ambiguous and need 'a critical point of reference'. Hence, Jesus' identification 'with outcasts, the poor, sinners, and the disabled provides' the criterion that is needed; Jesus' compassion embodies the principle of 'universality through a historically particular

---

[14] Brendan Byrne, *Lifting the Burden: Reading Matthew's Gospel in the Church Today*, (Strathfield, NSW: St. Pauls, 2004), 57.

[15] Byrne, *Lifting the Burden*, 193.

[16] *The Bible and Morality*, 68.

intermediary'.[17] Or, as William Spohn suggests elsewhere, Jesus is the 'concrete universal' of Christian ethics.[18]

Which brings us to the third distinguishing feature.

Narratives

Sight and moral perception take paradigmatic form in the parable of the Good Samaritan (Lk 10: 29-37). This provides an instance of how Covenantal Ethics is anchored not only in a *person* but also in concrete experience though the third specifying factor—*narratives*. This parable unfolds in the interplay of authentic and distorted understandings of Covenantal Ethics and does so around two 'moments'.

Recognition

This is a story about attention that leads (or does not lead) to *recognition*.[19] The priest and Levite are privileged members of society.[20] They also represent the 'religious fundamentalism of their times'[21] seeing faithfulness to the Covenant as fulfilled in conformity to rituals that were relatively unimportant. This focus led them, and others, to neglect the Hebrew tradition of showing compassion to the poor and marginalized. They notice the wounded man but pass by. Blinded by ethnic and religious prejudice, they do not 'recognize' this one individual and his situation (with its moral claims). He is a non-person, not a human being needing help.

Again, this is compounded by their fear of attack by bandits if they stop to help together with their unwillingness to be 'defiled' by touching the victim. The same lack of recognition extends to the Samaritan himself. For the Jews, he is culturally

---

[17] Elizabeth K Tillar, 'Critical Remembrance and Eschatological Hope in Edward Schillebeeckx's Theology of Suffering for Others', *Heythrop Journal* 44 (2003):15-42, at 24.

[18] William C Spohn, *Go and Do Likewise: Jesus and Ethics* (New York: Continuum, 1999), 2.

[19] There has been an explosion across disciplines about the structure of personal and group identities based on the notion of 'intersubjective recognition'. This has bearing on Pope Benedict XVI's remarks in *Caritas in Veritate* (par 67) about how increasing global interdependence has prompted a 'strongly felt need' for various reforms (e.g., United Nations, economic institutions, and international finance) to enhance solidarity.

[20] This section is indebted to the very fine discussion in Gerald A Arbuckle, *Humanizing Healthcare Reforms*, (London and Philadelphia: Jessica Kingsley Publishers, 2013), 78-81. He draws on Bruce J Malina & Richard L Rohrbaugh, *Social–Science Commentary on the Synoptic Gospels*, (Minneapolis, MN: Fortress Press, 1992) and John J Pilch and Bruce J Malina, eds. *Biblical Social Values and their Meaning* (Peabody, MA, Hendrickson, 1993).

[21] Arbuckle, *Humanizing Healthcare Reforms*, 79. While 'fundamentalism' may be a term more relevant to modern religious phenomena, Arbuckle's usage is analogically appropriate.

and religiously inferior, excluded, even hated. He is further marginalized by his 'shady' profession, a trader in oil. Finally, it must not be forgotten that the inn in the story is a 'den of thieves' and the innkeeper is the head thief.[22] The Samaritan, as with the 'unjust' steward, knew the ways of the world. He bribed the innkeeper but clearly indicated 'I'll be back!'

And so, to the second 'moment' in the story.

Subversion

How specifically does this story instantiate Covenantal Ethics? By exploring distorted understandings of the Covenant and its ethical demands it uncovers what is authentic in the Hebrew tradition. In this, it uses two types of *subversion*. One is through the contrast of inside/outside. The story offers a model of true faithfulness and an authentic Covenant ethic embodied in a person—the Samaritan—who is perceived by the Israelite community to be an *outsider*. He is culturally, religiously, and occupationally inferior and unclean—yet is the one who truly 'belongs'. This raises the question of the true Covenant together with the nature of the Covenant community and its membership, anticipated in Jer 31: 31-4.

Subversion takes another form when Jesus, in answering 'who is my neighbor', inverts and re-frames the question. The original question refers to 'neighbor' in the objective sense, namely, who counts, who belongs to God's people and, hence, qualifies to be an object of neighborly love. At the end of the parable, Jesus responds by turning the original question back on itself. 'Which of these proved himself a neighbor…?' Here, 'neighbor' is seen in the subjective sense. What matters is the attitude and heart that is *neighborly* and, inevitably, has a scope of concern that is universal. The Good Samaritan embodies the identity, right perceptions, and appropriate dispositions of authentic Covenant Ethics. While representing a specific (and alien) culture, he points beyond it. He is, in fact, a faithful Israelite, a true disciple.

This brings us to the next stage in the discussion.

A Church in Disgrace: Learning from Covenantal Ethics

The Australian Royal Commission is one of many international projects.[23] These have generated commentaries adding to the many studies from the early twentieth

---

[22] Arbuckle, *Humanizing Healthcare Reforms*, 80 citing Malina & Rohrbaugh, *Social-Science Commentary*, 346-8.

[23] See Linda Hogan, 'Clerical and Religious Child Abuse: Ireland and Beyond', *Theological Studies* 72:1, (2011): 170-186. She notes, for instance, John Jay College: *The Nature and Scope of Sexual Abuse of Minors by Catholic Priests and Deacons in the United States 1950-2002* (Washington, DC: U.S. Conference of Catholic Bishops, 2004 and a Supplementary Report (2006); *Commission to Inquire into Child Abuse (Ryan Report)*, (Dublin: Stationary

century by social scientists and theologians.[24] Since the Royal Commission, relevant bodies and protocols have been established nationally and within dioceses in the Catholic Church in Australia. Recognizing the need for a new era of co-operation, transparency and honesty, the Church set up a *Truth, Justice, and Healing Commission* to advise its bishops, to run its dealings with the Royal Commission and, importantly, to work with victims of clergy sex abuse.

What emerged was that the sexual abuse revelations involve a range of issues: a growing appreciation of the damage done to victims; the theology of sexuality, clerical celibacy, cover-up by episcopal authorities, ecclesial structure, systemic dysfunction, the distortions of a culture etc. These set the scene for the remainder of this chapter.

In the light of the two ethical traditions explained above, Covenantal Ethics, as an overall framework, appears to be more consonant with the present situation (as it is for issues of suffering, poverty and solidarity facing the global community in general) while including elements from the Sapiential tradition.

As we have seen, the community 'is a fundamental datum of moral life according to the Bible'.[25] Covenantal Ethics, grounded in the gift of God, embraces the various dimensions of relationship, and gives special preference to those who suffer injustice, here the victims of sexual abuse. Again, in the current circumstances, any appeal to the Church itself in its tradition or in its Episcopal representatives as repositories of wisdom risks being, at the least, foolish and, at the most, offensive. The Church's moral authority and credibility have been damaged. It is a time for the Church to listen.

In using Covenantal Ethics as a hermeneutical lens to understand and respond to this crisis for the Church, five signposts suggest themselves: covenant identity as gift; recognition of, and solidarity with victims; listening to learn; the transpersonal power of evil as demonic; the functional analogy with the destruction of the Temple.

(sic) Office, 2009). Report and Executive Summary is available at http://www.childabusecommission.com/rpt/pdfs/. *Report into the Catholic Archdiocese of Dublin (Murphy Report* (Dublin: Stationary (sic) Office, 2009).

[24] For instance, in the USA, Joseph P Chinnici, *When Values Collide: The Catholic Church, Sexual Abuse and the Challenges of Leadership* (Maryknoll, NY: Orbis, 2010); Philip Lawler, *The Faithful Departed: The Collapse of Boston's Catholic Culture,* new ed. with preface (2008; New York: Encounter, 2010). In Ireland: Tony Flannery. C.Ss. R, ed. *Responding to the Ryan Report,* (Dublin: Columba, 2010); John Littleton and Eamon Maher (eds), *The Dublin/Murphy Report: A Watershed for Irish Catholicism?* (Dublin: Columba, 2010).

[25] *The Bible and Morality,* 187.

So, to first signpost.

Identity as Gift

Commentators agree that the sexual abuse crisis touches the very identity of the Church. Arbuckle reminds us that any culture in crisis, needing change, must return to its founding story and values.[26] The first lesson from our Hebrew roots, then, is to engrave on our awareness (and memory) that the Covenant (and the community's identity) is a *gift* from God.

Yet, human history and biblical narratives tell the story of humans who do not do justice to the gift of God—in wickedness, weakness, and failure. As a Church, we are part of that story. This is who we are. We must own and reclaim this as part of our identity. We cannot rely on ourselves. We can only beg for forgiveness and for the original gift to be renewed, appreciating what the Bible attests—that 'God's "giving" is followed by his "forgiving"'.[27]

Recognition of Victims

The second lesson is, with the LORD, to hear the cry of the poor—to be affected by *victims*—in the perspective of the Prophets. Hearing is remembering—another way of describing faithfulness to the Covenant: 'I will never forget you my people'. This is fully realized in God's response in Jesus, in his sacrificial death, which, as Ormerod points out 'carries the weight of a religious and moral imperative to put an end to sacrificial violence and the creation of victims'.[28] In the Hebrew Scriptures, another word for sin is 'to forget'. To forget who we are is to be unfaithful to what is revealed in Jesus' death and resurrection. It is an erosion of the Church's very identity, a distortion in its culture. Just as Jesus, the risen Victim, identified with all victims, so too must be his Church.

In the light of past failures, the most basic task is for the Church, in its authorities and communities, in its very culture, to learn 'to identify with the victim'.[29] This is about *recognition*. In the language of the virtues, being true to our identity entails a set of perceptions and dispositions that lead us to be affected, understand, respond and act as people who have put on 'the mind of Christ' (consistent with Browning's definition of culture noted earlier).

---

[26] Arbuckle, *Humanizing Healthcare Reforms*, 161.

[27] *The Bible and Morality*, 111.

[28] Neil Ormerod, 'Clergy Sexual Abuse: What Difference Did Vatican II Make?' in Neil Ormerod et al., eds. *Vatican II: Reception and Implementation in the Australian Church* (Mulgrave, Vic: Garratt Publishing, 2012), 213-225, at 225.

[29] Ormerod, 'Clergy Sexual Abuse, 225.

Again, as Ormerod implies, *solidarity* will require a much wider range of people listening to, and being 'with', victims in their pain (beyond members of the Church appointed Commission). Such a consideration cannot be separated from the agonizing possibility, if not, reality: namely, the responsibility of bishops, clergy, and laity 'who colluded, whether actively or passively, with a system that allowed the rape and abuse of children'.[30]

It is also a call to theologians to be part of this process during and not just after the Royal Commission (cf., representative studies noted later in this chapter). The tools are there, as in tapping the work of Edward Schillebeeckx or Dorothy Soelle on theology and suffering. These writers remind us that it is particularly in times of crisis, in negative contrast experiences, that hope is the antidote to suffering. 'It is those contrast experiences which make hope real, since hope then becomes so necessary'.[31] There is also suffering's *subversive* aspect as the 'dangerous memory' in that, as Robert Gascoigne reminds us, 'although it is suffering that most confounds our search for ethical intelligibility, it is likewise suffering that is the most profound source of insight and conversion'.[32] For all that, Australian Archbishop Mark Coleridge reminds us in an interview in 2010: '…the challenge for me was to see their faces and to hear their voices and that was not easy'.[33]

Listen and Learn

This brings us to a third guidepost for the Church—*listen and learn*. This is captured by Bishop Kevin Dowling of Rustenburg, South Africa. He made headlines in suggesting that 'church leadership, instead of giving an impression of power, privilege and prestige, should rather be experienced as a humble, searching ministry together with its people'.[34]

Such an approach could reveal the face of wisdom. Like Solomon, this entails the quest for a discerning and responsive heart. The Church will need to change radically 'if such a humble, searching ministry is to be its hallmark' concludes

---

[30] Hogan, 'Clerical and Religious Child Abuse', 186.

[31] Tillar, 'Critical Remembrance', 27.

[32] Robert Gascoigne, 'Suffering and Theological Ethics: Intimidation and Hope', in James F Keenan, SJ, ed. *Catholic Theological Ethics in the World Church: The Plenary Papers from the First Cross-cultural Conference on Catholic Theological Ethics* (henceforth *CTEWC*) (New York: Continuum, 2007); 163-6, at 163.

[33] 'Where is the fire of Pentecost? Sexual abuse, the Catholic Church, and culture', Interview by Margaret Coffey with Archbishop Mark Coleridge, Professor James Ogloff, Brendan Callaghan, SJ, Professor Karen Terry, Professor William Marshall, Professor George Rousseau and Dr. Alistair Blanshard, on ABC Radio National, *Encounter*, 23.5.2010.

[34] Kevin Dowling, 'Catholic Church Teaching Finds Church Leadership Lacking', *National Catholic Reporter*, July 8, 2010 cited in Hogan, 'Clerical and Religious Child Abuse', 185-6.

Linda Hogan.[35] It means embracing vulnerability and a sense of powerlessness that shares the powerlessness of the victims. Hogan cites McDonagh's conclusion (confirming what is implied in Ormerod's comment), that:

> bishops and the wider Church must first be evangelised by the abused, brought to some deeper and fuller meaning of the gospel by the abused before they presume to lead in the evangelising of others.[36]

Again, the past decade has confirmed the extent of the crisis and its devastating effects worldwide. While the figure of 5% for sexual abuse amongst clergy is no greater than its occurrence in other groups within the community, it is still commonly described as 'staggering', 'horrendous' 'incomprehensible', particularly in the light of betrayal of the trust placed in priests and in the Church.

Relevant here are the comments made about Benedict XVI's Pastoral Letter to the Catholics of Ireland. While Bernard Treacey, O.P. acknowledges his appreciation, with others, of the tone and 'register' of the Pope's words, he notes that:

> there is a sense...of a writer overwhelmed by the enormity of what he has had to confront, both in the horror of abuse and in the dereliction of duty among church leaders to whom it was reported.[37]

In Australia, Archbishop Mark Coleridge is of similar mind. When asked by interviewer Margaret Coffey how he sees the situation here in Australia, he offers an extended reflection, even if 'a work in progress'. About the 'enormity' of the sexual abuse question he observes:

> The Church may also have underestimated the power and subtlety of evil. This may seem strange to say of the Church which is often regarded as taking evil and sin more seriously than do other Churches and Christian communities.
>
> But it is evil we are dealing with in the case of sexual abuse of the young; and it is an evil which is not just personal.

---

[35] Hogan, 'Clerical and Religious Child Abuse', 186.

[36] Hogan, 'Clerical and Religious Child Abuse', 187, citing McDonagh, 'Between Evangelising and the Priesthood', in *Dublin/Murphy Report,* 113-120, at 113.

[37] Bernard Treacey, O.P., 'Learning with Pope Benedict', *Doctrine and Life* 60:5 (May-June, 2010): 2-3, at 2. Cited in Hogan, 'Clerical and Religious Child Abuse', 178. In the intervening decade, initiatives under Pope Francis have been taken to further address this issue, e.g., changes in Canon Law; *The Pontifical Commission for the Protection of Minors* established in 2014; the 2021 International Symposium 'Faith and Flourishing: Strategies for Preventing and Healing Child Sexual Abuse'.

It is a power which reaches beyond the individual; it seems more metaphysical than moral. A supra-personal power seems to take hold of human beings who are not in themselves wholly evil. But they are in the grip of a power which they can, it seems, do little to understand or control; and it is a power which is hugely destructive in the lives of those they have abused and in their own lives.[38]

This brings us to the fourth benchmark from our Jewish heritage.

Evil: A Transpersonal Power?

What Archbishop Coleridge is trying to articulate may find an analogical equivalent with the world-view prior to, and in, Jesus' time, one reflected, in striking form, in Mark's Gospel. There, the *transpersonal power of evil* is the realm of the *demonic*. This notion sits uneasily with the modern sensibility. More importantly, it must be carefully understood in the present discussion of sexual abuse. Coleridge's description of the present is paralleled by that of fellow scripture scholar Brendan Byrne looking into the past.

In both the ancient and biblical worlds, people spoke of 'demonic possession'. This described 'when they felt themselves held captive from within by forces and compulsions over which they had no control'. These were 'transpersonal forces that robbed them of freedom of choice, stunted their human growth, and alienated them from God, from life in community, and from their own individual humanity'.

Byrne suggests that, in today's world, the manifestations of the demonic are in the many 'captivities' whether personal, social, or economic, under which people labor. It is also manifested in the 'multiple forms of addiction that burden us as individuals and as societies—huge, transpersonal forces that control us and make us their slaves'.[39]

I noted above how this is an analogy. The destructive evil in abuse of the young (a criminal act) cannot simply be reduced to Byrne's 'captivities' and 'multiple forms of addiction' (often about self-harm that is not criminal). Again, Coleridge is not attempting to address any correlation between the recidivist rate and the compulsive nature of sexually abusive behavior nor trying to minimize personal or institutional responsibility. He is wondering aloud (tentatively): how can evil be so powerful that it can almost take on a life of its own and shape an individual's attitudes and actions? By implication—how can that also apply to a community such as the Church?

---

[38] 'Where is the fire of Pentecost', *Encounter* (toward end of the transcript available on the ABC website).

[39] Brendan Byrne, SJ, *A Costly Freedom: A Theological Reading of Mark's Gospel* (Strathfield, NSW: St Pauls, 2008), xi-xii.

This reminds us, once again, how social systems and Church communities are cultures. As such, they subtly shape, often without our conscious awareness, how we think, feel and act. So, we must consider the possibility that unseen, unnameable, evil can so infiltrate ecclesial cultures that abusive behavior is made easier for a perpetrator.

Further, the Church must recognize the empirically grounded research that has verified corruption of Catholic institutional culture in various parts of the world (e.g., some seminaries and chanceries). Whether unseen or observable, such processes can also influence how the abuse, once revealed, is subsequently handled by church or secular authorities. It can involve what may be tantamount to silent, even if unwitting, collusion, as noted earlier.[40]

Like a massive tsunami that engulfs all in its path and, as it recedes, leaves not only destruction but everything (and everyone) stained—both innocent and guilty can be caught up in something so much bigger than themselves. Ultimately, what the Jewish story anticipated was embodied in personal form in Jesus. He alone has the power to set us free from such 'demonic' forces and from our own weakness or unwillingness to acknowledge any collusion with them.

As a Church, then, we must throw ourselves at the feet for the crucified Lord, again captured well by Archbishop Mark Coleridge in response to the announcement of the Royal Commission.

> We can forget that evil is an awesome power…we can forget that the only power greater than evil is the love of God which raised Jesus from the dead…denial is long behind us and defensiveness is futile…the only way forward now is to face the full horror of what has happened, and to do so humble and courageously as men of faith who have entrusted our lives to Jesus crucified and risen.[41]

The enormity of the crisis brings us to the fifth and final lesson from the Jewish tradition.

---

[40] See n. 30. Relevant here are more recent studies on clericalism as part of ecclesial culture, and, of an even more pernicious aspect of that culture, namely, hierarchicalism—the impunity of the hierarchy from transparency and accountability and any associated vulnerability. See James F Keenan, SJ, 'Hierarchicalism', *Theological Studies* 83:1 (2022): 84-108. Also, Daniel J Fleming, 'Overcoming silence: Fraternal correction, hierarchy, and the abuse crisis in the Australian Catholic Church', in eds. Mathias Wirth, Isabel Noth, Silvia Schroer, *Sexual Violence in the Context of the Church: New Interdisciplinary Perspectives* (Berlin/Boston: Walter de Gruyter, 2021), 75-91.

[41] Archbishop Mark Coleridge, *Letter to the Clergy of the Archdiocese of Brisbane*, Nov. 19, 2012.

Destruction of the Temple: A Functional Analogy

If we tap the Hebrew/Christian memory, what can we learn from public disasters that befell Israel, for instance, the destruction of the Temple by the Babylonians? This event offers a *functional analogy,* a striking parallel with what is happening for the Church today. Walter Brueggemann reminds us that, for Israel:

> the temple had come to be the point of reference for all life. Its destruction thus meant the *loss of a center,* a profound public *disorientation,* in which *public meanings and values* are *nullified* or at least severely placed in *jeopardy.* [42]

The language used here encapsulates something of the situation today for the Church locally and internationally. Brueggemann notes how public energy in Israel's prayer focused on the destruction of the Temple—the collapse of their 'known world'. They resorted to the psalms of communal lament. Nevertheless, we are reminded that 'after the trauma of the collapse of the monarchy and the exile, God's power renews the religious community of Israel'.[43] For us, such a process requires, as Brueggemann suggests, 'an imaginative identification of a 'dynamic analogy', for 'the points of contact with our own experience'.

As Catholics, what is happening with sexual abuse involves a public sense of 'loss, hurt and rage that we have in common' yet is something in which 'we have an immediate, direct, and personal stake'.[44] Like the loss of the Temple, it almost certainly will involve the end of the world we have known concerning the Church.

In the light of this, are we perhaps prone to 'loss of public awareness and public imagination?' While transparency and accountability are central, we need to think about this crisis *theologically* as with other public events and disasters.

Further, we need to find ways of *praying publicly* about it—to grieve, repent and lament together. Somehow, we need to ritualize forgiveness—asked from and received from victims. We need specifically designed liturgical gatherings, beyond the Eucharist or Ash Wednesday, to engage the sense of loss, hurt, guilt, shame, disorientation and even rage. As Brueggemann points out:

> … it is stunning to think that prayer of this kind might indeed by the point of entry into the larger world of faith, where the Lord of the nations governs.[45]

---

[42] Walter Brueggemann, *The Message of the Psalms: A Theological Commentary* (Minneapolis: Augsburg, 1983), 67; my emphasis.

[43] *The Bible and Morality,* 176.

[44] Brueggemann, *The Message of the Psalms,* 68.

[45] Brueggemann, *The Message of the Psalms,* 68.

Or as Tiggar has observed, 'it is those contrast experiences which make hope real'.[46]

Conclusion

This chapter outlined the general and specific characteristics of 'Covenant' noting the place of justice and of victims. Highlighted were Covenant's focus on relationship, gift, inclusive scope, and identity. It then examined how 'Covenant' can act as a hermeneutical window to consider the sexual abuse crisis facing the Church and we suggested five signposts: covenant identity as gift; recognition of, and solidarity with victims; listening to learn; the transpersonal power of evil as demonic; the functional analogy with the destruction of the Temple.

Often, the Church's public face shows a dominant concern for credibility. In the light of the victims' pain and anger and of the justified public outrage, what is being asked now, and the benchmark against which all is measured, is authenticity, humility, and honesty. Most importantly, the Church (and all its members) need a more sensitized capacity to be moved by a situation of evil, to recognize its moral claim and to respond accordingly. What matters is nurturing a culture of trust, a 'heart change' so that 'things come naturally and spontaneously, because you feel it'.[47] The language used in *Truth, Justice and Healing Commission* is a good start. There is needed a deepened and more realistic reclaiming of our identity.

As noted earlier, any culture in crisis or needing change must return to its founding story and values. This could well be achieved by drawing on our Jewish heritage. Further, Desmond Tutu reminds us that healing and forgiveness will be possible 'only if the depth of the damage and the awfulness of the abuse are acknowledged, and if we are prepared to deal with the real situation'.[48]

We must start at the feet of the victims. At times, this may involve lying beside the victim traveler abused by the robbers before we can be the Good Samaritan. Again, as in the parable, the 'true' Israelite was an outsider, so too with the sexual abuse issue, prophetic voices from outside the Churches accompany, even enable, the cry of victims. Most importantly, before even thinking about evangelizing, even if under the rubric of the "New Evangelization', we must first be evangelized.

---

[46] See above n. 31.

[47] Dioceses of Parramatta and Wollongong, *Creating a Safe Church from Within: Summary Report*, September 2018, 15, citing Fr Hans Zollner SJ.

[48] Desmond Tutu, *God Has a Dream: A Vision of Hope for Our Time (*London: Ebury, 2004), cited in Hogan, 'Clerical and Religious Child Abuse', 186.

Our catholic tradition speaks of the four marks of the Church—one, holy, catholic, apostolic. As one theologian reminds us, through this experience, we are learning about the fifth mark— sinful.

Perhaps these final thoughts from the Jewish tradition offer an appropriate end to this chapter:

> The story is told of a Rabbi who was missing from the Synagogue on the evening of the Day of Atonement. The Synagogue was filled with all the Jewish people of the Town, waiting to commence the service on this most holy day. They sent a messenger to search for the Rabbi and he was found rocking the cradle of a crying child. The parents had left it behind to go to the Synagogue. To attend to the little crying Child has priority before the needs of the Community; the balance in Judaism is weighed in favour of the individual soul.[49]

---

[49] Kenneth Arkwright, 'The Essence of Judaism in the Perspective of History' available at www.ccjwa.org/Documents/Articles/**jewishnessinhistory**.pdf

VIRTUE AT WORK

4
Jesus – 'Our Wisest and Dearest Friend': Aquinas and Moral Transformation

The first section of this book spent time with conscience: in its primordial form; in the contested issue of religious freedom; finally, about distorted conscience and evil at the institutional level in relation to sexual abuse and the Catholic Church.

We move on to consider conscience in its wider setting, which, as noted earlier, embraces the virtues, the other powers of human nature and, most importantly, the redeeming, healing and elevating presence of Christ and the Holy Spirit.[1] The angle of approach now shifts to examining specific exemplars of virtue in action. The phrase 'Christ and the Holy Spirit' is the cue for this present discussion—the first of four chapters in the second part of the book. [2]

Recent studies have tried to assess the role of Christ in the moral theology of Thomas Aquinas. For some, that role, as reflected in the *Summa Theologiae*, is 'not inconsiderable', especially in the Third Part (*Tertia Pars*) where Jesus is presented as both model and savior.[3] Close analysis of the *Summa*, particularly of the relationship between the Christology (whether implicit or explicit) of the First (*Prima*), Second (*Secunda*) and Third Parts of the *Summa* and their respective Prologues, helps to clarify Aquinas' intentions. Brian Shanley observes that:

> Aquinas does not always signpost the deep connections as much as one would like, yet they are there to an attentive reader. Perhaps, if Aquinas had lived to finish the *Summa*, he might have gone back to make the connections clearer.[4]

---

[1] See Introduction, n. 1 citing Levering, *The Abuse of Conscience*, 207.

[2] This chapter was originally published as '"Jesus—Our Wisest and Dearest Friend": Aquinas on Moral Transformation', *New Blackfriars* 97: 1071 (Sept), 2016: 575-610.

[3] Joseph Wawrykow, 'Jesus in the Moral Theology of Thomas Aquinas', *Journal of Medieval and Early Modern Studies* 42:1, Winter (2012): 13-33, at 13. See also Patricia M Clark, 'The Case for an Exemplarist Approach to Virtue in Catholic Moral Theology', *Journal of Moral Theology* 3:1 (2014): 54-82, at 61 and 54.

[4] Brian Shanley, 'Aquinas's Exemplar Ethics', *The Thomist* 72:3 (2008): 345-68, at 368-9. Also, D Stephen Long, 'The Way of Aquinas: Its Importance for Moral Theology'. *Studies in Christian Ethics* 19:3 (2006): 339-356. For readers not conversant with the standard form of referencing of the *Summa,* there are three sections in the *Summa Theologiae*: the Second Part further divided into a First and Second Part (*Prima Secundae* and *Secunda Secundae*). For the sake of consistency, I will use the Latin terminology.

I would like to build on these discussions as guided by the title above, namely, Jesus as our 'wisest and dearest friend'. This phrase is found towards the end of the *Prima Secundae* of the *Summa* where Aquinas treats of the New Law of the Holy Spirit. There is traceable thread between this discussion and that found in the *Tertia Pars* on Christ as a moral exemplar. Both have a firm Scriptural content. Both are revelatory of moral standards and of the relational framework of moral living.

I will, first, offer some foundational considerations. Second, I examine the evidence supporting Aquinas' original description of Jesus as our 'dearest friend' and as further disclosed in the *Tertia Pars*. This leads to an investigation of Jesus as 'wisest' —the Incarnate Word and Wisdom. I probe this sapiential aspect further in terms of the gifts of the Holy Spirit, specifically, that of wisdom, and, in particular, as construed in recent work on the second person perspective and Joint Attention.

Foundational Considerations

In the Prologue to the *Prima Secundae,* Aquinas surveys what he has done. He has discussed God (the 'exemplar'), the exercise of divine power, and how the human person, created according to the divine 'image' (*ad imaginem Dei*), reflects the divine goodness through the capacity for reflection, self-direction, and freedom.

The Prologue's wording concerning 'exemplar' and 'image' must be understood in the light of his earlier discussion of 'image' in relation to the procession of the Word. Whatever implies procession or origin in God belongs to persons, hence, image is a personal name when used of God.[5] 'Exemplar' is a more 'proper' description of the Trinity in whose 'image' humans are made.[6]

Whereas the Son is the 'perfect image of the Father', so humans are made 'in the divine image' in having a certain tendency to perfection, namely, realizing the

---

[5] *Summa Theologica,* 1.35.1 (Henceforth *ST*).For my referencing of the *Summa*, I have consulted the Latin/English (Blackfriars) version of the English Dominican Province (London: Eyre and Spottiswoode, 1963-1975) and the *Summa Theologica of* St. Thomas Aquinas, 2nd rev. ed. 1920, translated by Fathers of the English Dominican Province in the on-line version www.newadvent.org/summa/ and the new translation by Alfred J Freddoso, on-line version at http://www.nd.edu/~afreddos/summa-translation/TOC.htm accessed 20/11/2015. Translated passages from the *Summa* are from the English Dominican New Advent version unless otherwise indicated. Summaries or paraphrases are this author's.

[6] *ST* 1.35.1 ad 1 which notes Augustine's comment about the Trinity as the 'image' to which man was made.

image by sharing the life of the Son.[7] This is the final causality aspect implied in exemplar causality reflected in the three stage movement of the human as 'image' by nature, grace (virtue) and glory.[8] The formal causality is implied in that humans are created to know and love and, through knowing and loving God, we share in God's own life. We are both beatified and deified. As Shanley sums it up: it is 'entering into the very knowing and loving that is the Trinitarian life of God'.[9]

Again, Aquinas explains that the exemplar principle is appropriated to the Son by reason of wisdom and in relation to creation.[10] Creation can only be understood through a right knowledge of divine persons, namely, that it emerges not by necessity but from the Word prompted by the love in God. Only on this basis can we 'think rightly concerning the salvation of the human race accomplished by the Incarnate Son, and by the gift of the Holy Spirit'.[11]

This is anticipated at the start of the *Prima Pars* where Aquinas looks ahead to Christ who, in his humanity, is the way along which we journey to God (*tendendi in deum*).[12] With the *Tertia Pars* Prologue, Aquinas is now in a position to explore how Jesus Christ not only redeemed us from our sins, but 'showed us in his own person (*in seipso demonstravit*) the way of truth, whereby we may attain the blessings of eternal life by rising again'.[13] This is expanded when Aquinas offers reasons for the Incarnation being for our good: firstly, 'for the sake of right action, in that he has given us an example in his own life' and, secondly, 'for the sake of a full participation in divinity, in which lies our beatitude and the end of human life, and this is bestowed on us through the humanity of Christ'. [14]

The wording here is instructive. The Incarnate Word, as embodying God's goodness in his humanity, is our savior and teacher. In his own person we find the exemplar of the way to live and develop 'in the image' of Jesus whose life we

---

[7] *ST* 1.35.2.

[8] *ST* 1. 93. 4.

[9] Shanley, 'Aquinas's Exemplar Ethics', 350.

[10] '...the exemplar principle is appropriated to the Son by reason of wisdom and in relation to creation, in order that, as it is said (Psalm 103:24), "Thou hast made all things in wisdom," it may be understood that God made all things in the beginning—that is, in the Son; according to the word of the Apostle (Colossians 1:16), "In Him"—viz. the Son—"were created all things"'. *ST* 1.46.3 resp.

[11] *ST* 1.32.1 ad 3.

[12] *ST* 1. 2. prol.

[13] *ST* 3. prol.

[14] *ST* 3. 1. 2. Rendition as in Shanley, 'Aquinas's Exemplar Ethics', 354.

share through baptism. Clark notes that the call made in Christ to participate in the divine life 'is made possible only by the mystery of the Incarnation: by the words and deeds of Jesus as they occurred in human history'.[15] This sentence captures the main content of the *Tertia Pars*. Responding to Jesus as exemplar is not so much through 'imitation' understood in relation to some external standard or model. As we shall see, *imitatio* is best captured by the word 'identification'.

In the *Tertia Pars,* the prominent role played by the person of Jesus in his teaching and actions as narrated in the Gospels is indicative of Aquinas' purpose. It is not simply to expound the meaning of the Christ Event, especially of his Passion and death. Aquinas aims to arouse his 'audience' or readers to a personal engagement with, and commitment to, the person of Jesus and, hence, to accompany Him on his Way.

The latter section of the *Prima Secundae* with its treatment of the New Law is picked up again in the Prologue to the *Tertia Pars* noted above and, in the articles, concerning Jesus' life, teaching, passion and death. From here we see that Jesus, in his person, is not only a paradigm of the moral life but is also an 'exemplar' in the metaphysical sense of the word.

For Aquinas, faith entails identifying with Jesus as the exemplar, namely, the human person is made to be 'ad imaginem', participating in the divine life through Christ, the Incarnate Word. This movement involves a call to respond to a personal relationship which takes the form of friendship. We trace this thread in Aquinas' use of the Gospels in relation to two articles in the *Prima Secundae*.

Jesus as our 'Dearest Friend'

The foundation of the New Law, which is primarily 'inscribed in our hearts', is 'specifically and dominantly' found in the grace of the Holy Spirit given to those who believe in Christ. Such grace comes to us through the Incarnate Word.[16] For Aquinas, the written or external aspects of the Law, as found in the Gospels, for instance, are secondary (though not superfluous). They help dispose the intellect through faith (concerning truth) and the affections (through the ordering of affections) to be fit to receive the grace of the Holy Spirit. From this emerges behavior (effects of 'spiritual grace') or the works of virtue as exhorted to in diverse ways in the New Testament.[17]

---

[15] Clark, 'The Case for an Exemplarist Approach', 79.

[16] *ST* 1.2.106.1.

[17] *ST* 1.2.106 ad 1.

Again, Aquinas says, citing Augustine, that the Sermon on the Mount contains 'the whole process of forming the life of a Christian' in that Christ, in his teaching on true happiness, orders our interior movements concerning oneself and one's neighbor in relation to beatitude. Resultant action requires volition (the ordering of desires and choice concerning what ought to be done or avoided) and also intention concerning the 'end', namely, the proper goal and the guiding or overarching motivation to reach it.[18] This suggests another aspect to the intentionality of the act of faith construed as the virtue of 'the first intention' (*virtus primae intentionis*) concerning the ultimate end whose force 'perdures and of itself informs every desire of the believer and every decision of his'.[19]

The twelve articles on the Law (Old and New) in the *Prima Secundae* are, understandably, anchored in the Scriptures. In these two representative articles above, Aquinas adumbrates key elements of the moral life that he develops more comprehensively in the *Prima* and *Secunda Secundae*. These involve the centrality of integral knowledge (wisdom) and ordered affections (love) that guide action. There is, then, an inter-play of the cognitive, affective, and behavioral in the moral life embodied, as we shall see, in the virtues. More significantly, it is inherently inter-personal, which is our next consideration.

Friendship and Virtue

For Aquinas, friendship is the best model to express our relationship with God. As Wadell notes:

> we only truly love God when we have learned to be God's friend, and to be God's friend our relationship with God must be marked by the qualities integral to friendship.[20]

The first quality is benevolence in which one wishes what is good or best for a friend. Second, friendship entails mutual and reciprocal love. This means that love changes us. In loving God, we become more like God. Friendship's third mark is that, through this bond of love, each becomes for the other, another self. 'We can see ourselves in them because we know we too have been formed, shaped, defined by the same love'.[21]

When discussing the commandments and counsels of the New Law, Aquinas

---

[18] *ST* 1.2.108.3.

[19] Livio Melina, *Sharing in Christ's Virtues: For A Renewal of Moral Theology in the light of* **Veritatis Splendor** (Trans. William E May: Washington DC: Catholic University Press of America, 2001), 111 citing *ST* 1.2.1 6 ad 3.

[20] Paul J Wadell, C.P., *Friendship and the Moral Life* (Indiana: University of Notre Dame Press, 1989), 130-141. Wadell presents an extensive treatment of Aquinas on friendship as the basic model of the Christian moral life.

[21] Wadell, *Friendship and the Moral Life,* 137.

encapsulates his discussion by observing that Christ is 'our wisest and dearest friend' (*Sed Christus maxime est sapiens et amicus*) and explains it further.[22] In this regard, Melina points out that action is regulated in the context of the New Law principally through Christ guiding us by his counsel, as one would do with a friend rather than by precepts as one would do with servants (See Jn 15:15). 'In the dynamism of friendship, the beloved becomes the rule of the lover. Through affective union, what our friend wants will begin to appear fitting and connatural to us'.[23] Friendship with Jesus, then, both *informs* and *forms* us. It also entails growth in virtue—a matter that requires a brief comment.

For Aquinas, virtue in the full sense is only found in the infused virtues (theological and moral). Aristotelian dispositions are virtues only in the restricted sense. Aquinas introduces the category of virtue by using Augustine's definition of virtue from Peter Lombard's *Sentences*. 'Virtue is a good quality of mind, by which we live righteously, of which no one can make bad use, which God works in us, without us'.[24]

Aquinas explains that God working virtue 'in us without us' does not mean that God works virtue in us without our consent. What is essential to the notion of virtue is that it is infused by God. Virtues that order a person to good (to human flourishing) as defined by divine law (i.e., beatitude), cannot be caused in us by habituation. (i.e., developed by our own efforts).[25] On that basis, for Aquinas, 'without the infused virtues, there are no virtues'.[26] Virtues, in the fullest sense, direct a person to happiness with God.

This brings us to the key questions: how does Aquinas draw on Jesus' life together with his presence in the Church and the sacraments in the *Tertia Pars* to instruct our minds and foster our desire to walk the Way with 'our wisest and dearest friend'? Further, in Aquinas' treatment, how is God at 'work in us, without us'? Our focus moves, then, to Jesus in his Passion and as teacher.

---

[22] 'We must therefore understand the commandments of the New Law to have been given about matters that are necessary to gain the end of eternal bliss, to which end the New Law brings us forthwith: but that the counsels are about matters that render the gaining of this end more assured and expeditious' (*ST* 1.2.108. 4).

[23] Livio Melina, *The Epiphany of Love: Towards a Theological Understanding of Christian Action* (Grand Rapids, Michigan; UK, Cambridge: Eerdmans, 2010), 17. This phrase ('connatural') was clarified in chapter one and will be pursued later in this chapter.

[24] *ST* 1.2.55.4 as in Andrew Pinsent, *The Second-person perspective in Aquinas' ethics: Virtues and gifts* (New York: Routledge, 2012), 13.

[25] *ST* 1.2.63.2.

[26] Pinsent, *The Second-person perspective*, 13.

Jesus in his Passion

Amongst the reasons offered for the fittingness of Jesus' Passion for our salvation, the first is that the Passion reveals the depth and scope of God's love and that we are 'thereby *stirred* to love Him in return and herein lies the perfection of human salvation'.[27] The centrality of divine love is a persistent theme in Aquinas' discussion of Jesus' Passion, sufferings, and death. We read that Jesus underwent the Passion from love for his Father and neighbor.[28] To ensure a 'living faith' or charity, Jesus' Passion is applied both to our minds and hearts and that Christ's Passion 'excites' our charity as a cause for the forgiveness of sins'. The correlative of divine love in Jesus' Passion is the conquest of sin and evil.[29]

Again, this pattern of love is evident during Jesus' ministry. For instance, the Transfiguration stems from Jesus's 'loving foresight' (*pia provisione*) that the disciples not only know the Way and its goal but that, through their brief taste of eternal joy, would still be drawn to it by desire, despite the hardship and suffering it involved.[30] Earlier, in his temptations, Jesus wants to strengthen us, offer an example but, importantly, to be in solidarity with us, as the compassionate high priest, in order to fill us with confidence in his mercy.[31]

Finally, and relevant to our purposes here, Christ's suffering on the cross is an example of virtue, citing Augustine: 'God's Wisdom became man to give us an example in righteousness of living'.[32] This reflects Aquinas' earlier comment: 'in his Passion Christ offers himself to us as the perfect model of all the virtues'.[33]

How is this emphasis on the Passion and divine love to be understood? Being 'in Christ' and adopting Christ as exemplar of the moral life is not simply a matter of being like Him in our actions. Through our participation in the divine nature in Christ,[34] we identify with Christ, 'putting on his mind' such that, as Clark notes, 'Christ *himself* becomes the principle of one's agency'.

---

[27] *ST* 3.46.3; my emphasis.

[28] *ST* 3. 47. 2 ad 1.

[29] *ST* 3. 49. 1.

[30] *ST* 3. 45. 1.

[31] *ST* 3. 41. 1.

[32] *ST* 3. 46. 4.

[33] *ST* 1.2. 46.3.

[34] *ST* 1.2.62.1.

Further, Jesus in the paschal mystery indicates the 'manner in which certain acts may *reveal* rather than merely conform to standards of human goodness and moral perfection'.[35] The Passion is revelatory of the core quality of what is true and good, namely, Christ's gift of himself, of love realized in the form of redemptive suffering. Through discipleship, and especially, though the sacraments, we 'are united and conformed to the person of Christ himself'.[36] We are called to share in the self-giving love of our 'dearest friend'.

In the Eucharist, we share in the very action of Jesus on the cross and, through freely consenting to his Eucharistic action, we allow ourselves 'to be permeated and informed by it'.[37] Our moral life is directed and animated by friendship with Jesus where 'the beloved becomes the rule of the lover'. With Him, we are called to the 'no greater love' of laying down one's life for one's friends.

For Aquinas, then, God befriends humanity in the person of Christ, principally through His reconciling and atoning work and through his continuing presence in the Church, specifically in the sacraments. Friendship means that one person can 'atone' for another. This applies to Christ and the Church since 'the head and members are as one mystic person (*una persona mystica*)'.[38] It is in the Church, especially in the sacraments and, most importantly, in the Eucharist, that Christ's formative presence is at work. For Aquinas, Christ is present in the Eucharist in the manner of his Passion since it was his Passion that restored humanity to friendship with God. The Eucharist is the sacrament of charity and the proof of friendship.[39] But the Passion is complemented by another aspect— the next concern.

Jesus as Teacher

The role of teacher is another feature of Christ as exemplar. The pedagogical dimension is implied above in Jesus' role as counsellor and guide as too in the exemplary role of his Passion as a 'model of virtue'. Again, the Holy Spirit, as the Spirit of Jesus, speaks from within as a teacher (*Magister interior*) but is also working in the Church and its sacramental life. As Aquinas points out, Jesus has received the fullness of the Spirit but it is given to us only in 'moderation', hence,

---

[35] Clark, 'The Case for an Exemplarist Approach', 61 and 54.

[36] Clark, 'The Case for an Exemplarist Approach', 62.

[37] Melina, *The Epiphany of Love,* 36.

[38] *ST* 3. 48. 2 ad 1.

[39] *ST* 3. 73. 1.

we need external instruction.[40] Our focus here is on one particular facet of Jesus as teacher.

Aquinas says that Jesus' choice of the teaching /listening/response pattern was most suited for his 'doctrine' to be 'imprinted on the hearts of his hearers' as one having power.[41] The link between teaching and friendship with Jesus is captured in Aquinas' comment that 'the true sign of friendship is that a friend reveals the secrets of his heart to his friends'.[42] That means that we must listen and learn. Earlier, Aquinas reminds us that Jesus is an example to all through faith and that 'faith comes from hearing'.[43]

Anthony Kelly notes that Aquinas 'insists on the biblical priority of hearing, for, in all revelatory experiences, hearing precedes the seeing—even in the original experiences of seeing related to the risen Jesus'.[44] While, at times, hearing the Word of God is superseded by a seeing and a touching (as in 1 Jn 1:1-3), Kelly makes a comment that is pertinent to our discussion of the inter-personal nature of moral life in Jesus:

> It remains, however, that the experience of hearing is still basic in the economy of faith since, while sight and touch play their parts, they are less able to register either the excess of God's self-giving or to underline the essential self-surrendering receptivity of faith. *To hear the word of God places the hearer in a profoundly interpersonal context of relationships which occur in time, as a call and response.*[45]

The summons to a shared self-surrender with Jesus entails, as with true friendship, a response to an invitation rather than a command. Yet it is central in the call/response dynamic. While, as Melina suggests above, 'our dearest friend' 'principally' counsels and advises rather than 'commands', it is still true that 'the beloved becomes the rule of the lover'. For Aquinas, friendship can generate imperatives if it is to endure and grow.[46] Further, this personal relationship as a

---

[40] Melina, *Sharing in Christ's Virtues,* 186 citing St. Thomas Aquinas, *Super Ep. ad Romanos*, Ch 12, Lect.1, no. 971.

[41] *ST* 3. 42. 1

[42] St Thomas Aquinas, *Commentary on St John,* 15, lect. 4. N. 2016 cited in Paul Morrissey, 'The Sapiential Dimension of Theology according to St. Thomas', *New Blackfriars* 93:1045 (May 2012): 309-323, at 315.

[43] *ST* 3. 42. 2 ad 1.

[44] Anthony J Kelly, 'Faith as Sight? Toward a Phenomenology of Revelation', *Australian eJournal of Theology* 19:3, December (2012):180-194, at 185 citing *ST* 3.55.3 ad 1.

[45] Kelly, 'Faith as Sight', 185; my emphasis.

[46] See n. 22 above.

form of self-surrender within friendship with Jesus, involves, as noted earlier, a participation in 'God's Wisdom [who] became man to give us an example in righteousness of living'.[47]

This brings us to Jesus as our 'wisest' friend.

Jesus as Our 'Wisest' Friend

Martin Rhonheimer, in his analysis of Aquinas on the law of practical reason, explains that human reason as:

> constituting the natural law, is a conscious, intelligent, free, responsible partaking in the power and wisdom of the divine reason, and thereby also a 'sharing' as well in the divine providence and governance of the universe.[48]

Again, for Aquinas, created wisdom shares in uncreated Wisdom.[49]

Aquinas sees discipleship with Jesus as grounded in our participation in the Incarnation, but with a specific focus, namely, in relation to our human share in divine wisdom and, specifically, in the Word as Wisdom.[50] This is explained by Aquinas:

> Now the Person of the Son, who is the Word of God, has a certain common agreement with all creatures, because the word of the craftsman, i.e., his concept, is an exemplar likeness of whatever is made by him. Hence the Word of God, Who is His eternal concept, is the exemplar likeness of all creatures. And therefore as creatures are established in their proper species, though movably, by the participation of this likeness, so by the non-participated and personal union of the Word with a creature, it was fitting that the creature should be restored in order to its eternal and unchangeable perfection; for the craftsman by the intelligible form of his art, whereby he fashioned his handiwork, restores it when it has fallen into ruin. Moreover, He has a particular agreement with human nature, since the Word is a concept of the eternal

---

[47] *ST* 3. 46. 4.

[48] Martin Rhonhemier, (Trans from the German by Gerald Malsbary), *Natural Law and Practical Reason: a Thomist View of Moral Autonomy* (New York: Fordham University Press, 2000), 11-12. See ST 1.2.90.1; 1.2.91.2: 94.2 ad.1; 1.103. 6 and 8.

[49] *ST* 1. 43. 3 and 4.

[50] *ST* 3. 52. 2. Also, there are three levels of wisdom for Aquinas: philosophical (human), theological and supernatural (gift). This is explored by Morrissey, 'The Sapiential Dimension', 311-318. See *ST* 1.1.1; and 2.2.45.

Wisdom, from Whom all man's wisdom is derived. And hence man is perfected in wisdom (which is his proper perfection, as he is rational) by participating the Word of God, as the disciple is instructed by receiving the word of his master.[51]

As noted earlier, through creation, human beings as 'image' participate in God (the metaphysical exemplar) through knowledge, love and freedom expressed in self-directed action.[52] Again, they share in divine wisdom and providence (through prudence). But, as the above text indicates, the Incarnation involves another level of participation, namely, the possibility of direct union with the person of the Word. Christ's humanity mediates grace as the 'instrument of the Godhead'. As Word, He is Wisdom itself. Now, as the Word made flesh, He makes wisdom accessible and achievable for us.[53] Further, Christ 'is the means by which creation is drawn into full participation in the life of the Triune God'.[54] As Shanley explains, the New Law of Christ 'is a deeper entering into divine providence, indeed a sharing in it precisely as Trinitarian: returning to the Father through the Son and in the Spirit'.[55]

Our concern here is not so much on participation in the Incarnation but on Jesus as divine Wisdom. As the final sentence of the text above indicates, this has clear implications for hearing the teaching, heeding the counsel, and being guided by the 'rule of the lover'—by Jesus, our 'wisest friend'. This applies also to virtue as God working in us 'without us'. On these matters, we are helped by recent studies on Joint Attention and the gifts of the Holy Spirit.

Second Personal Perspective, Joint Attention, and the Gift of Wisdom

I will briefly outline the 'traditional' presentation of the gifts, with specific focus on the gift of wisdom, and then explore the relevance, to our topic, of studies in Joint Attention.[56]

---

[51] *ST* 3. 3. 8.

[52] *ST* 1. 2 prol.

[53] A paraphrase of a comment of Michael Sherwin, OP, 'Christ the Teacher in St. Thomas's Commentary on the Gospel of John', in Michael Dauphinais and Matthew Levering, eds. *Reading John with St. Thomas* (Washington: Catholic University of America, 2005), 175 cited in Morrissey, 'The Sapiential Dimension', 316.

[54] Clark, 'The Case for an Exemplarist Approach', 70 and *ST* 3. 1. 2.

[55] Shanley, 'Aquinas's Exemplar Ethics', 368.

[56] Relevant sources here are Pinsent, *The Second-person perspective,* and Eleonore Stump, *Wandering in Darkness: Narrative and the Problem of Suffering* (Oxford: Clarendon Press, 2010). For an extensive discussion and evaluation see Tom Ryan, 'Second Person Perspective,

Pinsent proposes that, for Aquinas, moral perfection grounded in God 'working virtue in us without us' gives an essential role to the gifts (and the beatitudes and fruits of the Spirit). The gifts are perfections disposing a person to be attuned to, and to follow, the divine impulse or instinct of the Holy Spirit. These dispositions surpass all the Aristotelian or divinely infused moral virtues. With the theological virtues (faith, hope and charity) as their ultimate foundation, for Aquinas, the gifts are not secondary but essential to salvation and, hence, to the moral life.[57] The gifts accompany grace in Baptism and are not for the 'more advanced' in virtue.

Again, it is true that in Christ, just as there are found all the virtues[58] so too are found the seven gifts of the Holy Spirit to 'a pre-eminent degree'.[59] But, as noted earlier, our capacity is such that the Spirit is given 'in moderation'. Given our creaturely status, the effects of sin and our resistances, our share in the divine life is, understandably, imperfect, and fragile. The gifts are meant to remedy these influences that can impede our growing into the divine likeness.[60]

The Seven Gifts of the Holy Spirit

When Aquinas speaks of the cognitive gifts, namely, those allied to the intellect (wisdom, counsel, understanding and knowledge), he is referring to intellect in terms of practical reason (*ratio practica* or *ratio affectiva*).[61] Their specific objects (truth under the aspect of good or value to be pursued) involve evaluation and appreciative knowledge.

Aquinas' account of the four cognitive gifts suggests two aspects to their kind of 'knowing'. Through understanding, we are enabled to grasp as true something proposed to us and 'withdraw' from is opposite. In order to 'grasp or 'withdraw' we must be enabled to make the appropriate judgment and that depends on the matter under consideration: for created things, it is the gift of knowledge; for divine things, it is wisdom; for individual actions, it is counsel. [62]

As Anthony Kelly notes, Aquinas presents:

Virtues, and the Gifts in Aquinas's Ethics', *Australian eJournal of Theology* 21:1 (April 2014): 49-62.

[57] *ST* 1.2.68.2.

[58] *ST* 3. 7. 2.

[59] *ST* 3. 7. 5.

[60] Shanley, 'Aquinas's Exemplar Ethics', 361.

[61] The other three appetitive or affective gifts are fear, piety, and courage.

[62] *ST* 2 2.8.6. Also, Pinsent, *The Second-person perspective*, 39.

> ... the gift of grace as saturating every aspect of the cognitive and conative life of faith. The seven gifts are given to enable the graced subject to respond to the movement of the Spirit and to act in a manner that is beyond the human measure.[63]

He goes on to say that:

> ...intelligence must be receptive, waiting, as it were, on the gift from above, in order to know and to act in a way that respects the irruptive and transformative character of the Spirit's action. Each gift is an aspect of transforming grace of the Spirit. Each gift specifies a particular receptivity within Christian consciousness to the Spirit's 'suprarational' action. Consequently, the notion of these gifts of the Spirit leads to a healthy deconstruction of a one-dimensional rational or calculative mode of thinking, while suggesting other domains of spiritual perception.[64]

Aquinas is consistent in the different texts where he explains what is specific about the gifts. The gifts dispose a person to be 'amenable' or readily moveable (*disponitur ut efficiatur prompte mobilis*) by divine inspiration or *instinctus*.[65] The objects of both the gifts and the virtues are co-extensive. The difference lies in the manner of operation.

With the virtues, a person is moved promptly and easily by her own reason. It is a person-object process, captured in the blend of final and formal causality noted earlier (self-movement in knowing and loving).

With the gifts, alternatively, the person is moved by God (the Holy Spirit) with regard to the object of one's attention. As Pinsent sums it up: in the gifts 'Aquinas is describing a triadic person-God-object scenario in which one's stance to the object is "moved" by God, in some sense yet to be understood'[66] (a phrase to be considered later).

Again, unlike the parallel virtues, in none of the gifts do we know or arrive at truth through the process of deliberation. For example, when Aquinas describes the gift of knowledge, he contrasts it with the 'demonstrative reasoning' of the intellectual virtue of knowledge to arrive at sure judgment about the truth. Aquinas proposes that in God 'there is a sure judgment of truth, without any discourse, by simple intuition'. The gift of knowledge is a participated likeness of God's knowledge. Through this gift, one is moved by God to a knowing that is

---

[63] Kelly, 'Faith as Sight?', 187, Citing III Sent d. 34, q. 1 a. 1; ST 1.2. 70, 4.

[64] Kelly, 'Faith as Sight', 188.

[65] ST 1.2.68.1 and Pinsent, *The Second-person perspective*, 32.

[66] Pinsent, *The Second-person perspective*, 32.

a share in the divine knowledge that is 'absolute and simple'.[67] Again, we find here the triadic person-God-object pattern at work on a particular object that is the focus of one's attention. Further, this judgment is evaluative or appreciative in character, one that moves the will to a certain 'stance', or as Stump describes it, to 'a conative attitude prompted by the mind's understanding'.[68]

On this matter, more can be said—the next task.

Second Personal and Joint Attention

Recent studies of second personal experiences and second personal relationship can illuminate Aquinas' approach to the moral life.[69] For Stump, the necessary condition for a minimal second personal experience is a personal conscious interaction between two persons that is immediate, namely, a mutual presence. There is the recognition by one person of the other as a 'you'.[70] Stump's necessary conditions reflect studies of those suffering from autism spectrum disorder which is characterized by diminished social interaction and communication. In other words, autism involves an impaired ability to form 'second person' (or I-you) relationships.[71]

Further, within a mutually shared second personal relationship there is a phenomenon called *triadic joint attention* whereby both individuals can simultaneously have his or her attention fixed on some third object, event, or state of affairs. Each person's attitudes and responses to the third 'object' can be shared in a manner that is direct and intuitive. It is a 'sharing of minds'. Pinsent argues that this form of interactive relationship can offer an insight into the interaction

---

[67] ST 2 2.9.1 ad 1. Also, Pinsent, *The Second-person perspective*, 39.

[68] Eleonore Stump, 'The Non-Aristotelian Character of Aquinas's Ethics: Aquinas on the Passions', *Faith and Philosophy* 28:1 (2011): 29-43, at 41.

[69] See above n. 56 for studies by Stump and Pinsent that draw on advances in neuroscience (differences in left [analysis] and right brain [affective and metaphoric] activities) and, importantly, on research into social cognition with its relational and embodied context. Also, for the second-personal perspective and its fundamental role in the various forms of recognition of persons and the moral claims they entail, see Stephen Darwall, *The Second-Personal Standpoint: Morality, Respect, and Accountability* (Cambridge, MA: Harvard University Press, 2006).

[70] Stump, Wandering in Darkness, 75–6.

[71] Given that those with autism 'do not easily identify with other persons or appropriate their psychological orientation', they have difficulty using the second-personal pronoun 'you', namely, 'in grasping the grammatical meaning of the second person.' See Pinsent, *The Second-person perspective*, 128, n. 56. In the same work, Pinsent cites research that confirms the phenomenon of 'pronoun reversal', namely, that 'children with autism often refer to themselves as "you" and the person they are speaking with as "I"' (48).

and 'sharing of minds' between God and the person in the setting of a graced relationship and of God working 'in us without us'.

Research has shown that children with autism spectrum disorder are often unable to be 'moved' by the other person such that, from a basic form of affective response, the child can identify with the 'other' and so engage in 'joint attention' of another object or event.[72] Pinsent (and Stump) suggests that such a condition can be seen analogically in terms of a person's 'spiritual autism'—the inability to be 'moved' affectively by the divine other and, hence, share a graced relationship with God. [73]

On this basis, Pinsent probes texts in Aquinas where the infused non-Aristotelian virtues (theological and moral) and gifts heal and remove a person's spiritual autism. One is, thus, enabled to enter and pursue a relationship with God which is radically different in character and consequences from Aristotelian accounts of virtue. This is a disposition which 'God works in us without us'.

The Gift of Wisdom Reinterpreted

The virtues and the gifts are interrelated and complementary dispositions in Aquinas' moral theory. First personal dispositions (such as the virtue of wisdom) do not require a shared stance or inter-personal relationship. Alternatively, second personal dispositions involve the shared experience of embodied relationship, namely, a mutual presence of another and an acknowledged shared stance. The person so identifies with the other that they take on something of the other's psychological disposition, namely, their ways of perceiving and their dispositions to be moved and respond affectively.[74]

For Aquinas, then, with the virtue of wisdom, a judgment is made in relation to the benchmark of first personal flourishing (growing *ad imaginem* through self-direction on freedom), albeit within the context of the gift of grace.[75]

---

[72] It must be remembered that those with this disorder are, often, highly intelligent. Again, 'spectrum' is a crucial word; there can be a gradation of responsive abilities from individual to individual. Much work has been done in more recent years in this area not only in research but in assisting families and educators in constructive methods in helping children with autism.

[73] Pinsent relates his discussion of autism (a relational and affective deficit) to Aquinas' view that the infused virtues and gifts as dispositions can be present in children and in the intellectually impaired (*ST* 2.2.47.14 ad 3). See Pinsent, *The Second-person perspective*, 131, n. 95. Again, in this matter, we are reminded how all analogies 'limp'. The spiritual 'inability' noted above might have its source in defective cultural or familial factors in terms of faith and the workings of divine grace, hence, a matter of culpability that is diminished, even, removed. But it can also be grounded in a deliberate rejection of, or resistance to, divine grace, a matter of free choice, perhaps through bad habits that have been allowed to develop—a contrast with the autism spectrum disorder as a condition that is not chosen.

[74] Pinsent, *The Second-person perspective*, 62.

[75] *ST* 1.2. prol.

Alternatively, since the gifts are a disposition to being 'moved', they entail an interaction with another personal agent resulting in a shared stance towards some object—an expression of inter-personal flourishing or, in Aquinas' terms, of friendship.

The gift of wisdom, then, is qualitatively different from the virtue of wisdom. It is a disposition, within friendship with God, seeking to be associated with God by a kind of 'union of the soul'. From the action of the Holy Spirit, the person is disposed to be 'amenable' or 'readily moveable' by divine inspiration'.[76] Here, wisdom's judgment comes from a 'meeting of minds' in which there is a 'connaturality' for such judgments from love through union with God, a sharing of the divine instinct. In other words, the personal conviction grounded in love is such that we are moved to judge about a right response and action where one's desire and choice are at one.[77]

Wisdom as Taste: A Multidimensional Gift

Pinsent's treatment of the gifts recognizes their soteriological function. A reading that takes into account Aquinas' discussions elsewhere helps to throw light on their christological and ecclesial nature. As noted earlier, for Aquinas, such aspects are central in our participation in the divine nature and moral growth with Christ as exemplar. The gift of wisdom, for instance, is a share in Christ's wisdom in whom all the gifts are found to an 'exemplary degree'. By partaking in the divine nature in Christ, we are called to put on 'the mind of Christ'.

Hence, the gifts of the Spirit attune the believer's mind and heart to existence in our 'new creation' in Christ and to 'the divine milieu in which faith must now live'.[78] They enable one to be responsive to the divine gift and action of being 'moved' such that one's identity, perceptions and dispositions are shaped and informed by those of Jesus.

With the gift of wisdom, in relation to a common object, event or situation, a shared stance with God comes an intuitive judgment or 'a sure estimation that something ought to be adhered to and its opposite withdrawn from' that simulates the will. Citing Stump's phrase noted earlier, it is a shared 'conative attitude prompted by the mind's understanding'.[79]

---

[76] Pinsent, *The Second-person perspective*, 32 citing ST 1.2. 68.1.

[77] 'In this way, therefore, wisdom that is a gift has its cause in the will, namely charity, but has its essence in the intellect, whose act is to judge rightly'. ST 2.2.45.2.

[78] Kelly, 'Faith as Sight', 189.

[79] Pinsent, *The Second-person perspective*, 40. See Stump, 'The Non-Aristotelian Character of Aquinas's Ethics', 29-43, at 41.

But this has an ecclesial dimension based on union with Christ whose formative and collaborative influence finds its fullest expression, for Aquinas, in the Eucharist—as we have seen earlier. We have noted how Aquinas sums up the relationship between Christ and the Church in these terms: 'the head and members are as one mystic person (*una persona mystica*)'.[80] This is the context of the mutual presence and joint attention expressed in the gift of wisdom. As Kelly explains, the gift of wisdom

> ...is at once a tasting and an attunement to the reality of the crucified and risen One mediated in the life of the Church. It amounts to a feeling for the totality of the divine economy centered in Christ.[81]

One is moved by the Spirit to taste with the divine taste. Because of our union with Incarnate Wisdom, that wisdom which is uppermost among the gifts brings a sharing in Christ's 'taste' for divine things and in his judgment about divine realities.

Further, participation of the graced person in the Word of God Incarnate who is Wisdom together with amenability to be 'moved' by the Spirit has an inescapable Trinitarian dimension. As noted earlier, Shanley sums up the Christian moral life as a return 'to the Father through the Son and in the Spirit' and continues:

> We enter most deeply into the life of the Trinity when charity is crowned with the gift of wisdom resulting in a deep affective affinity (*compassio sive connaturalitas*) for the things of God as our own, and the resultant ability to judge them aright on that basis (*recte judicium propter connaturalitatem*).[82]

In understanding, loving, and judging as God does, one grows into the image of God (*imago Dei*), of the triune God, *Dei Trinitatis* and, one could rightly add, a person becomes *imago Christi*.

Finally, the gift of wisdom subverts and relativizes our human understandings in that it is a participation in divine Wisdom whose paradigmatic, personal, and supreme expression is the cross. It is God's 'wise foolishness' that conquers all 'human prudence' as Paul reminds us writing to the Corinthians and, as noted earlier, the cross gives us an example of virtue.[83]

---

[80] See n. 38 above.

[81] Kelly, 'Faith as Sight', 189 citing *ST* 2.2. 45.2.

[82] Shanley, 'Aquinas's Exemplar Ethics', 368 citing *ST* 2.2.45.2.

[83] Melina, *The Epiphany of Love,* 62.

Aquinas sees the timing of the Passion as subject to the divine will but within the overarching direction of divine wisdom.[84] Earlier, he draws on Gregory of Nyssa's comment that the shape of the cross extending to the four points of the compass is a metaphor of Christ as universal Savior. The Word as divine Wisdom is expressed in 'the power and the providence diffused everywhere of Him who hung upon it'. [85]

Conclusion

The discussion in this chapter revolved a phrase used by Aquinas, namely, of Jesus as 'our wisest and dearest friend'. Hopefully, with these considerations, we can better 'signpost the connections' concerning the role of Christ in the moral theology of Aquinas. Central are the role of the Word as embodied Wisdom and the soteriological emphasis of Jesus as exemplar, especially in the redemptive love of his Passion and as teacher. These aspects help to illuminate both the unity of the *Summa Theologiae* and Aquinas' sapiential approach to moral transformation, particularly, through the gifts of the Holy Spirit and, specifically, that of wisdom and its mode of operation as a form of joint attention in a second person relationship.

Our investigation has also drawn attention to the Christological and ecclesial aspects of this process. When all this is viewed within the overall matrix of friendship, of the New Law as personalized in Jesus, and of the formative action of the Holy Spirit, then, Aquinas' dictum on Christ as our 'wisest and dearest friend' offers a distilled 'taste' of the moral life that is both rich and appealing.

The theme of exemplars continues in the next chapter where we explore wisdom as loving knowledge in Dag Hammarskjöld's *Markings*.

---

[84] *ST* 3. 46.9.

[85] *ST* 3. 46. 4.

5
Wisdom as Loving Knowledge in Dag Hammarskjöld's *Markings*

Consistent with an approach to virtue through the lens of models and exemplars we come to our next topic. It is based on a recent resurgence of interest in the second Secretary-General of the United Nations, Dag Hammarskjöld and, specifically, in his personal journal *Markings*, published after his death (1961).[1] Studies generated by the publication of Hammarskjöld's diary, often present the word 'Yes' as a central theme bringing unity to his relationship with God and its ethical demands.[2]

Inspired by this recent trend, I engaged with the text of *Markings*, beyond the handful of passages often quoted in the public domain. In the process, I became conscious of an aspect of Hammarskjöld's religious consciousness that warranted further attention, hence, this discussion.[3] The chapter has five stages: first, the various forms of love present in Hammarskjöld's reflections are outlined; second, after a briefly explaining one facet of the spiritual senses, it probes a representative text on the process of knowing and loving God; third, it analyses key passages in *Markings* concerning wisdom as a virtue; fourth, in the light of the theology of the gifts of the Holy Spirit and contemporary approaches based on the second person perspective, the gift of wisdom is examined which leads to some concluding observations.

---

[1] Se Roger Lipsey, 'Dag Hammarskjöld and Markings: A Reconsideration', S*piritus: A Journal of Christian Spirituality*, 11:1 (2011): 84-103, at 85; and *Hammarskjöld: A Life* (Ann Arbor: The University of Michigan Press, 2013).

[2] 'For all that has been—Thanks! To all that shall be—Yes!' The ethical implications of Hammarskjöld's faith are again captured in his words 'The only value of a life is its content —for *others*' and 'In our era, the path to sanctification necessarily passes through action'. Dag Hammarskjöld, *Markings*, translated by W H Auden and Leif Sjöberg (London: Faber & Faber, 1964), 87. Also, Bernhard Erling, *A Reader's Guide to Dag Hammarskjöld's Waymarks* (St. Peters, Minnesota, 1987) available at http://www.daghammarskjold.se/wp-content/uploads/2014/08/rg_to_waymarks.pdf

[3] Originally published as: 'Wisdom as Loving Knowledge in Dag Hammarskjöld's *Markings*', *Spiritus: A Journal of Christian Spirituality*, 17:2 (2017): 228-245. This advanced further the theological treatment in Thomas Ryan, '"Yes!" And "Thou" in Dag Hammarskjöld's *Markings*: A Theological Investigation', *Irish Theological Quarterly* 81:2 (2016): 119-137.

The 'Yes' of Love

Hammarskjöld's faith, his 'Yes' to God of 1953 (noted above) indicated, as Aulén notes, that 'something new had come; it meant union with God, living in the hands of God, receiving rest and strength from him—and thus it also meant new integrity for the 'I', ('the wonder: that *I* exist'[4]) integrity instead of chaos, freedom instead of the bondage of self-centeredness'. Yet, even until the last prayer of his final year, it was 'a faith at battle with the risks of returning chaos and ever threatening self-centredness'.[5]

For Hammarskjöld, central to faith is the 'union of God to the soul' (St John of the Cross).[6] Union with, and life in, God were centered on *Imitatio*, a key idea arising from the Gospels and Hammarskjöld's acquaintance with the medieval mystics. *Imitatio* is the invitation to fellowship and discipleship with Jesus the 'Brother'. It is fulfilled paradigmatically in Jesus in sacrifice as self-surrender to God and to others through forgiveness and in love unto death.

Authentic self-realization, then, is only found in self-transcendence, in self-surrender. Self-surrender, as a sharing in the divine life in Christ, is inseparable from responsibility for others within the framework of one's vocation.[7] For Hammarskjöld, it was a call to serve the world and mankind which he saw as a 'service to God'. The love of God, revealed in Jesus, the cross, sacrifice and forgiveness, is 'ultimate reality'.[8]

As revealed in *Markings*, these faces of love are reflected in a prayer from *Markings* that captures the Trinitarian texture of his consciousness of loving union with God and its centrifugal orientation.

> Thou who are over us,
> Thou who art one of us,
> Thou who *art*—
> Also within us,
> May all see Thee—in me also,
> May I prepare the way for Thee,
> May I thank Thee for all that shall fall to my lot,

---

[4] *Markings*, 102.

[5] Gustaf Aulén, *Dag Hammarskjöld's White Book: The Meaning of Markings* (Philadelphia: Fortress Press, 1969), 145.

[6] *Markings*, 91. Aulén, notes that the translation of the Swedish word as 'marriage' gives the wrong impression. It suggests that Hammarskjöld might have understood the union as a form of the Bride Mysticism that, in fact, he never refers to (Aulén, *White Book*, 42).

[7] Aulén, *White Book*. 148.

[8] Ibid., 148, 151.

May I also not forget the needs of others,
Keep me in Thy love
As Thou wouldest that all should be kept in mine.
May everything in this my being be directed to Thy glory
And may I never despair.
For I am under Thy hand,
And in Thee is all power and goodness.

Give me a pure heart—that I may see Thee,
A humble heart—that I may hear Thee,
A heart of love—that I may serve Thee,
A heart of faith—that I may abide in Thee.[9]

Noteworthy is the Trinitarian sense of the first four lines where Father, Son and Holy Spirit are addressed, respectively, as 'over us', 'one of us' and 'within us'.[10] Erling notes the chiastic pattern of the following lines where we find an inverted mirror of that pattern: of the indwelling Spirit 'in me' to be visible to others, of preparing the 'way' of the Son (like John the Baptist) and gratitude to the Father as creator and guide of one's destiny.[11] This is repeated in the final stanza but centered now in the heart: to hear as 'under' the Father; to serve in imitative love of the Son; to 'abide' in God through the Spirit. This Trinitarian prayer offers a compressed expression of Hammarskjöld's spirituality and its moral impulse. This brings us to our next consideration.

Love and the Spiritual Senses

The Trinitarian prayer above has a religious context and content, one that is clearly interpersonal, participative, and oriented towards action. Hammarskjöld's journal entries, with their affective texture and mastery of rhythm and images, reflect a man of a poetic sensibility.[12]

In the texts that follow, this needs to be kept in mind. Further, as with any literary text or work of art, meaning is not only stated (in the words) but also suggested (in images, metaphor, or symbols) and associated with tone and mood. Meaning can be conveyed by what is said or not said, by polyvalent and tensive symbols, by understatement or by silence. We read 'between the lines', aware

---

[9] *Markings*, 93.

[10] Lipsey, *Hammarskjöld: A Life,* 197.

[11] Erling, *A Reader's Guide,* 113.

[12] WH Auden, a friend of Hammarskjöld, notes the 'extraordinary extent of Hammarskjöld's knowledge and understanding of poetry', *Markings,* 14.

there can be a 'surplus' of meaning or that some things are just inexpressible and can only be intimated.

With this in mind, *Markings* discloses more concerning love and Hammarskjöld's consciousness of God's presence in his life. One text from 1955 is strikingly representative of how Hammarskjöld's religious consciousness is in continuity with a long-standing tradition. Before examining that text, some background may be helpful.

The Spiritual Senses

In understanding and articulating the presence of God, analogous recourse to the 'spiritual senses' has deep roots from early in the Christian tradition.[13] A specific focus from that wider discussion offers an investigative window and hermeneutical tool, particularly as this investigation progresses.

In the mediaeval period writers such as Thomas Gallus and Thomas Aquinas hold that, concerning our rational capacities of knowing and loving, *intellectus* is oriented towards truth and *affectus* towards the good. Regarding the spiritual realm, it is *affectus* that tastes, touches, and smells and *intellectus* that sees and hears. Priority here is given to *affectus* in experiencing divine things.[14] The 'certainty of the intellect' (in sight) rests on the 'security of the affect' (affective response in faith).[15]

For Aquinas, 'taste' best describes the experience of divine goodness. Unlike touch, which entails contact from the outside, taste enables us to have 'inside knowledge', namely, 'from inside what we are tasting', namely, God 'within us'.[16] In spiritual things, something is first tasted and then seen.

Again, there is an acknowledged overlap or co-inherence of these modes of 'apprehension', namely, of love and knowledge. This is encapsulated in the words

---

[13] The expression 'spiritual senses' is first attested in the works of Origen (c. 184–254 CE) who constantly calls on his reader to reconceptualize the sensual language of the Bible and place it on a 'spiritual register'. At various times he uses all five senses to describe the relationship of the human being with God. They all point to a 'divine sense' or a special mode of perception. See the extended discussion in Paul Gavrilyuk and Sarah Coakley, *The Spiritual Senses: Perceiving God in Western Christianity* (New York and Cambridge UK: CUP, 2012), Introduction, 5; 22–31.

[14] Boyd Taylor Coolman, 'Thomas Gallus' in Gavrilyuk and Coakley, *The Spiritual Senses*, 140-158, at 147.

[15] Richard Cross, 'Thomas Aquinas', in Gavrilyuk and Coakley, *The Spiritual Senses*, 174-189, at 188.

[16] Thomas Aquinas, *Postilla super Psalmos* 33,8 cited in Tony Kelly C Ss R, *The Bread of God; Nurturing a Eucharistic Imagination* (Pymble, NSW: HarperCollinsReligious, 2001), 89.

of Gregory the Great (cited by Aquinas) that 'love itself is a form of knowing' (*amor ipse notitia est*).[17] As Andrew Louth sums it up:

> The soul wants to know God more and more because it loves him, and loves him because it knows that he is supreme Truth and Beauty. Love and knowledge of God are united in the kind of knowledge we have of God, namely wisdom, *sapientia*.[18]

Here, Aquinas offers a needed caveat. Whatever the degree to which we come to know and love God in this life it is, nevertheless, a union with one who is beyond our comprehension and as one unknown. We do have a natural desire to see God and to find the light. But given the limitless radiance of God, our human knowledge of God is still vespertilionine: since the bat cannot bear the sunlight, it engages with its environment through radar-like soundings.[19] Further, McIntosh reminds us that it could be said that in 'mystical contemplation it is not the mystic who knows and loves but rather the mystic is the one *known* and *loved* by God'.[20]

We return to Hammarskjöld.

Images of Loving Knowledge

Consider this 1955 text in *Markings*.

> He had no need for the divided responsibility in which others seek to be safe from ridicule, because he had been granted a faith which required no confirmation—a contact with reality, light and intense like the touch of a loved hand: a union in self-surrender without self-destruction, where his heart was lucid and his mind loving. In sun and wind, how near and how remote—. How different from what the knowing ones call Mysticism.[21]

Erling argues that this forms a separate text in the Swedish version and also in Hammarskjöld's original manuscript. This clearly separates it from the

---

[17] Gregory the Great, *Homelia in Evangel.* 27:4, cited in Thomas Aquinas, *Catena Aurea Vol. 4 St John* Cap. 15: v.15 (London: St. Austen Press, 1999), 486. 'For while we love the heavenly things we hear, we know them by loving, because love is itself knowing'.

[18] Andrew Louth, 'Bernard and Affective Mysticism', in Benedicta Ward, SLG, ed. *The Influence of St Bernard* (Oxford, SLG Press, 1976), 3. Wisdom and its association with 'taste' will be explored later in this chapter.

[19] Summa *Theologiae* 1.12.13 and 1.1.12.1 (henceforth *ST*).

[20] Mark A McIntosh, *Mystical Theology: The Integrity of Spirituality and Theology* (Malden MA: Blackwell, 1999), 70; italics in original.

[21] *Markings*, 100.

previous three lines which it is agreed refer to the person of Jesus.[22] On that basis, contra Aulén, Erling (with van Dusen and Lipsey) holds that this text is about Hammarskjöld himself.[23] How can this be evaluated?

The text is certainly consistent with earlier passages in his journal that give insight into Hammarskjöld's religious consciousness. The passage's language and mood resemble other entries where Hammarskjöld describes his experiences of the 'unspeakable' by drawing on nature and human experience rather than using explicitly religious idiom or images. It is almost as if spirituality is hidden within the secular. For all that, Hammarskjöld can still observe that 'a landscape can sing about God' (89).

In this entry, with the nature imagery there is an accompanying sense of personal relationship and closeness that converges with our comments above about touch and the primary role of affectivity— 'like the touch of a loved hand'. The contact with reality is immediate— 'light and intense', requiring no confirmation. The intellect's 'certainty' is underpinned by an affective 'security'.[24]

Further, the recipient is passive, receptive to the action of God, to a gift (faith 'that had been granted'). Its fruit is union, bringing self-surrender without self-annihilation (the move from union to *agape* but also the finding of the true self). From here comes his sense of a unified rather than 'divided' responsibility. Again, there is intimated the mutual co-inherence of knowledge and love ('heart was lucid and his mind loving').[25] Overall, the mood conveyed is one of serene receptivity.

Mystery as immanent/transcendent or kataphatic/ apophatic is suggested in 'sun and wind, how near and how remote'.[26] While the use of sun (light) and wind imagery may not be explicitly Christian in intention here, their suggestive

---

[22] 'He broke fresh ground—because, and only because, he had the courage to go ahead without asking whether others were following or even understood', *Markings*, 100.

[23] Aulén's reason is that Hammarskjöld's usual practice was to use the second person when referring to himself (*White Book*, 27). Yet, there are passages where Hammarskjöld alternates between 'he' and 'you' (see *Markings*, 65, 88-9) or speaks of something in objective mode which is clearly consonant with his own spiritual experience (e.g., concerning 'mystical experience', *Markings*, 108).

[24] Earlier, Hammarskjöld speaks of a knowing 'without knowing' in a '*vision* in which God *is*' underpinning self-surrender. *Markings*, 83; italics in original.

[25] Aulén does not modify this translation. Erling's rendition is 'clarity of feeling and warmth of understanding', Erling, *A Reader's Guide*, 131.

[26] Aulén, *White Book*, 43.

quality is certainly consistent with Hammarskjöld's use of those images elsewhere to capture his experience of reality and of God (to be clarified later).

His final ironical comment about the 'knowing ones' betrays his understanding of 'Mysticism', namely, that it is not an escape from life. From the medieval mystics Hammarskjöld had learned that love meant an overflowing of strength when one lives from true self-oblivion in service of others together with openness to life, whatever it brings.[27] In this, Hammarskjöld returns to the morally responsible orientation of mysticism with its 'concrete and sober commitment to humanity and this world' that has a 'long ancestry'.[28]

Later in 1955, he outlines his understanding of 'mystical experience', as 'Always: *here* and *now'*, a mystery constantly present for one 'free from self-concern' that matures 'before the receptive attention of assent'.[29] This balances the earlier passage. Now there is more emphasis on the everyday nature of 'mystical experience', namely, that is not a matter of special experiences for special people. In this, Hammarskjöld is distancing himself from more privatized and elitist trends emerging with the modern period.

Where does this awareness of being 'touched' by God lead? It brings us to the virtues.

Virtue and Wisdom

While virtues such as faithfulness, courage, humility, and patience are expressed in Hammarskjöld's various entries, there is also the presence of one significant virtue, specifically, wisdom. Coming to know 'the only real thing, love's calm unwavering flame...'[30] creates a union and singleness of heart, hence, giving light that transforms how we perceive reality, oneself, and one's actions. This underpins Hammarskjöld's search for a moral path (virtue) and for wisdom, reflected in his 1959 entry from Psalm 51: 6, 'thou require truth in the inward parts, and shall make me to understand wisdom secretly'.[31]

---

[27] Aulén, *White Book,* 43.

[28] Frans Maas, *Spirituality as Insight: Mystical Texts and Theological Reflection* (Leuven: Peters, 2004), 52.

[29] *Markings*, 108; italics in original.

[30] *Markings,* 139, 140.

[31] *Markings,* 147.

Concerning virtue, in 1956, Hammarskjöld, citing Eckhart, refers to 'habitual will'.[32] Trust between God and the very core of a person embodied in the 'yes' of loving surrender is encapsulated in the term 'habitual will'. In this meeting of wills, there is a collaborative relationship that is not a loss of human freedom but its fullest expression. It also denotes an openness to, and creative influence on, the 'wills' and lives of others. 'Re-transformed into instinct' in the passage suggests the will's habituated tendencies to true values that we call virtues, namely, good dispositions that are second-nature and, in a sense, 'instinctive'.

Specifically, for the virtue of wisdom, we look to 1958:

> Only in man has the evolution of the creation reached the point where reality encounters itself in judgment and choice...Only when you descend into yourself and encounter the Other, do you then experience goodness as the ultimate reality—united and living—*in* Him and *through* you.[33]

Here, 'the Other' reflects his reading of Rudolf Otto and the idea of 'Wholly Other'. Using the language of encounter, Hammarskjöld conveys his movement beyond the frontier of 'the unheard-of' (where 'desire is purified into openness') into a more immediate and embodied consciousness of the mystery of being and its revelatory power. Hammarskjöld appears to blend the language of interpersonal relationship and that of the Unitary God in alluding to goodness as a transcendental property of being ('the ultimate reality'). Elsewhere, there is a parallel use of beauty (to be explored later).

Wisdom as Participatory and Centrifugal

This passage above suggests, first, the participatory nature of the 'experience' of goodness. It is the sharing of, and between, two subjects. The resultant shaping of one's rational capacities, as reflected in this and further entries (examined below), converges with a similar approach in the Christian tradition found, for instance, in the virtue ethics of Thomas Aquinas. As 'one' in God, we share in the wisdom and providence of the divine exemplar through affective consciousness, namely, an appreciation of God as the absolute center of value, of good as the 'ultimate reality'. Again, as discussed previously in this book, we are images of God (the exemplar) in judgment, freedom, and the capacity for self-direction, especially through practical wisdom.[34]

---

[32] *Markings,* 117; Erling, *A Reader's Guide,* 56:31.

[33] *Markings*, 139; italics in original.

[34] See *ST* 1.2.91.2 and 1.2 prol.

Second, Hammarskjöld's longing for wisdom is further specified later (1959). He speaks of encountering the world from a 'point of rest at the centre of our being' where 'to be *one* or *whole,* namely, single hearted, is:

> ...to experience reality, not *in relation to ourselves,* but in its sacred independence. It is to see, judge and act from the point of rest in ourselves. Then, how much disappears and all the remains falls into place.[35]

A persistent concern for Hammarskjöld is to be attentive, to listen to his inner movements and to the reality of the world around him—whether social, political or in creation. There is an ongoing search for purity of heart, of being open to, and receptive to, reality, 'the receptive attention of assent' of the mystical attitude noted earlier. Here, it is couched in terms of bringing a 'single heart' from the center of one's being.

Seen within the spiritual tradition, this personal stance is resonant with Simone Weil's focus on cultivating the 'faculty of attention' in which 'we open ourselves to what is objectively there'. In this way, we become 'supple to reality' and 'have penetrated the object'. Truthful knowledge emerges from the 'spiritual activity of waiting'. 'We do not obtain the most precious gifts by going in search of them but by waiting for them'. Appeal to Weil's view of attention is made by Iris Murdoch (also by Rowan Williams). Murdoch writes that the direction of attention is, contrary to nature, outward, away from the self...towards the great surprising variety of the world'. It is only when I look at something objectively am I taken beyond myself into contact with reality. 'I am disabused of my selfish projections'.[36]

For Hammarskjöld, this attentive openness, without filters or projections, brings insight into reality when experienced in its 'sacred independence'. Wisdom's secrets should acknowledge the autonomy of earthly realities (the secular realm) together with their claims concerning truth and goodness in moral evaluation and action from God's perspective.

Attention and Dark Impulses

Further, when we stand 'in the righteous all-seeing light of love that we can dare to look', this enables a way of 'recognising' and gaining 'full insight' into that

---

[35] *Markings,* 148; italics in original. Aulén suggests 'single-hearted' or 'simplicity' as best capturing the Swedish word rather than 'humility' (Aulén, *White Book*, 68).

[36] Benjamin Myers, *Christ the Stranger: The Theology of Rowan Williams* (London/New York: T & T Clark, 2012), 110-111 citing or paraphrasing Iris Murdoch, *The Sovereignty of Good* (UK: Routledge and Kegan Paul, 1970), 46-76 and Simone Weil, *Waiting for God* (New York: G.P. Putnam's Sons, 1951).

'dark, counter-centre of evil in our nature' (Original Sin) and reach a point of self-forgiveness.[37] This is associated with the need to 'purify the eye of [your] attention until it becomes utterly simple and direct'.[38]

Self-criticism and a probing attention to self-centeredness and duplicity are evident from the start of *Markings*. In 1941-2, we see Hammarskjöld engaging with the 'dark, counter-centre' with its impulse to cruelty, falsehood, spite, and self-absorption. Twice he uses the image of the wolf to express the predatory, ruthless, even, fierce side of himself. Nevertheless, he is determined 'to gaze steadfastly' into this aspect of himself until he has 'plumbed its depths'.[39]

However, this determination to be attentive to his 'dark' side does not seem to maintain the same stringency as the journal progresses. Later, while he feels shame for his defects, he also has a sense of gratitude and a growing sense of God's ever-present forgiveness and, even, as noted above from 1957, of self-forgiveness. He displays awareness that his sinful failures and resistances underline an emptiness that only God can fill. In the last analysis, using an image of the stage and the stage-manager, it is God who is in charge.[40]

Overall, such insights from two to three years before his death mark a significant stage in Hammarskjöld's evolving consciousness. His union with God deepens his sensitivity to the importance of being attentive and receptive. In this way, perceptions, dispositions, judgments, choices, and actions find their true objects and meaning through the life of the virtues.

There is, then, a resonating of one's being with that of God (the Other) by sharing the divine 'ethical space'. By being 'in' Him, what is truly good can be discerned and enacted in cooperation with God ('*through* you'), in practical wisdom. This is to be self-effaced in the Light 'so that it may be focused or spread wider'.[41] Hammarskjöld's is, like that of Aquinas, a sapiential vision with appreciative knowledge animated and directed by love's 'calm unwavering flame'.

What has been said above underpins two other excerpts noted earlier: 'The only value of a life is its content—for *others*' and 'In our era, the path to

---

[37] *Markings*, 128.

[38] *Markings*, 95.

[39] *Markings*, 36-7.

[40] For these aspects see, respectively, *Markings*, 110, 133, 84, 98.

[41] *Markings*, 133.

sanctification necessarily passes through action'.[42] There is a continuum of the mystical and the ethical.

We turn now to another perspective on wisdom.

Wisdom and Second Person Perspective: An Applied Approach

Before approaching further texts in *Markings,* we need to return to ideas developed earlier concerning the gifts of the Holy Spirit, with particular reference to the gift of wisdom and the second person perspective.[43]

In the life of faith, the gift of divine grace permeates the cognitive, affective, and conative aspects of personhood and their influence on interpersonal relationships. In contrast with the virtues, through the gifts of the Spirit, one is disposed to be readily moveable by the Spirit to act in a manner that is beyond human measure. One is attuned to the divine milieu of a shared relationship and enabled to judge and act in a modality that is intuitive and immediate.

The traditional analogy to capture the different modes of the virtues and the gifts is the progress of a boat. The use of oars to move the boat forward represents the role of the virtues. Putting up the sails to be propelled by the wind represents the work of the gifts—the impulse and action of the Holy Spirit. With the virtues, it is our effort, albeit under the grace of God. With the gifts, it is God's work but with our cooperation.[44]

As explained in the previous chapter, recent studies on second person perspective and Joint Attention offer further refinements in regard to understanding the gifts.[45] The analogy of the affective response entailed in the mutual presence and Joint Attention between, for instance, and parent and a child, has been applied to the modality of the gifts. There is a shared attitude and response to a common object or state of affairs. The mutual love or friendship in union with God brings a shared response of love together with a common understanding and response to values that underlie moral judgments. As noted earlier, grace enables us to share in the divine subjectivity, the divine knowing and love and in the Trinitarian relationships.

---

[42] *Markings*, 140 and 108. Aulén prefers 'sanctification' to 'holiness' because of its stronger sense of God's action and its centrifugal character (Aulén, *White Book*, 100).

[43] See chapter four, 69-74.

[44] It is a misunderstanding to see this analogy in sequential mode—the virtues are operational first and, then, at a certain stage of advanced virtue, the gifts come in to play. In reality, the gifts are given with the grace of Baptism, hence, are at work from the very start. The precise relationship between the virtues and the gifts is beyond this discussion.

[45] See above, 73-74.

How is this applicable in our discussion here?

Images of Light and Love at Work

With this as background, we can now approach a 1956 passage in *Markings* that is strikingly consonant with this traditional approach to the gifts, even using the principal analogy used to capture their modality. While commentators do not indicate whether Hammarskjöld was aware of the theology of the gifts and its associated boating metaphor, his appeal to it is enlightening.

> The *Wind* bloweth where it listeth—
> so is every one that is born of the spirit. (John III, v 8)
>
> And the *light* shineth in darkness,
> And the darkness comprehended it not. (John I, v 5)
>
> Like wind—. In it, with it, of it. Of it, just like a sail, as light and strong that, even where bent flat, gathers all the power of the wind without hampering its course.
> Like light—. In light, lit through by light, transformed into light. Like the lens which disappears in the light it focuses.
>
> Like wind, Like light.
> Just this—on these expanses, on these heights.[46]

Erling suggests this entry possibly reflects 'an experience on a cliff overlooking the sea'.[47] Hammarskjöld cites and comments on two passages from John's Gospel building on two symbols for God that, as noted earlier, he uses elsewhere. For example, wind and light prompt Hammarskjöld to ponder God's greatness and how good it is, despite one's smallness, to be caught up in that which alone is great'.[48]

In the scriptural section of the text above from two passages in John's Gospel, the interplay of the affective and the cognitive is intimated (the hermeneutical window explained earlier). In affective mode, the wind clearly refers to the person of the Holy Spirit, with the implied scriptural connotation of love. Hammarskjöld sees himself as a sail in relation to the wind, hence, guided by divine love. In this, both the sail and the wind become wholly identified. Even when it is 'bent flat' ('bound to the earth' in Erling's rendition),

---

[46] *Markings,* 112; italics in original. Erling, *A Reader's Guide*, 56:16.

[47] Erling, *A Reader's Guide*, 156-7.

[48] *Markings,* 137. Erling's rendition is 'In your wind—. In your light—. How small is everything else, how small are we— and happy in that which alone is great' (*A Reader's Guide*, 57:52).

the sail can harness the power of the wind while not impeding or constraining it. It is a collaboration done in love.

The cognitive aspect is conveyed in the second symbol where the light represents the incarnate Word from the Gospel's Prologue, who, as the light in the darkness, is a divine beacon of truth ('the Light of the world', cf., John 8:3). Hammarskjöld sees himself, again, as so identified with the light that he acts like a 'lens that focuses the light to new strength and intensity, but is not itself seen'.[49]

A year later (1957) there is the corresponding passage where Hammarskjöld describes sanctity as 'either to be the Light, or be self-effaced in the Light, so that it may be born, self-effaced so that it may be focused and spread wider'.[50] Intimations of growing light and insight are evident from 1952. He likens being sustained by the strength and power from the air to a glider or like water for a swimmer together with the illuminating vision of being part of a magnetic field, in a timeless present, part of the Communion of Saints.[51]

The symbol of light used in this passage from John, its association with truth and its embodiment in the person of the Word could be seen as the culmination of developing mystical intensity and its associated insights. Five years earlier in 1951 Hammarskjöld has a breakthrough experience after a night in the mountains. He is unable to form a clear image of the One causing the experience and prompting the accompanying insight. That mysterious reality is hidden. He draws on nature and its images—the doorway to the 'beyond' and the inexpressible. He moves from the dark of night into the 'pale gold of a new day'. He is drawn by 'Light without a visible source'. All of this is convergent with the caveat noted earlier from Aquinas.[52] The spiritual awakening, the moment of insight comes suddenly (an answer to his original question and hope, to reach the destination where 'life rings out' in 'a clear pure note in the silence').[53]

> Then—all of a sudden—the first blackbird's piercing note of call, a reality outside yourself, the real world. All of a sudden—the Earthly Paradise from which we have been excluded by our knowledge.[54]

---

[49] Erling, *A Reader's Guide*, 157. See also entry in 1957, *Markings,* 133 in similar vein.

[50] *Markings*, 133.

[51] *Markings*, 84.

[52] See n.19.

[53] *Markings*, 31.

[54] *Markings*, 74.

This is not an insight from rational knowledge. It is a flash of meaning that 'rings true'. This resonating call from beyond is 'something touching and tempting'...physical and concrete like a bird's call'.[55] It still leads Hammarskjöld to wonder about the visible and the invisible, about the frontier bordering the beyond in whose depths are found beauty, harmony, and inexpressible truth:

> Where does the frontier lie? Where do we travel in those dreams of beauty satisfied, laden with significance but without comprehensible meaning? Etched into the mind far deeper than the witness of the eyes. Where all is well—without fear, without desire. [56]

Later, in 1956, from the text we have seen on the wind and the light, Spirit and Word, there is intimated an answer to his question here. Hammarskjöld's sense of the inter-penetration of light and lens is underpinned by the physical and embodied expression of the call from beyond, one that touches him and is alluring. The light may still not have a visible source, but now it takes the visible form of a personal revelation in Jesus, the Word made flesh. The truth, the axis of meaning, is now a person within history.

Modality of the Gifts

Again, Hammarskjöld is attempting to express an 'irreducibly simple experience' ('just this') through the compression of image and emotion in poetic and descriptive mode rather than through explanatory and theological language. Lipsey says that Hammarskjöld is thinking 'about two wills and their relation'.[57] Granted his use of synecdoche, this is true, up to a point. It is consistent with our elaboration above of the controlling metaphor used of the gifts of the Holy Spirit in the Catholic theological tradition, namely, the Spirit symbolized as the wind acting on the sails to drive a boat forward.

However, in Hammarskjöld, it is not just a matter of 'will power' in a relationship, but the will as expressing personal love that seeks what is mutual and unifying. It is the person of the Spirit, of divine love that 'guides the boat' of spiritual progress. This is strengthened by the symbolic interaction of light and lens to capture the simultaneous presence and action of the Word and the association with truth.

The interplay of wind/love (Spirit) with light/truth (Word), then, intimates the interpenetration of the affective and the cognitive (suggested in the 1955 text: 'his heart was lucid and his mind loving'). It points to a maintaining of the 'alliance'

---

[55] Maas, *Spirituality as Insight*, 82.

[56] *Markings*, 76.

[57] Lipsey, *Hammarskjöld: A Life*, 262.

between intellect and will, knowledge and love, theology, and experience', noted by Denys Turner.[58]

The fuller significance of the passage here, then, must be seen in terms of the sense of union, of mutual co-inherence of persons—Word, Spirit, and Hammarskjöld—that forms its context in his spiritual development. It is a growth in knowing and loving *of* God and *from* God. Further, the use of prepositions (in, with, through and of) is suggestive of the Trinitarian dimension in Hammarskjöld's religious consciousness as reflected in the pattern of his prayers (noted at the start of this chapter).

Again, the implied sense of touch (especially of 'being touched' by God) from the metaphor of the wind on the sail must be balanced by that of taste as associated with wisdom (mentioned earlier). Reflecting on the meaning of his fellowship with God (Christmas Day 1955), Hammarskjöld cites the *Imitation of Christ*. The passage speaks of tasting God 'in Himself or in His works' which brings a sense of the 'infinite distance between the creature and the Creator'. The passage ends with a prayer to be enlightened that leads to being 'transported out of herself by the excess of her happiness' so that [the soul] 'binds herself to Thee with all her powers and in all her motions'.[59]

In the following entry, he expresses his own personal experience of tasting and finding joy in God:

> You take the pen—and the lines dance. You take the flute—and the tones shimmer. You take the brush—and the colors sing. In this way everything becomes meaningful and beautiful in that space beyond time which you are. How then can I keep anything back from you?[60]

Erling rightly observes this is a celebration of God 'as the source of beauty'. The Creator that Hammarskjöld encounters is One who 'enlivens in a person every kind of competence, the ability to write, to make music, to paint. Everything becomes meaningful and beautiful because eternity interpenetrates time'.[61] Truth is mediated by the apprehension of beauty. In the next entry Hammarskjöld offers a vision of creation and eternal life as an expression of the interchange between time and eternity.

Again, in 1959, his entry is in haiku form:

---

[58] Denys Turner, *The Darkness of God: Negativity in Christian Mysticism* (Cambridge, UK: CUP, 1999), 224.

[59] *Markings*, 105.

[60] Erling, *A Reader's Guide*, 55:54.

[61] Erling, *A Reader's Guide*, 142.

> Beauty. Goodness.
> In the wonder's here and now
> Became suddenly real.[62]

While wonders do occur, Hammarskjöld does not want to base faith on them.[63] Here, he returns to his earlier insight that wonder is our primary impulse about mystery; it drives our quest for meaning.[64]

What emerges from these texts associated with taste is a strongly internalized sense of beauty, a form of knowing 'from the inside', noted earlier about taste. It is through this that the author is touched and drawn by what is 'meaningful' in the world (its truth, its goodness) in a movement of self-transcendence. As noted earlier, the taste for divine things in the gift of wisdom is normally associated with the appreciation of the good. In discussing wisdom as a virtue, we explained Hammarskjöld's awareness of an intimate appreciation of, and sharing in, divine goodness as a center of value. These texts, seen cumulatively, indicate the interpenetration of the transcendentals of beauty and goodness as doorways to the truth in Hammarskjöld's apprehension of God and of reality. This confirms a point noted earlier that beauty, with goodness (and truth), are properties of being, of reality that Hammarskjöld not only is touched by and tastes but is called to share.

Interweaving of Goodness, Truth, and Beauty

The co-inherence of goodness, truth and beauty is distilled in a passage that immediately precedes the passage on wind (Spirit) and light (Christ) explained above.

> A poem is like a deed in that it is to be judged as a manifestation of the personality of its maker. This in no way ignores its beauty as measured by aesthetic standards of perfection, but also considers its authenticity as measured by its congruence with an inner life.[65]

The three criteria suggested above for evaluating a poem also apply to our human actions: the aesthetic, the authentic and the ethical. One could couch these in three questions: does the poem have integrity, harmony and proportion in its form that enables it to bring light (insight) to the reader? Is the poem a sincere and honest expression of the poet's innermost response to life? What sort of personality is being revealed, namely, the character of the poet?

In these three questions can be found a compressed expression of the interplay and co-inherence, successively, of the beautiful, the true and the good

---

[62] *Markings*, 158.

[63] *Markings*, 125.

[64] *Markings*, 33.

[65] *Markings*, 112.

as much in human action as in a poem. If beauty is the truth that shines out, namely, it manifests itself, goodness is truth appreciated as a value to be pursued. For Hammarskjöld, the criterion of the authentic life (as true, good, and beautiful) is one lived for others. This is captured in one phrase: when one reaches a point of being able to give without expecting a response, then '...Love has matured and, through dissolution of the self into light, [it] becomes a radiance...'[66]

Taste, then, for Hammarskjöld, is an 'inside' knowing of beauty and of goodness that opens up to truth. Here is found the gateway to mystery with its summons to self-transcendence. Nevertheless, his taste for God prompting the desire to act as God would act in relation to the world mirrors what was discussed earlier about Hammarskjöld's insights into wisdom as an element in his religious consciousness. There, it was couched in terms of virtue and the first-person modality. Now wisdom can be seen as the gift. It is a sharing in the divine 'taste.' From the Spirit's wind acting on the sail, there emerges a common attitude, a shared judgment about true value and subsequent action. With the second person perspective and the role of Joint Attention, the context is more explicitly interpersonal. Within friendship, a divine-human cooperation is prompted and guided by the action of the Spirit. It is the realization of Hammarskjöld's comment: 'Not I but God in me'.[67]

Again, one cannot ignore how, in 1955, in addressing issues of conflict, Hammarskjöld reveals his awareness of the need to somehow 'enter into' the subjectivity of the ''other'. He wants to shift:

> the dividing-line in my being between subject and object to a position where the subject, even it is in me, is outside and above me—so that my *whole* being may become an instrument for that which is greater than I.[68]

For him, faith is being '*one* in God and God [is] wholly in you'.[69] Its expression is in the polyvalent and participatory symbolism of wind (truth, the Word) and light (love, Holy Spirit). In this, Hammarskjöld is again expressing an entering into 'the subjectivity of the 'other' but now it is of the Trinitarian 'Others'.

---

[66] *Markings*, 112.

[67] *Markings*, 127.

[68] *Markings*, 64; italics in original. See also Erling, *A Reader's Guide*, 53.

[69] *Markings*, 139.

Summary

Our discussion indicates Hammarskjöld's appreciation of the sharing of subjectivity reflected in the identification with the movement of the Spirit (wind on the sail). It is intertwined with the presence (and action) of the Word through Hammarskjöld's use of the symbol of light in relation to a lens.

On this matter, it should be noted that the role of Christ in the work of the Spirit through the gifts is often muted. As Anthony Kelly points out, the gift of wisdom is 'at once a tasting and an attunement to the reality of the crucified and risen One mediated in the life of the Church'.[70] Because of our union with Incarnate Wisdom, that wisdom which is uppermost amongst the gifts brings a sharing in Christ's 'taste' for divine things and in his judgment about divine realities.

Hammarskjöld's blend of wind and light addresses this issue poetically and, by implication, theologically (while acknowledging his distinctive understanding of the community of the Church). The gift of wisdom is a share in the wisdom of Christ, who, has been given the Spirit 'without reserve' (Jn 3: 33) and, for Aquinas, possesses all the gifts 'to a pre-eminent degree'.[71]

Finally, Hammarskjöld's yearning for fellowship is paralleled by a particular approach to the Church (beyond this discussion here). But one passage adumbrates, even anticipates, a divinely-oriented future. It offers an insight into Hammarskjöld's hopes about the destiny of humanity and creation. It is seen, in God's company, as reaching down into the silent depths of the mystery of reality:

> In a dream, I walked with God through the deep places of creation; past walls that receded and gates that opened, through hall after hall of silence, darkness and refreshment—the dwelling place of souls acquainted with light and warmth—*until, around me, was an infinity into which we all flowed together and lived anew,* like the rings made by raindrops falling upon wide expanses of calm dark water.[72]

Conclusion

This chapter made soundings in the journal entries of Dag Hammarskjöld. It started with an outline of the various forms of love found in his reflections. After explaining an aspect of the spiritual senses, we did an exegesis and an interpretation of a text in *Markings* (from the Gospel of St John) on the process

---

[70] Anthony J Kelly, 'Faith as Sight? Toward a Phenomenology of Revelation', *Australian eJournal of Theology* 19:3, December, 2012: 180-194, at 189 citing *ST* 2.2.45.2.

[71] *ST* 3.7.5.

[72] *Markings,* 105; my emphasis.

of knowing and loving God. The chapter then analyzed key passages in *Markings* concerning wisdom as a virtue. Finally, the gift of wisdom was investigated in the light of the theology of the gifts of the Holy Spirit and contemporary approaches based on the second person perspective.

In *Markings*, with its blend of image, compressed emotion, and distilled insight, we have the reflections of a very private man. Scholarship has uncovered many of the sources that shape and inform Hammarskjöld's religious consciousness and spiritual quest. Our considerations have (hopefully) illuminated convergences within a long-standing tradition.

On the textual evidence, Hammarskjöld's articulation of wisdom, as loving knowledge, emerges from the author's groping and growing awareness of being known and loved by God. Again, through his use of image, symbol, and language, he is enabled to integrate the voluntarist and intellectualist strands that have, at times, been separated in that tradition.

For that, we are indebted to Dag Hammarskjöld.

In the next stage of our discussion of 'Virtue at Work', we offer a wider framework for considering the role of personal witness, namely, one related to moral development and the pedagogy of grace.

That is the next task.

6
Witness, The Pedagogy of Grace and Moral Development

The calibrations of virtue discussed in the two previous chapters were interwoven with pointers to personal witness and its role in the moral life. That topic sets the scene for this chapter. It will also shift the spotlight to the contemporary scene and the person of Pope Francis.

Three recent phrases of Pope Francis warrant attention and guide this chapter. First, there is his call for 'witnesses of God's love' in his tribute to modern martyrs. The second is 'the pedagogy of grace' and the work of the Spirit explained in his Apostolic Exhortation *Amoris Laetitia* (2016). The third phrase, from the same document, signals his discussion of 'accompaniment' in the process of moral discernment within the Church.

With these as guideposts and drawing on recent studies in moral philosophy and psychology, this chapter unfolds in five steps: a) setting the scene; b) witness in relation to moral understanding and intersubjectivity; c) intersubjectivity and conscience; d) a pedagogy of grace—Holy Spirit and non-believers; e) a pedagogy of grace in relation to moral development.[1]

Setting the Scene

'We do not encounter moral goodness or divine grace in the abstract but wrapped up in specific people and complex situations', as William Spohn reminds us. Some encounters lead nowhere, some strengthen our resolve in difficult circumstances, but some 'have an inviting quality that promises deeper value and meaning'.[2] Consider this well-known example.

In the early 1960's, aged seventeen, philosopher Raimond Gaita worked as a ward-assistant in a psychiatric hospital in Australia. The young Gaita speaks of admiring 'enormously' the dedicated psychiatrists who, devotedly, cared for the patients, so many of whom had lost self-respect or meaning in their lives and were judged to be 'incurable'.

One day, a religious sister came to the ward. Gaita was initially struck by her 'vivacity' but that changed when she spoke to the patients. As he says:

---

[1] This chapter was originally published as Daniel J Fleming and Thomas Ryan, 'Witness, Pedagogy of Grace and Moral Development', *The Australasian Catholic Record* 95:3 (July) 2018: 259-272.

[2] William C Spohn, 'The Formative Power of Story and the Grace of Indirection', in Patricia Lamoureux and Kevin J O'Neil, C.Ss. R, eds. *Seeking Goodness and Beauty: The Use of the Arts in Theological Ethics* (Lanham, MD: Rowman and Littlefield, 2005), 13-31, at 13.

> Then everything in her demeanour towards them—the way she spoke to them, her facial expressions, the inflexions of her body—contrasted with and showed up the behaviour of those noble psychiatrists... she thereby revealed that even such patients were, as the psychiatrists and I had sincerely and generously professed, the equals of those who wanted to help them; but she also revealed that in our hearts we did not believe this.[3]

This is a cautionary tale for us, as much as it was for Gaita and for the psychiatrists. We may be sincere, well-intentioned, and convinced of the value of the other person, especially those afflicted in some way. Yet, our behavior can reveal that, at a deeper level, we may not have really appreciated the worth of the person, of someone as an equal, namely, with a conviction that has personal or 'felt' significance.

Based on this incident, Gaita develops the case that the moral life has its grounding in the power of affective response such as love or remorse (he uses a further story for this) to reveal the value of other human beings. As Wynn expresses it:

> ...this account suggests that moral understanding, at its deepest and most effective in action, may be lodged in our felt responses to others (how we think of them 'in our hearts'), rather than in some more discursive account of their significance.[4]

Gaita does not see the religious sister's love as revealing a religious warrant or offering a form of independent justification. In saying that the patients were 'rightly' our equals and the objects of non-condescending treatment, 'I can only appeal to the purity of her love...(which) proved the reality of what it revealed'.[5] From the point of view of speculative intelligence, he suggests he is 'going around in ever darkening circles'. He sharpens his focus further in saying:

> Nothing I can say will diminish this affront to reason. Love, goodness, purity, beauty—the last being, as Simone Weil said, the word that first comes to mind when we think of saintly deeds....[6]

---

[3] Raimond Gaita, *A Common Humanity: Thinking about Love, and Truth and Justice* (Melbourne, Australia: The Text Publishing, 1999), 17-19.

[4] Mark R Wynn, *Emotional Experience and Religious Understanding: Integrating Perception, Conception and Feeling* (Cambridge, UK: Cambridge University Press, 2005), 30-1.

[5] Gaita, *A Common Humanity*, 21.

[6] Gaita, *A Common Humanity*, 22.

Gaita himself goes on to observe:

> our sense of the preciousness of other people is connected with their power to affect us in ways we cannot fathom and against which we can protect ourselves only at the cost of becoming shallow.[7]

Building on this incident, Gaita proceeds to elaborate and defend his moral theory. Our purpose here is more limited. Together with the cue offered above by Wynn, the event's 'inviting quality' warrants further probing for any 'deeper value and meaning'. We can approach this, first, in terms of witness, moral understanding and intersubjectivity; second, intersubjectivity and conscience; third, concerning the pedagogy of grace in relation to the Holy Spirit and, finally, to moral development.

Witness, Moral Understanding and Intersubjectivity

In teasing out the event and its effects on him, Gaita's primary focus is the religious sister's love. It is a spontaneous response that finds immediate echoes, not only in him, but, arguably, for any observer, whatever their culture or religion. As Wynn suggests, Gaita's love-based account could serve as a kind of 'natural law' approach grounded on love rather than happiness, rationality, autonomy, or flourishing. Its strength is the inclusive scope of a love that is evoked by the 'sheer humanity of the other' and not 'premised on a particular human achievement' such as autonomy or the exercise of rational capacities.[8]

Again, the religious sister's form of moral understanding can rightly be described as 'emotional intelligence' or, as 'connaturality' in the language of the Thomistic tradition. It is consistent with 'an intimate attunement of human consciousness to the realm of aesthetic and moral values'.[9] Further, it brings to mind Aquinas' view that 'beings' are revealed not in what they *are* but in what they *do* and always in an interactive context.[10]

Similarly, Gaita, in citing Simone Weil, alludes to the medieval transcendentals of 'being' (existence or *esse*), especially beauty and goodness, as universal aspirations of humanity. In so doing, he points to a further dimension of

---

[7] Gaita, *A Common Humanity*, 26-7.

[8] Wynn, *Emotional Experience and Religious Understanding,* 41.

[9] Anthony J Kelly's review of R J Snell, *The Perspective of Love: Natural Law in a New Mode* (Eugene, OR: Pickwick, 2014) in *Studies in Christian Ethics* 29:4, (2016): 506-8, at 507. See, also, comments on emotional intelligence in chapter one of this present book.

[10] Fergus Kerr, *After Aquinas: Versions of Thomism* (Oxford, UK: Blackwells, 2002), 48-9 citing *Summa Theologiae* 1.105.5.

the love revealed in this incident. It not only involves a form of empathetic identification of the religious sister with the patients. Perhaps Gaita senses that, particularly through the very beauty of the sister's response, a new horizon as enhanced or enriched existence opens up, disclosing the inter-subjectivity or 'sociality' of consciousness itself?[11] In other words, his resonating with this incident is about 'being'—in its beauty, truth, goodness, unity, but also in its inherent relatedness and expansiveness that, in this instance, through love, reveals itself in what it *does*.

Further, in Gaita's account, we can see intimated, in the religious sister's attitude and its impact on him, a consciousness of the person (patient) as subject and as a center of value. This can be further investigated drawing on other sources. The first stage is through an appeal to Martin Buber as seen by Andrew Tallon (mentioned in the first chapter).

Perspectives on Intersubjectivity

In Martin Buber's philosophy of dialogue and intersubjectivity, the key aspect is the category of 'the between'. Andrew Tallon views this category within the framework of intentional consciousness understood in terms of three forms of intentionality—the cognitive, affective, and volitional. Tallon suggests that, in explaining 'the between' in Buber, it is helpful to have recourse to the concept of 'affective intentionality' (which Tallon sees as another expression for 'connaturality' which mediates between a being's nature and its action).[12]

Tallon argues that, for Buber, 'the between' must be designated as an 'encounter', namely, 'an affective consciousness that keeps the distance that makes relation possible', namely, an 'intending by the I of the Thou in an actual, present relation (I-Thou)'. 'Experience', alternatively, for Buber, is a 'cognitive consciousness that absorbs the otherness...making others the same as my ideas or images of them'.[13] Where space becomes intentional through embodiment, the

---

[11] Oliver Davies, *A Theology of Compassion: Metaphysics of Difference and the Renewal of Tradition* (United Kingdom: SCM; USA: Grand Rapids MI, Eerdmans, 2001), 232-3.

[12] Andrew Tallon, *Head and Heart: Affection, Cognition, Volition as Triune Consciousness* (New York: Fordham University Press, 1994), 29, 8. Tallon offers a phenomenological development of the Thomistic model of intentionality. For a helpful explanation of connaturality (as ontological and as habitual) and its application in the context of education see T Brian Mooney and Mark Nowacki, 'Aquinas on Connaturality and Education' in Thomas Brian Mooney and Mark Nowacki, eds. *Aquinas, Education, and the East* (Dordrecht: Springer, 2013), 27-45, at 32-8.

[13] It can be asked if this is necessarily the case? Can one envisage a cognitive aspect of encounter in which the 'distance' and 'otherness' experienced affectively is appropriated (and deepened) at a reflective and conceptual level?

'between' of encounter brings a sense of nearness that is' felt intersubjectively' as an 'ethical space'.[14]

Meaning, then, for Buber is neither in *you* or in *me* as free-standing subjects but *between* us. It is revealed in the moment of encounter as embodied, felt meaning, a resonating of one's being with that of another. Even before we 'know' it (at least logically, if not chronologically, in concepts, through cognitive intentionality), 'intersubjectivity is already ethical and valuable as sensed and felt in affectivity'. The immediacy of affective intentionality, as the immediate and interpersonal appreciation of value, 'opens the way to cognitive intentionality'.[15]

Elsewhere Tallon elucidates these ideas with reference to the continental philosopher, Emmanuel Levinas, whose work reflects deeply on the encounter with the 'Other' person and the ethical call that is made manifest therein. Following on from the argument developed above, Tallon argues that the encounter with the Other:

> is not something first understood in concepts or reached as a conclusion in judgements, nor is it freely chosen or decided on after deliberation. Rather, one is affected by meaning, one is commanded by proximity, held hostage by an experience, not after representation but before it, in presence, presentation, vulnerability, embodiment, in affectivity as its own kind of intentionality, its own access to meaning.[16]

In developing the line of thought in this way with Levinas, Tallon adds an additional level of ethical salience to the encounter with the Other. This is because, within Levinas' philosophy, it is not only that meaning is between *you* and *me*, it is that in this encounter I experience myself as called into question by you, held 'hostage' by your vulnerable presence, and suddenly aware at an affective level of your profound vulnerability. These loaded terms highlight the ethical responsibility that already exists within *my* encounter with *you*—an affectivity that is unchosen and prior to my thinking about it, but nonetheless constitutive of who I am.

---

[14] Tallon, *Head and Heart*, 39, 42.

[15] Tallon, *Head and Heart*, 42.

[16] Andrew Tallon, 'Nonintentional Affectivity, Affective Intentionality, and the Ethical in Levinas's Philosophy', in *Ethics as First Philosophy: The Significance of Emmanuel Levinas for Philosophy, Literature and Religion*, ed. Adriaan T Peperzak (New York: Routledge, 1995), 108.

Intersubjectivity and Conscience

Investigations elsewhere have explored the alignment between these observations and conscience, as understood in Catholic ethical teaching.[17] As is well known, in Catholic thought, conscience refers to three interrelated phenomena: the experience of a call to moral responsibility; the search for an appropriate response to that call; and the courage to commit to the outcomes of such a search.[18]

The affective experience of responsibility identified above relates most clearly to the first dimension of conscience, and provides a way in which to understand its function: as I approach the other person, I experience the saliency of the ethical call, and I am spurred on to respond through the second and third dimensions of conscience. The first movement of conscience is thus not one of grappling with moral principles at the level of cognitive intentionality, but rather of affective response. This dimension of conscience, and the encounter with the other person that stimulates it, remain our focus here.

That such an encounter, and the call to responsibility issued therein, occurs on the level of affectivity does not mean that rationality is absent, only that it is a second movement in ethics.[19] On this view, we can expect that ethical responses will also follow a similar pattern: first at the level of affectivity, and then at the level of cognitive intentionality. The account of the incident earlier with the religious sister and its significance for Gaita can be viewed through the lens of Tallon's elaboration of Buber and Levinas. What does it tell us?

We have here an immediate, embodied 'encounter' (see her demeanor, speech, facial and bodily expressions and reactions); her 'pure' love as response is self-

---

[17] See Daniel J Fleming, 'Primordial Moral Awareness: Levinas, Conscience and the Unavoidable Call to Responsibility', *Heythrop Journal*, 56:4, 2015: 604-618.

[18] Timothy E O'Connell, *Principles for a Catholic Morality* (New York: HarperOne, 1990), 103-119. In a later work, O'Connell aligned his understanding of conscience with a synthesis of information on the task of moral formation, see Timothy E O'Connell, *Making Disciples: A Handbook of Christian Moral Formation* (New York: The Crossroad Publishing Company, 1998), especially 36-7. Anthony Fisher uses a similar threefold distinction of conscience which is founded on the understanding developed in Vatican II and the *Catechism of the Catholic Church*, nos. 1777-1802. See Anthony Fisher, *Catholic Bioethics for a New Millennium*, (Cambridge: Cambridge University Press, 2012), 47-50. This part of his book also provides a brief and helpful overview of the history of reflection on conscience from Biblical times until now.

[19] Tallon, 'Nonintentional Affectivity,' 109. Cf. Levinas' comments that the 'intentional consciousness of reflection, in taking as its object the transcendental ego, along with its mental acts and states, may also thematise and grasp supposedly implicit modes of non-intentional lived experience. It is invited to do this by philosophy in its fundamental project which consists in enlightening the inevitable transcendental naivety of a consciousness forgetful of its horizon, of its implicit content and even of the time it lives through'. Levinas, 'Ethics as First Philosophy,' 80.

validating, a form of affective intentionality with its appreciation of the worth of the person; it is a 'nearness' felt between her and the patients as between subjects but also as an 'ethical space', namely, of personal value and equal regard; it is a resonance 'of one's being with another' ('felt intersubjectively') that, in turn, reverberates in the consciousness of Gaita, the teenage witness; it is a revelatory moment of affective intentionality prior to cognitive intentionality—an awareness of the preciousness of the human person affecting us 'in ways we cannot fathom'. It is thus prior to the kind of cognitive discourse that is normally associated with ethics.

This analysis has a good degree of explanatory power, for it helps to describe how it is that many people who would be identified as moral heroes have little or no formal training in ethics.[20] If responsibility can take the form of affective intentionality then cognitive intentionality 'comes in behind' as it were, to refine a movement that is already taking place.[21] This also helps to explain the apparent disjoint that Gaita identifies—in rational terms, one may be able to articulate ethical commitments, but the affective shape of one's response could reveal otherwise.

Pope Francis has reminded us that theological reflection does well to engage in the insights born out of the sciences.[22] With that exhortation in mind, it is worth noting here that the perspective we have been developing thus far aligns well with current insights from the fields of moral psychology and cognitive neuroscience. Whilst an in-depth study of these is beyond our scope, in short, such research has come to two main conclusions of relevance for our work. First is that at the neuroscientific level the human brain appears to be constituted in such a way as to be open to the *affect* of another's presence. In other words, the emotional centers of the brain are constructed in such a way as to heighten attention when

---

[20] A recent analysis of such moral heroes from the field of moral psychology casts this observation into light. See William Damon and Anne Colby, *The Power of Ideals: The Real Story of Moral Choice* (Oxford: Oxford University Press, 2015).

[21] This observation should be distinguished from neo-determinist moral psychology which holds that cognitive intentionality does nothing more than justify decisions made at an irrational/emotional level, a perspective advanced in Jonathan Haidt, 'The Emotional Dog and its Rational Tail: a Social Intuitionist Approach to Moral Judgment', *Psychological Review* 108, no. 4 (2001). A more subtle, and widely accepted, correlative view in moral psychology is that affective intentionality underpins cognitive rationality, but can also be formed by it (and in other ways). See for example Daniel J Fleming, "From Theory to Praxis: Challenges and Insights for Conscience Formation Today," in *Doing Asian Theological Ethics in a Cross-Cultural and an Interreligious Context*, eds. Yiu Sing Lucas Chan, James F Keenan and Shaji George Kochuthara, (Bengaluru: Dharmaram Publications, 2016), 291-304

[22] Pope Franics, *Evangelii Gaudium: The Joy of the Gospel* (2013), no. 242. http://w2.vatican.va/content/francesco/en/apost_exhortations/documents/papa-francesco_esortazione-ap_20131124_evangelii-gaudium.html, accessed 13/11/2017/

another person is encountered. Crucially, this occurs at a largely emotional level and so is prior to conscious reflection on it.[23]

Second, research has discovered that the brain 'thinks with feeling', meaning that the affective disposition of a person influences, guides, and directs their use of rationality.[24] Furthermore, moral motivation rests at the level of affectivity, not rationality.[25] In concrete terms, this means that the manner in which I respond to another on an *affective* level will direct the manner in which I think about them. Furthermore, that I can reason about the ethics of my encounter with another does not of itself guarantee my ethical response to them—my affectivity does. This provides yet another explanation of the encounter between Gaita and the religious sister recounted above.

The Theory of Triune Ethics

Relevant here is the work of the moral psychologist, Darcia Narvaez, who proposes a theoretical framework called 'Triune Ethics Theory'. Narvaez draws on research from cognitive and affective neuroscience to highlight three systems which relate to moral motivation and decision-making. The systems rest on evolved competencies concerned with safety/security (the first system), engagement/relationality (the second system) and cognitive intentionality (the third system).[26]

The first system, known in Narvaez's work as the safety system, is shared with all creatures and refers to the innate need to avoid threat and seek out safety. It might be referred to in common parlance as the 'fight or flight' system, and it is the most primitive part of the human brain.[27] When a person senses threat, their brain will revert to this system (in literal terms, more blood will be directed to it), meaning that emotion, motivation, and cognitive intentionality will be directed

---

[23] Refer to Tallon, 'Nonintentional Affectivity,' for a broad survey of these findings.

[24] A survey of this research can be found in Darcia Narvaez, *Neurobiology and the Development of Human Morality: Evolution, Culture, and Wisdom* (New York: W.W. Norton & Company, 2014). A parallel discussion on moral perception notes that '[It] takes finely tuned affectivity to perceive what is morally relevant in a situation'. See William C Spohn, *Go and Do Likewise: Jesus and Ethics* (New York: Continuum, 1999), 95.

[25] Darcia Narvaez, 'Neurobiology and Moral Mindset', In *Handbook of Moral Motivation: Theories, Models, Applications,* eds. Karen Heinrichs, Fritz Oser and Terence Lovat. (Rotterdam: Sense Publishers, 2013), 323-42.

[26] In Narvaez's work, the third system is referred to as the 'imagination system'. Narvaez's understanding of what constitutes imagination aligns with what we have been referring to as cognitive intentionality. This language has been used here for consistency.

[27] Darcia Narvaez, 'Triune ethics: The neurobiological roots of our multiple moralities', *New Ideas in Psychology* 26 (2008): 98. Also, Darcia Narvaez, 'Neurobiology and moral mindset', in *Handbook of Moral Motivation,* 324.

towards avoiding threat and securing safety. [28] This may express itself in aggressiveness (fighting), passivity or fleeing.

The second system is counter-functional to the safety system, meaning that it does not operate when the safety system is prioritized, and is known in Narvaez's work as the engagement system. It is underpinned by aspects of the human brain that have a more recently evolved heritage, which allow for social engagement from creature to creature—something that we share with more highly evolved creatures, such as primates and other mammals.[29] This system gives rise to empathy, engagement, the capacity for taking the perspectives of others and similar qualities to these.[30] When it is in operation, then emotion, motivation and cognitive intentionality will be directed towards values such as those we have highlighted above. Hence, the affective intentionality we are pointing towards is best cultivated when the engagement system is nourished. We will return to this point below when we discuss implications for pedagogy.

The third system aligns with what we have been referring to as cognitive intentionality. It is the most recently evolved aspect of the human brain, and makes possible our capacities for abstract reasoning and imagination. [31] Significantly, this system does not operate in isolation but does so in tandem with either the safety system *or* the engagement system (recalling that when one of these is operating, the other is not).[32] This observation underpins Narvaez's observation that feeling systems underpin cognitive intentionality, by motivating it and directing it to preference certain values (either safety and security or engagement). In this way, it supports the phenomenological account of affective intentionality that we have been developing to this point.

To make things more concrete, it is helpful to return to the incident from Gaita (concerning the religious sister) understood as an encounter between a self and an Other centered on affective intentionality and felt sense of value. It finds a parallel in the life of Dag Hammarskjöld, the second Secretary General of the United Nations (with a text discussed in the previous chapter of this book). Writing in his journal in 1955, Hammarskjöld reveals his awareness of the need to somehow 'enter into' the subjectivity of the ''other'. Lasting solutions in conflict, for instance, involve both a learning 'to see the other objectively' but, at the same

---

[28] Narvaez, 'Neurobiology and moral mindset', 325; Narvaez, *Neurobiology and the Development of Human Morality*, 166.

[29] Narvaez, 'Triune ethics', 100.

[30] Fleming and Lovat, 'When encounters between religious worldviews are a threat', 384-85.

[31] Narvaez, 'Triune ethics', 105.

[32] Narvaez, *Neurobiology and the Development of Human Morality*, 161.

time, to experience 'his difficulties subjectively'.³³ This expression of political wisdom is underpinned by an attitude of self-dispossession and of accountability to a transcendent 'subject' revealed in Hammarskjöld's earlier 1950 entry (but far removed from the autonomous ethic of Kant): 'Treat others as ends, never as means' and of shifting:

> the dividing-line in my being between subject and object to a position where the subject, even if it is in me, is outside and above me—so that my *whole* being may become an instrument for that which is greater than I.³⁴

Clearly, For Hammarskjöld, the movement of conscience as moral responsibility for the 'other' has a self-transcending impulse that resonates in his whole person. This brings us to the next phase of our investigation.

A Pedagogy of Grace: Holy Spirit and Non-Believers

Our discussion so far has focused on the phenomenology of one particular 'moral moment'. The aim has been to illustrate the disclosure of moral values through the role of witness that is both embodied and enacted. Wynn suggests that, while Gaita's approach does not 'trade on religious assumptions', its focus on unconditional love is 'congenial' from a Christian perspective. Wynn proceeds to discuss whether Gaita's account 'invites completion in Christian or other religious terms'.³⁵

However, in this next stage, our task here is different. It is to investigate the 'deeper value and meaning' of Gaita's approach from a theological perspective, namely, the Catholic theology of grace and its saving action in those who are non-believers.³⁶ Such a process suggests initial insights into the pedagogy of the Holy

---

³³ Dag Hammarskjöld, *Markings,* translated by W H Auden and Leif Sjöberg (London: Faber & Faber, 1964), 102. Hammarskjöld expands on this passage and quotes at length from Martin Buber in his speech 'The Walls of Distrust' delivered in 1958 at Cambridge University. See Gustaf Aulén, *Dag Hammarskjöld's White Book: The Meaning of Markings* (Philadelphia: Fortress Press, 1969), 74.

³⁴ *Markings,* 64; emphasis in original.

³⁵ Wynn, *Emotional Experience and Religious Understanding,* 41-2.

³⁶ For an extended discussion of this topic, see Thomas Ryan, 'Holy Spirit, Hidden God: Moral Life and the Non-Believer', *The Australasian Catholic Record*, 84.4 (2007): 444-458 and his *The Eyes and Ears of Conscience: Lessons of Encouragement* (Strathfield, NSW: St. Pauls, 2022), chapter seven.

Spirit in the quest for moral self-transcendence. In this, we have two further guides.

The first is Sandra Schneiders and her definition of spirituality. It is 'the experience of consciously striving to integrate one's life in terms not of isolation and self-absorption but of self-transcendence towards the ultimate *value* one perceives'.[37]

This definition is realized, in varying degrees, in exemplars who, prototypically, embody and enact a pattern of attitudes, responses and behavior that are both revealing and authoritative. In parallel with Gaita's example of the role of the witness, as an alternative to reliance on moral theory, Edith Wyschogrod argues the case for 'hagiographical ethics'. She defines:

> ...the saint—the subject of hagiographic narrative—as one whose adult life in its entirety is devoted to the alleviating of sorrow (the psychological suffering) and pain (the physical suffering) that afflicts other persons without distinction of rank or group or, alternatively, that afflicts sentient beings, whatever the cost to the saint in pain or sorrow. On this view theistic belief may but not need be a component of the saint's belief system.[38]

Our purpose here is not to debate the nature of 'saints'. Rather, prompted by the religious sister's witness to moral values highlighted earlier, it is to probe further the definitions above in terms of self-transcendence and moral exemplars.[39]

If we consider the pedagogy of grace, the foundational aspect in this process of moral self-transcendence is captured in the document of the Second Vatican Council, namely, *Lumen Gentium* 16 which highlights the salvific value of striving to lead a good life through commitment to conscience.[40] Further, the same

---

[37] Sandra Schneiders, 'Spirituality in the Academy', *Theological Studies* 50 (1989): 676-697, at 684; my emphasis.

[38] Edith Wyschogrod, *Saints and Postmodernism* (Chicago/London: University of Chicago Press, 1990), 34.

[39] On a discussion of saintliness and holiness as 'trans-religious' and 'cross-religious' concepts see Donna Orsuto, *Holiness* (London UK: Continuum, 2006), 192-3. Again, one wonders whether it is adequate to 'define' a saint purely in moral terms. As Adams asks, is there some form of 'ultimacy', of 'goodness flowing from a boundless source' that is larger than morality yet embraces it? See Robert Adams, 'Saints', *Journal of Philosophy* 81 (1984): 392-401, at 398.

[40] 'Those also can attain to everlasting salvation who through no fault of their own do not know the gospel of Christ or His Church, *yet sincerely seek God* and, *moved by grace*, strive by their deeds to do His will as it is known to them through the dictates of conscience. Nor does Divine Providence deny the helps necessary for salvation to those who, without blame on their part, have not yet arrived at an explicit knowledge of God and with His grace *strive to live a good*

Council explicitly says that the offer of grace (sharing God's life) is in terms of the paschal mystery and is the work of the Holy Spirit.[41] Such silent activity in the conscientious non-believer is revealed in the 'displacing of the ego (that) becomes a giving "place" to others'.[42] As a mode of living, its inbuilt momentum is towards developing in depth and scope. Alternatively, as the free acceptance of a gift, it 'symbolises our willingness to receive "the other", our willingness to enter into a world that is not of our own making'.[43]

Such an openness to an objective reality is exercised when one chooses to engage in an ongoing search for the truth about what is good. This implies a desire to understand not only what is good in so far as it is *true* but also to grasp what is *true in itself* in so far as it is good, namely, as a value to be pursued. The sincere effort to pursue the claims of a world 'not of our own making' is integral to the non-believer's positive response to the Spirit's offer to be 'associated' with the paschal mystery.

Again, since the Church is called to realize and witness to Christ's saving love in the world, the non-believer must be 'associated' with it in a hidden but real way ('in a manner known only to God').[44] In theological terms, this is understood in terms of the Church as the sign and instrument of God's Reign. In that sense, 'outside the Church no salvation' takes on a more expansive and positive meaning. As Ladislaus Boros notes, a universal negative proposition (*extra ecclesiam, nulla salus*) can be expressed affirmatively (*ubi salus, ibi ecclesia*)— wherever God's saving action (the Reign of God) is evident, then the Church is somehow present.[45] The Spirit's offer of grace to all people points inescapably, even if mysteriously, both to Christ and to the Church.[46]

---

life. Whatever good or truth is found amongst them is looked upon by the Church as a preparation for the Gospel'. *Lumen Gentium* 16 in Walter M Abbott SJ, ed. *The Documents of Vatican II*, (The America Press, 1965), 35; my emphasis.

[41] 'For since Christ dies for all men, and since the *ultimate vocation of man is in fact one, and divine*, we ought to believe that the *Holy Spirit*, in a way known only to God *offers to every man* the possibility of being *associated with this paschal mystery'. Gaudium et Spes* 22; my emphasis.

[42] Rowan Williams, *The Wound of Knowledge: Christian Spirituality from the New Testament to St. John of the Cross* (London: Darton, Longman and Todd, 1979), 12.

[43] Richard Lennan, 'Holiness, "Otherness", and the Catholic School,' *The Australasian Catholic Record* 82: 4 (2005): 399-408, at 401.

[44] *Gaudium et Spes,* par. 22.

[45] Ladislaus Boros, *Living in Hope* (London: Search Press, 1971), 47-8.

[46] See n. 40 and 41 above.

The final stage of this article turns from this theoretical overview of the phenomenon of affective moral intentionality to its practical implications for ministers and educators. The question which frames this next stage is, *what does this mean for how we educate for the Catholic ethical vision*? We undertake our answer to this question by having recourse to insights from the human sciences and from Pope Francis' writings.

A Pedagogy of Grace: Moral Development

Based on the insights developed above, the formation of the moral subject is clearly something that must attend both to their affective and cognitive dimensions. This takes any adequate attempts at moral pedagogy out of the realm of a purely abstract teaching of ethical principles in the context of an expert to amateur relationship. To put it bluntly: the religious sister in our opening example did not learn her affective disposition whilst sitting in a theological ethics class.[47]

Such an observation finds support in the educational sciences, particularly those which focus on moral education, which find that the best kinds of educational interventions that account for affectivity of moral dispositions intentionally frame themselves around that dimension. For example, classrooms which have an explicit focus on the cultivation of good relationships between teacher and students and between students tend to have a much greater impact on student moral formation. Interestingly, studies have demonstrated that such classroom environments also cultivate much higher achievements in the domain of cognitive intentionality, thus undermining any argument that in focusing on affection one does away with cognitive rigor.[48] The latter is only improved by the former. This aligns with Narvaez's approach earlier, highlighting the need to 'form emotions' so that the engagement system can work in tandem with cognitive intentionality in directing our embodied ethical disposition.

This focus on the affective side of moral pedagogy finds support in Pope Francis' writings, especially where he focuses in his presentation of the dual themes of accompaniment and the pedagogy of grace. These ideas may be framed with an excerpt from the Synod on the Family's *Relatio Synodi* which notes that 'God's indulgent love always accompanies our human journey; through grace, it heals and transforms hardened hearts, leading them back to the beginning through

---

[47] Even though this may have helped her to better understand it, rationalize it, and make it more enduring, a point to which we will return below.

[48] Terence Lovat et al., 'Project to test and measure the impact of values education on student effects and school ambience. Final Report for the Australian Government Department of Education, Employment and Workplace Relations (DEEWR) by The University of Newcastle'. (Canberra: Department of Education, Employment and Workplace Relations (DEEWR) 2009), 120. See also reference earlier in n.12 to Mooney and Nowacki, 'Aquinas on Connaturality and Education'.

the way of the cross'.⁴⁹ In presenting God's mercy to the world, the Church is called to effect such transformation by the same means, namely, through accompaniment.

To accompany means to 'remove our sandals before the sacred ground of the other (cf. Ex 3:5)' and has the purpose of 'making present the fragrance of Christ's closeness and his personal gaze'.⁵⁰ This gaze was the subject of reflection in the *Relatio*, which points out that Christ:

> looked upon the women and men whom he met with love and tenderness, accompanying their steps in truth, patience and mercy as he proclaimed the demands of the Kingdom of God.⁵¹

In this way, the Church's accompaniment should be 'steady and reassuring, reflecting our closeness and our compassionate gaze which also heals, liberates and encourages growth in the Christian life'.⁵²

In this context, it is helpful to recall the advice of Cardinal Newman in his discussion of the development of ideas: 'In a higher world it is otherwise, but here below to live is to change, and to be perfect is to have changed often'. ⁵³

Our discussion is about moral 'life', hence, the gradualism noted by Pope Francis and Pope St John Paul II is another way of talking about the processes that are integral to life—in whatever form. This applies to the search for what is true and good. It may, at times, involve misunderstandings, even, mistakes. What is central is the sincere seeking 'for the truth about the good' noted in *Veritatis Splendor* (par. 62).

A Purpose-Driven Task

This implies what we refer to as 'good will'—which raises another point. The search is purpose-driven, namely, it is teleological. Central here is the role of the will, evident in *Amoris Laetitia* (especially par. 303). It is unfortunate that

---

⁴⁹ The Synod of Bishops, *Relatio Synodi: The Pastoral Challenges of the Family in the Context of Evangelization* (2014), 14,
http://www.vatican.va/roman_curia/synod/documents/rc_synod_doc_20141018_relatio-synodi-familia_en.html accessed 13/11/17; cited in Pope Francis, *Amoris Laetitia: On Love in the Family* (2016), no. 62.,
http://m.vatican.va/content/dam/francesco/pdf/apost_exhortations/documents/papa-francesco_esortazione-ap_20160319_amoris-laetitia_en.pdf accessed 13/11/17.

⁵⁰ Francis, *Evangelii Gaudium*, par. 169.

⁵¹ *Relatio Synodi*, no. 12; Francis, *Amoris Laetitia*, par. 60.

⁵² *Evangelii Gaudium*, par. 169.

⁵³ Newman Reader—Works of John Henry Newman Copyright © 2007 by The National Institute for Newman Studies. http://newmanreader.org/works/development/chapter1.html accessed 20.6.2017.

contemporary usage seems to confine this function of human rationality to the power of choice, the making of a decision. Within the Thomistic framework (which Pope Francis is using), the will is an operation of the 'intellective appetite', namely, the affective wing of human cognition. The 'will' is as much about desire and love (*affectio*) as it is about choice *(electio)*. Pope Francis couches this in the language of the 'heart' and of love—from and towards God.

This returns us to Tallon's point earlier: intentional consciousness is more accurately described in terms of cognition, affection, and volition. In this, the gradual formation of attitudes, which can be viewed as the interplay of perceptions and dispositions (of cognitive and affective) is crucial in making judgments about the good and subsequent choices (volition). It is a gradual sensitizing in the appraisal and appreciation of what is salient in moral situations, namely, in the exercise of emotional intelligence (i.e., 'connaturality'). As Mooney and Nowacki point out:

> the knowledge arising from this form of connaturality need not be propositional. Rather, it may be a form of *knowing how* to perceive the salient moral features in circumstances that demand the exercise of a virtue.[54]

The accompaniment process that helps to foster this 'knowing how' is seen by Pope Francis in terms of Christ's closeness, the transforming effects of God's 'indulgent love' and of Christ's 'personal gaze'. In this context, Iain Matthew's words, discussing John of the Cross' *Canticle* and the gaze of the Risen Jesus, are relevant:

> 'Risen indeed', and so alive in each person's history, gazing into each one's story, not just benignly, but effectively. As John's own history had taught him, 'For God, to gaze is to love and to work favours'. His love acts. It makes us 'worthy and capable of his love'. *His gaze is his love and his love does things.* God's gaze works four blessings in the soul: it cleanses her, makes her beautiful, enriches and enlightens her.[55]

The reference to the fourfold 'blessings' on 'the soul' resonates with the transcendentals of 'being' noted earlier in this article—as true, good, and beautiful. It also indicates we have come full circle in our discussion.

---

[54] Mooney and Nowacki, 'Aquinas on Connaturality and Education', 34; italics in original.

[55] Iain Matthew, *The Impact of God: Soundings from St John of the Cross* (United Kingdom: Hodder and Stoughton, 1995), 140; my emphasis.

Conclusion

Spurred on by reflection on Raimond Gaita's personal encounter with moral goodness in a religious sister, experienced at the level of affective intentionality and reflected on cognitively thereafter, this chapter has undertaken an extended study of the meaning of such encounters and the corresponding implications for our theologies of grace and approach to the moral life. The discussion considered four aspects: first, witness in relation to moral understanding and intersubjectivity; second, intersubjectivity and conscience; third, a pedagogy of grace and the action of the Holy Spirit; finally, a pedagogy of grace in relation to moral development.

We have demonstrated the importance of construing moral dispositions not only in volitional and rationalistic terms—which are the most frequent frameworks through which theological ethics approaches the moral life—but also and especially in affective terms, which allows for a fuller appreciation of the moral life.

We have shown that such an approach is congruent with insights from the sciences. Further, it is aligned with Pope Francis' calls for a Church which accompanies, and which thereby provides, the condition of possibility for disciples to grow in their affective and moral life.

We come, next, to the final chapter in this section of the book ('Virtue at Work') and turn our focus to one individual in the Scriptures, namely, Joseph, the husband of Mary and foster-father of Jesus. Joseph illustrates conscience in action within the setting of the virtues. Importantly, he embodies the attitudes and dispositions associated with wisdom and moral integrity.

7
Joseph in Matthew's Gospel: Conscience and Moral Integrity

Our discussion in the previous two chapters revolved around words such as 'witness', 'wisdom' and 'moral development'. In this chapter, we combine these aspects with our earlier focus by examining a case study in moral integrity and the calibrations of conscience.

In this instance, our attention turns to the Christian Scriptures, and, specifically, Joseph, the husband of Mary (the mother of Jesus), as he is presented in the Gospel of Matthew.[1]

At the end of 2020, Pope Francis 'surprised us all again' with his letter entitled 'With a Father's Heart' (*Patris Corde*) and by dedicating the year 2021 to St Joseph. The words 'surprised us all' are not unwarranted.[2] They suggest a sense of rediscovery, of a renewed awareness of something (or someone) taken for granted.

As we know, titles such as 'Patron' (of the Church, of Workers, of a Happy Death) or 'Protector' (of the Family), or 'Guardian of the Redeemer', are used of St Joseph within the church's devotional life. But Francis' concern goes beyond that of devotion. He is presenting an extended theological reflection on St Joseph, one that builds on the four dreams that open Matthew's Gospel. In essence, we can look to St Joseph as the man-of-dreams to teach 'us that amid the tempests of life we must never be afraid to let the Lord steer our course'.[3]

Taking our cue from Francis, I would like to bring into sharper focus one aspect of what is found in his letter. Building on the infancy narrative that begins Matthew's Gospel, I propose a perspective on St Joseph that offers a more detailed, and perhaps a richer, portrait of the man-of-dreams. He embodies a model of both conscience 'at work' and discipleship with Jesus that characterizes Matthew's Gospel (as encapsulated in the title of this chapter).

---

[1] The original form of this chapter was: Thomas Ryan, '"Joseph was a Good Man": Conscience, Mercy, and Wisdom', *The Australasian Catholic Record* 99: 1 (January, 2022): 18-31.

[2] They are found in the reflections on the feast of St Joseph in 2021 from Rev. John Larsen, SM, Superior General of the Society of Mary,
https://maristfathers.org.au/images/Reflection_from_the_Superior_General_2109_ENG-c.pdf, accessed 27 September 2021.

[3] Francis, Apostolic Letter *Patris Corde,* 8 December 2020, 4,
https://www.vatican.va/content/francesco/en/apost_letters/documents/papa-francesco-lettera-ap_20201208_patris-corde.html, accessed 26 September 2021.

I will approach the task in five stages: first, Joseph as a just man wrestling with a moral quandary; second, lessons about conscience we can learn from Joseph; third, insights gained from Joseph's precarious (and violent) historical context and its impact on him; fourth, the placing of Joseph as a man of integrity within the overall Jewish story; fifth, a brief correlation between Joseph as a model of wisdom and past and present perspectives. This will lead to some final observations.[4]

A Volatile Situation: A Moral Dilemma?

We know that each Gospel presents Jesus in a certain light: the suffering Son of Man (Mark); the compassionate and universal Savior (Luke); the Word made flesh (John). In Matthew, we find that Jesus is viewed as the definitive interpreter of the Torah, one who, as a teacher (rabbi), is the model of how to live the Law. He is the 'new Moses' in the sense that, as the unique Son of God, his is an 'authority far beyond that of Moses or any oral tradition purported to derive from him'.[5]

With the mention of Torah (Law), some words of explanation are needed.

Torah and True Righteousness

The word 'Law' as a rendition of Torah must be carefully understood. The Torah presumes the covenant between God and his people Israel, which is, essentially, a gift of divine love. The Torah is an integral part of that gifted relationship. It is not a juridical but a theological concept, expressed as the way (*derek*), a journey entered to remain 'in [the] state of covenant'.[6] It is the path for walking together with God, one that has God as our destiny. Further, the Way (or the Law) achieves its purpose in Jesus. He embodies God's values, God's way of living. The way to God is realized and modelled in a person; discipleship, then, is a personal relationship with Jesus.

How does Jesus embody the Way? He is the one who is truly 'righteous' (just), namely, he does what God wants—to live in and foster right relationships, first with God and then with others, with society and with creation. These are captured in the attitudes and dispositions of the Beatitudes, in Matthew's Sermon on the Mount. The supreme test of true 'righteousness', as explained above, is the type of fruit that it produces (Mt 7:15-20): doing the will of our Father in heaven

---

[4] I am indebted to the ACR Board members who made very helpful suggestions in the peer review of this article.

[5] Brendan Byrne, *Lifting the Burden: Reading Matthew's Gospel in the Church Today* (Strathfield, NSW: St Pauls, 2004), 5.

[6] Pontifical Biblical Commission, *The Bible and Morality: Biblical Roots of Christian Conduct* (Vatican City: Libreria Editrice Vaticana, 2008), 30–1.

through the dual commandment of love, and 'what Jesus will later refer to as the Torah's "weightier" commandments: justice, mercy, and faith ... At the Great Judgment ([Matt] 25:31-46) only these will count'.[7] Pennington sums it up:

> The 'righteous' person, according to Matthew, is the one who follows Jesus in this way of being in the world. The righteous person is the whole (*teleios*) person (5:48) who does not only do the will of God externally but, most importantly, from the heart.[8]

We noted earlier how Pope Francis approaches Joseph as an interpreter of dreams and that, in allowing the Lord to 'steer our course', we open ourselves to God's saving purposes, the divine dream for humanity. In the Matthew account, Joseph is called to be led by God along the Way through four dreams, concerning, respectively: Mary's pregnancy and God's call; the journey to Egypt; the return to Israel; the instruction to live not in Judea but in Nazareth (Galilee).

Let's consider what happens for Joseph prior to the first dream.

Joseph, Conscience, and the Torah

In describing how Jesus Christ came to be born, the text speaks of how his mother Mary 'had been engaged to Joseph', but that, before they lived together, 'she was found to be with child from the Holy Spirit' (Mt 1:18, NRSV).[9] 'Found to be' or 'came to be' anchors a statement of fact made by the narrator for the sake of the reader of the Gospel.[10] We then read: 'Her husband Joseph, being a righteous man and unwilling to expose her to public disgrace, planned to divorce her quietly' (1:19).[11]

These opening sentences need to be viewed in the light of what has preceded them in the gospel text. The earlier genealogy (1:1-17) offers a theological context that illuminates the sort of situation in which Mary finds herself and that, somehow, she must manage in an ongoing way. Five women are mentioned across the generations: Tamar, Rahab, Ruth, the wife of Uriah (Bathsheba) and, finally, Mary. An aura of sexual impropriety surrounds the first four women either in their

---

[7] Byrne, *Lifting the Burden*, 71.

[8] Jonathan T Pennington, 'Joseph the Just and Matthew's Matrix of Mercy: The Redefinition of Righteousness', *Journal of Moral Theology* 10:1 (2021): 40–50, at 44.

[9] All my biblical excerpts in this article are from the *New Revised Standard Version* of the Bible.

[10] Of the phrase 'found to be', Brown notes: 'This need not have the sense of a secret discovered by a busybody. A weakened sense in which "found to be" simply means 'was' is to some extent present in English as well as Greek: "He found himself in the country."' See Raymond E Brown, *The Birth of the Messiah: A Commentary on the Infancy Narratives of Matthew and Luke* (Garden City, NY: Doubleday, 1977), 124.

[11] 'Righteous' (Greek dikaios) is variously translated, for instance, as 'good' (J B Phillips), 'right-minded' (Knox), 'upright' (Christian Community Bible, Catholic pastoral edition).

behavior (the prostitute Rahab) or in how they have been treated (Tamar, Ruth, Bathsheba).[12] Despite these settings of human scandal, within the story of salvation they are presented as models of being faithful, whatever it had cost them.[13]

This is the sort of context where the situation of Mary, the mother of Jesus, is situated. And, about this, Brendan Byrne is candid:

> No false piety should make us shrink from this plain implication of the story. From Joseph's point of view Mary is in a truly dreadful situation. If exposed to the full rigour of the Law, she is liable to be stoned as an adulteress (Deut 22:23-4). Even if such rigour no longer applied, she is vulnerable to public shame and lifelong humiliation.[14]

The first four women, then, offer a biblical precedent for 'God's channelling the stream of salvation through an episode or relationship fraught with or *thought to be fraught* with sexual impropriety'.[15] The relationship between Joseph and Mary was truly a marriage. They were not just 'engaged' in the modern sense. The dilemma of Joseph ('good', 'upright', 'righteous') was in knowing that Mary was pregnant from relations with someone other than himself; hence, it would appear, she is guilty of adultery. From a 'big picture' perspective, Mary's pregnancy 'from the Holy Spirit' (Mt 1:18, 20) will be the climax 'of divine interventions bringing the line of salvation out of situations that appear at first sight morally deviant'.[16]

Such knowledge, or larger perspective, is not available to Joseph, as it is to the reader of the Gospel and subsequent believers in Jesus. At this stage, no angel has appeared to Joseph in a dream—Matthew is not writing for readers who knew the Lucan story of the Annunciation to Mary (Lk 1:26-38). Joseph is not aware of any divine intervention ('through the Holy Spirit'). Joseph can only conclude that, in some way, Mary is pregnant because of sexual impropriety; in other words, she is guilty of adultery.[17] Such a reaction is understandable and consistent with his

---

[12] And, clearly, with Mary, the issue is firmly one of 'perceived' sexual impropriety.

[13] While in agreement with this comment, Elaine Wainwright, from a feminist perspective, points out that 'the anomalous or dangerous situation of each of the women, at a certain point, places her outside of a patriarchal marriage or family structure. Each one's actions threaten this structure further'. See Elaine M Wainwright, *Towards a Feminist Critical Reading of the Gospel according to Matthew* (Berlin: De Guyter, 1991), 68.

[14] Byrne, *Lifting the Burden*, 23. Concerning the 'rigour no longer applied', Byrne observes, 'As appears to have been the case in Jesus' time—though John 8:1-11 presupposes otherwise' (23, n. 10).

[15] Byrne, *Lifting the Burden*, 22-23; italics in original.

[16] Byrne, *Lifting the Burden*, 22.

[17] Byrne, *Lifting the Burden*, 23.

'being righteous' (a faithful Jew). Consider how it might have been for Joseph: to feel bewildered and perhaps even personally betrayed; at the same time, conscious of his love for Mary. Could we wonder if his inner turmoil also involved the possibility that Mary had been seduced, coerced, or, even, sexually assaulted?[18]

This points to the other side of his sense of moral responsibility. He is protective towards her. Rather than risk that Mary be exposed publicly with associated disgrace and punishment,[19] Joseph makes a sensitive appraisal of the situation: not to shame her but to end their betrothal quietly (without publicity). This is what he 'planned'. But the following verse 20 indicates this is not his final decision; he is still 'turning the matter over in his mind' (J B Phillips), 'agonized about this' (Anchor Bible)—a view of an ongoing rather than a completed process, an interpretation that is supported by Raymond Brown.[20]

As the account is written, Joseph's basic attitude and disposition about how to handle this difficult, even precarious, situation (personally and socially) is made evident to the reader *before* the first dream—in which he comes to learn of the divine act that has already occurred and receives his divine commission. His suspicions and fears about what might have happened to Mary are put to rest. Joseph is a good man, one of integrity and character, whose righteousness (true appreciation of the Law) is revealed in how he judges what is the right thing to do, what is God's will and desire about what to do in this situation confronting him 'here and now'. Appraisal and judgment are at the core of how conscience functions (illumined in Joseph's later decisions through the mediation of four dreams).[21] In this first stage, his judgment and ensuing actions find their overriding source in his sensitive and compassionate attitude toward Mary. Pope Francis points out that:

---

[18] 'The description of Joseph's embarrassment and his plans in verses 18-19 may presume his suspicion that Mary has been raped or seduced'. See Daniel J Harrington, 'Matthew', in *The Collegeville Biblical Commentary*, eds. Dianne Bergant and Robert J Karris (Collegeville, MN: Liturgical, 1989), 861–902, at 864.

[19] 'If exposed to the full rigour of the Law, she is liable to be stoned as an adulteress (Deut 22:23-4). Even if such rigour no longer applied, she is vulnerable to public shame and lifelong humiliation'. Byrne, *Lifting the Burden*, 23.

[20] '... as he was considering this'. See Brown, *Birth of the Messiah*, 128.

[21] In biblical literature, a dream is a normal means of communication between God and human beings. It can also function as a symbolic setting for coming to some form of understanding. A dream may not necessarily be associated with an angel. Consider two other examples of conscience as a moment of moral insight. First, Pilate's wife, from a dream that troubled her, urges her husband Pilate to have 'nothing to do' with 'that innocent man', i.e., Jesus (Mt 27:19). Second, in Abimelech's dialogue with God in a dream, he is assured he was misled by Abraham concerning Sarah such that Abimelech had acted 'in good faith', i.e., with integrity of heart (Gen 20:1-18).

> The nobility of Joseph's heart is such that what he learned from the law he made dependent on charity. Today, in our world where psychological, verbal and physical violence towards women is so evident, Joseph appears as the figure of a respectful and sensitive man. Even though he does not understand the bigger picture, he makes a decision to protect Mary's good name, her dignity and her life. In his hesitation about how best to act, God helped him by enlightening his judgment.[22]

The final phrase from Francis reminds us that God does not override human freedom. Joseph's judgment underpinned and guided his free response. Importantly, we have here a man guided by his conscience not so much despite (or in conflict with) the Law but as consonant with the fullest expression of the Law. Joseph, in so responding and acting, is righteous in the way that Jesus will later define righteousness throughout Matthew's Gospel: as marked by the highest virtue of a compassionate, forgiving, and merciful love toward others (modelled in Jesus himself). Joseph is a model, 'in an anticipatory way [of] the fulfillment of the Torah that Jesus will promote (5:17-20)'.[23] These qualities are further complemented by his courage. As Francis reminds us:

> Joseph had the courage to become the legal father of Jesus, to whom he gave the name revealed by the angel: 'You shall call his name Jesus, for he will save his people from their sins' (Mt 1:21). As we know, for ancient peoples, to give a name to a person or to a thing, as Adam did in the account in the Book of Genesis (cf. 2:19-20), was to establish a relationship.[24]

Some characters in Matthew (scribes and Pharisees) might view righteousness as focusing on justice and rights, condemning those who have done wrong according to God's Law. But prior to the first dream, and confirmed by the divine intervention, we find Joseph stands as the first exemplar in Matthew's Gospel of a deeper truth: that mercy, compassion, forgiveness, and love are the greatest commandments and, therefore, the greatest form of righteousness. Further, the portrayal of Joseph reminds us that conscience does not stand alone; it must be exercised through wise judgment (prudence) as informed and directed by the virtues and prayer.

---

[22] Francis, *Patris Corde*, 6.

[23] Byrne, *Lifting the Burden*, 23.

[24] Francis, *Patris Corde*, 1. Elizabeth Johnson reminds us that, hard though it may be 'for us moderns to understand', a declaration of paternity making a man the legal father 'had a strong force in this culture'. This would be all the more so when the child was conceived 'in what appeared to be dubious circumstances'. See Elizabeth A Johnson, *Truly Our Sister: A Theology of Mary in the Communion of Saints* (New York: Continuum, 2003), 193.

A More Inclusive Perspective

Recent scholarship offers a critical feminist and more inclusive approach to what we have discussed above. We see in verse 18 earlier how Mary is named as the one who will give birth to Jesus but not through the agency of a male. This verse heralds the power and presence that is of 'a spirit which is holy and it alerts the reader to the association of the divine with this story of a woman which threatens the prevailing ethos'.[25] This woman Mary continues the line of women highlighted earlier as models of faith and as channels of God's action in history.

Yet, the focus shifts to Joseph at verse 19. As Elaine Wainwright points out, the events are presented from his standpoint, one that can be viewed as androcentric. Mary here is passive, does not speak nor is spoken to, does not make decisions or act independently, 'nor do we gain any insight into her point of view'. How her conscience is at work is hidden from us. She is, in effect, marginalized.

For all that, 'her role, however, is crucial; so crucial that this story must be considered a "kernel" within the narrative because without the birth of Jesus from this woman, the story would not proceed'.[26] This critical approach offered by Wainwright reminds us that there are tensions and narrative clues that support a reading of Matthew 1:8-25 that 'offers a powerful critique of the androcentric perspective of the narrative with its focus on Joseph'.[27]

We come to our next consideration.

What Can We Learn from Joseph about Conscience?

First, Joseph's conscience as a 'righteous' man seems to incline him to obey the Law and have Mary subjected to the full force of the Torah. However, as we have seen, such a possible response is taken to a higher level by his compassion. He was 'upright *but* also merciful'.[28] In this, a deeper level of his appreciation of the right thing to do (his conscience) is the paramount factor.

Second, Joseph has the courage of his convictions in this most unexpected (and disturbing) set of circumstances. Divine revelation to him is through dreams—a common scriptural device for divine interventions, as noted earlier. They can be

---

[25] Wainwright, *Feminist Critical Reading*, 70.

[26] Wainwright, *Feminist Critical Reading*, 71.

[27] Wainwright, *Feminist Critical Reading*, 75. Alternatively, in the Lucan infancy narrative, Mary is center stage and far from being passive, silent, and 'marginalised'. The annunciation scene (Lk 1:16-38) can be read as a process of discernment, of divine freedom engaging human freedom through the pattern of openness, call and response—of conscience interacting with divine grace. For a discussion of the contrasting (yet culturally subversive) perspectives of these two accounts, see Johnson, *Truly Our Sister*, 226–40 (on Matthew) and 247–58 (on Luke).

[28] Brown, *Birth of the Messiah*, 127.

vehicles for God acting unobtrusively, behind the scenes. Our modern sensibility is more attuned to the role of dreams in our unconscious life since the time (and writings) of Sigmund Freud and of Carl Jung; they can be the gateway to our inner world that can be used by God in his saving plan. In daily life, we ourselves might be faced with a difficult decision and are not averse to saying 'I'll sleep on it'. Through dreams the deepest self can be at work through the interplay of images, memories, feelings, and possible scenarios to resolve the problem or issue.

Once the dreams enter Joseph's life, especially from his special commission in the first dream, he demonstrates not only how he is, like Mary, affectively receptive to God but is also flexible and open to change, especially in his understanding of what God is asking of him. The process in which Joseph engages illustrates how the word *conscience* literally means 'knowing with or together'. The Bible and Vatican II remind us that our conscience is where we encounter God. The language used is worth noting. Conscience is a holy place, a sacred site, our 'most secret sanctuary' (hence, inviolable), where each person is 'alone with God whose voice echoes in [our] depths'.[29] It is there that we listen attentively in order to respond and act.

But 'conscience' has a second meaning: as our basic moral sensitivity that needs to be nourished and fostered. That means I have a responsibility to do that—to seek to know what is true and what is good and to do so in an ongoing manner. Fidelity to conscience binds together the human family (and Christians) 'in the search for the truth' such that 'the more a correct conscience holds sway, the more persons and groups turn aside from blind choice and strive to be guided by objective norms of morality'.[30]

In the 'true listening' of obedience, Joseph does not resist an ongoing process of learning about the ways of God and their impact on him and, naturally, on Mary and the unborn child. This implies that Joseph has an evolving appreciation of how to discern what is right and wrong, to be open to modify his judgment in light of new information. In other words, we see in Joseph that conscience is not a static reality. It follows the pattern (and need) of life itself: it must develop in scope and depth, especially, in the fine-tuning of moral sensitivity, attitudes and dispositions through the practice of the virtues.

Third, Joseph appears at the start of Matthew (and Luke) and then disappears. We never hear one word spoken by Joseph, even in the four dream sequences. But his presence (and influence) persists in the person of his foster son, Jesus. Jesus as an adult will commend the very virtues that Joseph manifests here, such as giving priority to mercy over justice (Mt 5:7); of practicing righteousness in secret rather than for the praise of others (Mt 6:4, 6, 18). Importantly, what Joseph gives

---

[29] Second Vatican Council, *Gaudium et Spes*, 16, in *The Documents of Vatican II*, ed. Walter M Abbott (Boston: America Press, 1966).

[30] *Gaudium et Spes*, 16.

witness to anticipates what is expressed in more specific terms in the call to universal love and to forgiveness of others, including enemies, in Mt 5:38-48.

Fourth, the Gospels speak of Joseph as a carpenter. He was a *tektōn*, a craftsman in wood or stone.[31] But, in the Talmud, it is suggested that the words 'carpenter' and 'son of a carpenter' could also be metaphors to signify someone who was learned in the Torah (the Law or the Way).[32] Pope Francis notes how, in Joseph, Jesus saw 'the tender love of God' and how he was guided by Joseph in childhood tasks, in his education and in his growth in wisdom.[33]

If Joseph is the model of Jesus' righteousness at the very start of Matthew's Gospel, one could well wonder how much Jesus, in his upbringing, was influenced by Joseph (together with Mary) in how he came to understand the Law. Later in this same Gospel (13:53-58), Jesus' 'wisdom' and 'miraculous powers' cause astonishment when he returns to his home town. A faith response to where these gifts came from is impeded by 'hometown familiarity with himself and his family'.[34] From the Lucan tradition, we are offered a further insight when the young Jesus engages the doctors of the Law in the temple and 'all who heard him were amazed at his understanding and his answers' (Lk 2:47). Michael Fallon makes the point that:

> When we consider that it would have been Joseph who introduced him [Jesus] to the law, we might have some insight into the origins of Jesus' own understanding of the law, as an essentially limited expression of God's will and as always requiring discernment rather than blind compliance.[35]

But Joseph's moral struggle was not just personal: it had a social and political aspect that was both precarious and close to home—the next consideration.

---

[31] We must be careful of drawing parallels with, for instance, blue-collar workers, the lower middle class, or a skilled tradesman of an advanced market economy. Joseph and his family belonged to the artisan class, to 'the poor who had to work hard for their living'. This was a family that 'lived on the economic underside of a two-sided system' where there was no middle class. See Johnson, *Truly Our Sister*, 148–9.

[32] Pennington, 'Joseph the Just', 48, citing Géza Vermès, *Jesus the Jew: A Historian's Reading of the Gospels* (London: Collins, 1973), 21–2.

[33] Francis, *Patris Corde*, 3.

[34] Byrne, *Lifting the Burden*, 117.

[35] Michael Fallon, *The Gospel according to Saint Matthew: An Introductory Commentary* (Kensington, NSW: Chevalier, 2018), 44.

Context: Aura of Fear and Memories of Terror

Consider the volatile, even dangerous, aspects of what confronted Joseph (and Mary and the child). These are presented within a theological framework, consistent with the earlier genealogy, the story of Israel's faith, the divine plan, and the overall purpose of the Gospels as documents of faith. Nevertheless, such contextual realities provide a glimpse into the historical substratum of Matthew's Gospel. They embrace not only social and cultural issues (shame, disgrace, rejection) but the wider threat of hostile forces (represented by Herod, known for his cruelty).

These factors are distilled in Matthew chapter 2: the visit of the Magi, the flight to Egypt, the slaughter of the Innocents, and the return from Egypt to Nazareth. One commentary notes that these events are 'not otherwise known but are in character', namely, consistent with the Herod of history. Concerning the slaughter of the Innocents, it is pointed out that:

> the story may not be historical but possesses verisimilitude and is reminiscent of Pharaoh's command to kill the male offspring of the Israelites (Exod 1:16), a classic example of genocidal abuse of power. If the incident is historical, the number of children killed need not have exceeded 20.[36]

Raymond Brown's opinion, based on Flavius Josephus, is that this story (and its basis noted above):

> could plausibly be attributed to Herod, especially amid the horrors of the last years of his life. To ensure mourning at his funeral, Herod wanted his soldiers instructed to kill notable political prisoners upon the news of his death.

Herod's aim was that 'all Judea and every household weep for me, whether they wish it or not', which, Brown notes, is not far from 'Matthew's scriptural comment upon the Bethlehem scene in terms of Rachel mourning for her children'.[37]

Again, Brown considers as 'plausible' Matthew's 'insistence that the massacre at Bethlehem came out of Herod's fear of the birth of a rival king'. Josephus records that Herod put to death those Pharisees who 'predicted that Herod's throne

---

[36] Benedict T Viviano, 'The Gospel according to Matthew', in *The New Jerome Biblical Commentary*, eds. R Brown, J Fitzmyer and R Murphy (London: Geoffrey Chapman, 1989), 630–74, at 635–6.

[37] Brown, *Birth of the Messiah*, 227, citing Flavius Josephus, *War* I xxxii 6 #660, and *Antiquities* XVII vi 5 ##174–8. See also Johnson, *Truly Our Sister,* 242–5.

would be taken from him and his descendants, and that power would go to Pheroras (his brother) and his wife and any children born to them'.[38]

We will return to the historical layer later. We recall here that the overall purpose of the first two chapters of Matthew's Gospel is to introduce Jesus as the all-encompassing Savior—Son of Abraham, Son of God and Emmanuel, New Moses etc. Again, the events recounted are indicative of what will confront Jesus in his mission and reach a climax in his passion and death. They also reflect conflict and hostility confronting (and within) Matthew's community. The return of Joseph and his family to Nazareth in Galilee rather than to Judea (Herod's base of power) intimates the interplay of Judea and Galilee in Jesus' ministry. Overall, Herod and later powers of opposition will become tools of the divine purpose for humanity.[39] What can we learn about St Joseph from these matters?

We can turn to what Jesus says later in Matthew's Gospel in his instructions to the Twelve: 'See, I am sending you out like sheep into the midst of wolves; so be wise as serpents and innocent as doves' (Mt 10:16).

As we know, Jesus goes on to exhort the Twelve to be fearless in their faith in the face of rejection and persecution—a perennial reality in the struggle for justice and in confronting hostile forces. Importantly, in such situations, he assures them not to be worried or afraid about what to do or to say: they will be strengthened and inspired by 'the Spirit of your Father'. In all this, Jesus himself is intimating a recipe with three ingredients: prayer, discretion, and street-smartness.

Can the same also be said of Joseph? His protective role involves the judicious handling of a precarious, even life-threatening, situation. Like refugees today, 'they have no control over where they may safely live but face constant uprooting as circumstances determined by those in power change'.[40] Entrusted with his special mission, Joseph, by further divine guidance (the three remaining dreams), is the instrument through whom the security of Jesus' family is secured against hostile forces (Herod and state authorities). This is done without 'forceful resistance' on the part of Joseph and his family.[41]

---

[38] Brown, *Birth of the Messiah*, 227–8, citing Flavius Josephus, *Antiquities* XVII ii 4 #43.

[39] Underlying the theological perspective is a practical reality. Joseph, as a craftsman in the building trade, could well have settled in Nazareth because of access to work in the reconstruction of neighboring Sepphoris by Herod Antipas around this time. See Viviano, 'Gospel according to Matthew', 636.

[40] Byrne, *Lifting the Burden*, 31. Of Herod and the 'brutality gene' passed on to his son, Archelaus, Johnson observes that 'carnage, upheaval, loss of home and neighbors, children caught in a web of violence, parents in despair—this story was all too intelligible to readers in Matthew's time, and in our own'. See Johnson, *Truly Our Sister*, 245.

[41] Byrne, *Lifting the Burden*, 31. See also the parallel discussion in Johnson, *Truly Our Sister*, 245–7.

Consider, again, the historical record. In this instance, it concerns Roman power and its ruthless response to resistance or rebellion. Pagola mentions that in A.D. 4:

> general Varus burned Sepphoris and the surrounding villages, then completely destroyed Emmaus and finally took Jerusalem, enslaving innumerable Jews and crucifying some 2,000.

Pagola puts the spotlight on one specific family:

> Jesus was three or four years old at the time and living in the village of Nazareth, only five kilometres away from Sepphoris. We don't know how it affected his family. We can be sure that the brutal Roman intervention was remembered for a long time. Peasants in the small villages do not easily forget such things. The stories must have terrified Jesus. Later, when he described the Romans as 'rulers of the nations' who 'lord it over them' and 'are tyrants over them', he knew what he was talking about.[42]

This graphic account offers specific evidence about the reality facing Joseph as the one responsible for Mary and Jesus. Consistent with this is the element of safety. One can well imagine that when they returned to Galilee and lived out their lives in Nazareth, given all that had happened, Joseph would be conscious of the need to stay under the radar to avoid attracting unwanted attention on himself or his family.

In considering Joseph and how he acted prior to and after the birth of Jesus, then, we recall Pope Francis' words cited earlier: 'God helped [Joseph] by enlightening his judgment'. In other words, Joseph lived by his conscience according to the recipe noted above—the mix of being prayerful and wise, but also streetwise. In the light of what has been explained above, his persistence and courage should also be included amongst the virtues at work in his life.

The Man of Integrity: The Wider Context

The scene at the start of Matthew that we have discussed, while subject to a feminist critique and a more inclusive reading, does, for all that, reveal Joseph as a man of integrity. Importantly, he is portrayed as having a sensitivity that colors his moral awareness in how to handle a very difficult situation. Just as our parents were models for us as we grew up, so with Jesus. It could well be said that the Joseph we see prior to the dreams emerges as the right sort of person to marry and protect Mary and Jesus. Luke's Gospel speaks of Mary as 'full of grace', that 'the Lord is with (her)'. On that basis, she is called to a unique task as Mother of the

---

[42] José A Pagola, *Jesus: An Historical Approximation* (Miami, FL: Convivium, 2014), 33 n. 8, and 37. These events are cited from Flavius Josephus, *The Jewish War*, 75–9 (no further details given).

Savior. Could it also be suggested, from what we have seen, that Joseph was chosen for a special task too because he was 'graced', especially 'favored', and 'the Lord was with' him?

Within the Hebrew tradition, Pope Benedict XVI reminds us that St Joseph presents as the just man whose 'delight is in the law of the Lord' (Ps 1:2), as one who is in contact with the word of God. He 'is like a tree, planted beside the flowing waters, constantly bringing forth fruit' and that:

> For him the law is simply Gospel, good news, because he reads it with a personal, loving openness to God and in this way learns to understand and live it from deep within.[43]

Finally, if we consider Joseph in a broader context, he joins company with Simeon and Anna (in Luke's Gospel), who represent those faithful Israelites who cling, in trust and obedience, to the promises of the Jewish heritage. All three, with Mary, are among those women and men of the Old Testament who, in Henri de Lubac's words, were already people of the New Testament in that:

> living out the first phases of the one history of salvation with an extremely pure faith, possessed an orientation of soul or spiritual dynamism which spontaneously carried them beyond Jewish perspectives, though they might not have been aware of it.[44]

This brings us to a brief summary of our discussion.

Past and Present Correlations

We began with Pope Francis and how St Joseph reminds us that 'amid the tempests of life we must never be afraid to let the Lord steer our course'.[45] We have seen that there was more to Joseph than the role of a protector, guardian, or patron. As a significant example of how God works through human agents in the plan of salvation, Joseph is distinctive for his sensitivity, mercy, compassion, and, importantly, his courage.

But to return to five centuries before his time, namely, to Greece. Aristotle remarked that if we want to know what is right or wrong, then ask someone who is wise. Whether we describe Joseph as just, righteous, good, or a man of character, our considerations indicate that Joseph also meets Aristotle's criteria for being a wise person (*phronimos*). Further, St Joseph offers a case study of conscience 'at work', featuring: the deepest self open to, and in dialogue with,

---

[43] Joseph Ratzinger, *Jesus of Nazareth: The Infancy Narratives* (New York: Random House, 2012), 39–40.

[44] Henri de Lubac, *The Sources of Revelation* (New York: Herder and Herder, 1968), 38.

[45] Francis, *Patris Corde*, 4.

God; a context of the virtues; the habit of wise discretion (and any interior struggle involved); an openness to grow and learn; finally, the pattern of living by the courage of one's convictions.

Again, the power of moral witness can have both a private and a public face. Its familial aspect has been noted with Joseph's influence, for instance, on Jesus. Its unobtrusive side also draws the attention of Pope Francis, especially when considering the pandemic. From doctors, nurses, storekeepers to fathers, mothers, grandparents, and teachers—such people and their devotion remind us that 'no one is saved alone'. In such a context:

> Saint Joseph reminds us that those who appear hidden or in the shadows can play an incomparable role in the history of salvation. A word of recognition and of gratitude is due to them all.[46]

Conclusion

As I was writing this article, I stumbled on a book title that suggests a contemporary way of viewing Joseph but also a bridge linking past and present, hence, a fitting way to close.[47] It reminds us, once again, that conscience, wisdom, and compassion transcend time and place.

The book in question explores the word *mensch*. It is originally the German term for a 'human being'. Its Yiddish usage throws further light on someone who is 'good' or 'righteous' or 'wise'. A *mensch* denotes a person (man or woman) on whom one can trust to act with honor and integrity. But the term also suggests someone who is kind and attentive. It is difficult to imagine a higher Jewish compliment than to be described with that specific word.

Rabbi Neil Kurshan characterizes the word *mensch* as:

> responsibility fused with compassion, a feeling that one's own personal needs and desires are limited by the needs and desires of other people. A mensch acts with self-control and humility, always sensitive to the feelings and thoughts of others.[48]

In the light of what we have seen, it would be difficult to find a more appropriate (and closing) word that captures St Joseph as a model in the Christian life.

This concludes the second part of the book.

---

[46] Francis, *Patris Corde*, 2.

[47] Neil Kurshan, *Raising Your Child to be a Mensch* (New York: Atheneum, 1987).

[48] Kurshan, *Raising Your Child*, cited in https://www.thejc.com/news/all/what-is-a-mensch-1.64427, accessed 26 September 2021.

In the third section of this study, we turn our attention to worship and moral formation, starting with Evelyn Underhill.

WORSHIP AND MORAL FORMATION

8
Evelyn Underhill:
Spirituality, Liturgy and Moral Responsibility

I would like to start with two quotations. In 1936, Evelyn Underhill, the Anglican spiritual writer, opens a retreat with two comments. First, she notes that a retreat's aim is to 'wait on the Lord', to be spiritually nourished 'not for our own sakes but for the sake of the world'. Second, she observes that the more the Spirit, that the 'Life of God possesses us, the more fully and inevitably it will bring forth its fruits'.[1]

The premise guiding this chapter is that Evelyn Underhill's observations suggest possibilities for spirituality today. This is particularly in the light of two trends: first, many seem to pursue the spiritual path apart from, even in opposition to, Church institutions and corporate worship; second, some do so on the understanding that spirituality is a form of self-development with little or no relationship to others in moral responsibility.[2]

The chapter proceeds in four stages.

I will set the context by noting key aspects in Underhill's theological development. Second, guided by the two quotations from Underhill, the article will uncover four intersecting themes underpinning her spiritual/moral vision and its relationship to worship and liturgy. Third, I will test the possibility that Underhill's Spirit-based approach anticipates today's spiritual seeker outside either institutional religion, or Christianity, and may even offer something to those whose spiritual quest is pursued 'without God'. The chapter will conclude with some comments on the significance of Underhill's work in the past and present.

A Word on Evelyn Underhill: Context

We associate Evelyn Underhill with her magisterial study *Mysticism* (1911).[3] To judge her solely on that work is to do her an injustice, given that her overall corpus

---

[1] Evelyn Underhill, *The Fruits of the Spirit* (London: Longmans, Green and Co., 1942), 5.

[2] This chapter is a revised version of an article originally published as 'A Spirituality *For* Moral Responsibility: Evelyn Underhill Today', *The Australasian Catholic Record* 85:2 (April), 2008.

[3] Evelyn Underhill, *Mysticism: A study in the nature and developments of Man's spiritual consciousness* (New York: A Meridian Book, 1955). Since the first printing (1911), it has been through at least twelve editions. The Evelyn Underhill Association, the text of *Mysticism,* some of her writings, related articles and resources can be accessed online at http://www.evelynunderhill.org/

is vast. Further, her thought evolved significantly after 1911, especially under the influence of Baron von Hügel in the decade prior to 1925.[4] It is generally agreed that *The Spiritual Life* (1937) reflects Underhill's mature spirituality both personally and as a spiritual guide and teacher.

Over the past thirty years, particularly in the United States, Underhill has been the subject of an ongoing critical reappraisal, especially of her later works (those published between 1921 and her death in 1941).[5] The main thrust of scholarship highlights the Spirit as the theological foundation of Evelyn Underhill's spiritual teaching. This has been probed by various authors especially in relation to sacraments, worship, spiritual transformation with its moral dimensions and, finally, subject to feminist critique.[6]

There seem to be four features in Underhill's theological development. First, the Platonic tone of her early writing reflects an unresolved tension in the relationship of spirit to matter, the invisible to the visible worlds. At this stage, the spiritual journey for Underhill is predominantly a movement away from this world to the spiritual realm of true values. However, through von Hügel's influence, she achieves a more integrated, even sacramental view of reality—the visible mediates the invisible. She articulates its depth, scope, and dynamisms by her effective use of images and visual art.[7] Truth and values are not found apart

---

[4] We can trace the trajectory of its development between *Mysticism* (1911), through *The Life of the Spirit and the Life of Today* (1922), *The Golden Sequence* (1932), *Worship* (1936) and *The Spiritual Life* (1937). A recent and valuable contribution about von Hügel's influence on Underhill is Robyn Wrigley-Carr, *The Spiritual Formation of Evelyn Underhill* (London, UK: SPCK Press, 2020).

[5] Two significant books are Dana Greene, *Evelyn Underhill, Artist of the Infinite Life* (Notre Dame, Indiana: University of Notre Dame Press, 1998) first published in 1990; Annice Callahan, RSCJ, *Evelyn Underhill: Spirituality for Daily Living* (Lanham, MD: Oxford, UK: University of America Press, 1997).

[6] For instance, Todd E Johnson, 'Pneumatological Oblation: Evelyn Underhill's Theology of the Eucharist,' *Worship* 68:4, July 1994: 313-332; Also his outstanding doctoral dissertation *In Spirit and Truth: Pneumatology, Modernism and their Relation to Symbols and Sacraments in the writings of Evelyn Underhill* (Ann Arbor Michigan: UMI Dissertation Abstracts, 1996*)*; Michael Stoeber, 'Evelyn Underhill on Magic, Sacrament and Spiritual Transformation,' *Worship* 77:2, March 2003: 132-151; Terry Tastard, *The Spark in the Soul: Spirituality and Social Justice* (London: DLT, 1989); Grace Janzten, 'The Legacy of Evelyn Underhill,' *Feminist Theology* No. 4 (1993): 79–100; the reply to this of Stephanie Ford, *Evelyn Underhill's Mystical Theology in the light of the Feminist Critique of Grace Jantzen* (Ann Arbor Michigan: UMI Dissertation Abstracts, 2003*)*.

[7] See Marie Crowley, *Beyond the Fringe of Speech: The Spirituality of Evelyn Underhill and Art*. Ph. D thesis, Australian Catholic University, 2009. In many ways, Underhill's spiritual/ moral teaching is embodied in a cluster of controlling metaphors. See David Walker, *God is a Sea: The Dynamics of Christian Living* (Homebush, NSW: St Paul's, 1977). The author gives

from this world but are embedded and disclosed within it. For Underhill, the spiritual quest is no longer an escape from the world but the search for the transcendent within our world and an ensuing responsibility towards it.

Second, Underhill's theological position reflects her dissatisfaction with pantheism. Her yardstick is the transcendent not only as satisfying our deepest yearnings but as a personal reality that is, most significantly, inherently moral. Cosmic awareness of the divine in nature, while religious, is not sufficient. In a letter written in 1924 she observes that pantheism 'offers no real incentive or sanction for moral effort'.[8] The human soul in its partial and imperfect state requires a relationship with a personal object in order to be whole and complete. We 'need conviction of *personal* responsibility to a *personal* God' that is best met 'by *genuine* and preferably Christian theism'.[9] Later, she makes this more specific in terms of our need for divine healing and redemption'.[10]

Third, her view changes concerning the scope and membership of the spiritual pilgrimage. Writing in 1911, Evelyn Underhill sees the journey towards the Absolute as the task of the 'mystic'.[11] Later, in her 1936 retreat and published BBC talks, the quest is no longer the preserve of a special group under the heading of 'mystics'. Its call is aimed at every seeker of the True, the Good and the Beautiful. It is, then, a change in context from the extraordinary to the ordinary.[12] All people have the capacity to receive and share in this state of harmony with the spiritual universe.

Finally, Underhill arrives at a different perspective concerning the source of transformation. The mystical quest is not accomplished through human effort in tune with the evolutionary movement of history. It is a spiritual life beginning and sustained by a divine gift. It is a free and unconditional response to the Spirit's

---

a commentary on thirty images from the Christian spiritual tradition. Nine are images drawn from the writings of Evelyn Underhill.

[8] Charles Williams (ed. and Intro.), *The Letters of Evelyn Underhill* (Longman, Green and Co., 1945), 155.

[9] Ibid., 155; emphasis in original.

[10] Like Augustine, to have a deeply-felt need, 'through real, heart-breaking penitence and longing for a costly perfection' from God in Christ to give us the deep healing needed for true wholeness and full humanity'. Ibid., 182, letter to Z.A.

[11] The journey, ('mystical' not 'spiritual'), aims at a 'state of harmony with the spiritual universe, sometimes called "deification"'. Underhill, *Mysticism*, 102.

[12] Evelyn Underhill. *The Spiritual Life* (Homebush, NSW: Society of St. Paul, 1976). This book, with an introduction by David Walker, is a printing of what were originally four talks delivered by her on BBC radio.

presence and action so that each person finds their unique role 'in the great and secret economy of God'.[13] This self-forgetting participation in a movement to a reality larger than ourselves is the only gateway to the true freedom of the children of God.[14] It is primarily and importantly a journey of being transformed by the Other.

With this background in mind, we come to the underpinnings of the spiritual life and its processes as found in Evelyn Underhill.

Four Intersecting Themes of Underhill's Spiritual Moral Vision

Any spirituality has, at the least, an implicit theological framework. I will chart the intersecting themes in Underhill's project: the Spirit animates and guides the spiritual journey as a work of transformation; modified consciousness responds in Adoration, Communion (Adherence) and Cooperation with God; finally, the fruits of this process emerge in the form of a changed quality of perceptions and dispositions to respond and act. Binding them together is the fourth theme—the internal dynamism of the Spirit's action. It is centrifugal, moving towards the 'Other' and others through a different mode of relationships embodied in moral responsibility in the world.[15]

The Spirit as a Gift That Transforms

The hub of Underhill's mature spirituality is the Spirit, but more the Spirit of God than the Spirit of Christ. The Spirit is not simply a divine presence that is omnipresent but only vaguely experienced. The Spirit, for Underhill, is always personal, free, and loving, even if there are gradations in how the Spirit is actually felt and known.[16] It is the donative reality, the self-giving presence of God, immanent in creation, permeating and supporting it.

---

[13] Underhill. *The Spiritual Life,* 37.

[14] Ibid., 37. Johnson argues that the transition to an integrated understanding of her predominantly Spirit-driven spirituality is articulated most clearly in Evelyn Underhill, *The Golden Sequence: A Fourfold Study of the Spiritual Life* (London: Methuen and Co., 1932).

[15] Recent studies on Evelyn Underhill by Australian scholar Dr. Robyn Wrigley-Carr illustrate in practical terms how these themes are at work in Underhill's personal prayer, spiritual teaching, and retreat conferences. See Robyn Wrigley-Carr, *Music of Eternity: Meditations for Advent with Evelyn Underhill: The Archbishop of York's Advent Book 2021* (London, UK: SPCK Press, 2021) and her edited collection, *Evelyn Underhill's Prayer Book* (London, UK: SPCK, 2018).

[16] It can be experienced 'dimly' in creation, as inspiring goodness, and heroism, as most deeply at work in a person's interior life, or as perfectly embodied in Christ. Underhill, *The Golden Sequence,* 28-9.

The Spirit is the bridge between eternity and time, the transcendent 'Wholly Other' and the immanent, derived, limited world of creation.[17] The Spirit enables the supernatural to be immanent in nature. von Hügel helps Underhill to appreciate that Christianity's central conviction concerns the penetration of spirit into sense, of the Eternal into time, especially in the Incarnation in that it encapsulates 'the real prevenience and condescension of the real God...'[18]

God's essential characteristic is as one who stoops down to the human level and whose manifestation in the Spirit and in Christ emerges from the 'depths of Absolute Being, yet (is) charged with the self-giving ardour of Absolute Love'.[19] Christ not only embodies the divine self-gift. He sums up in himself humanity and creation's response in his own self-giving to his Father in perfect submission to God's Spirit through a life of sacrifice and surrender'.[20] For Underhill, the Christian life as responding to and living in the Spirit, is a share in the life of the sacrifice, surrender and self-giving of Christ to God his Father.[21]

Within creation there is the human being, special and unique.[22] Human existence is characterized by an inbuilt yearning capacity to interact with reality. It is the Spirit that is the innate spark inviting the human spirit to open itself to the Real, be receptive to God and the divine purposes.[23] In explaining this, Underhill cites von Hügel who says that:

God's Spirit ever works in closest penetration and stimulation of our own; just as, in return, we cannot find God's spirit simply separate from

---

[17] 'Wholly Other' is found in her works, for instance in the Introduction to *Mysticism* (12th. ed. 1930). Its usage is particularly associated with Rudolf Otto, an author who had been read by Underhill, as *Mysticism* indicates.

[18] 'God and Spirit' published in *Theology* in 1930 and included in Dana Greene (ed. and Introduction), *Evelyn Underhill: Modern Guide to the Ancient Quest for the Holy* (Albany, NY: State University of NY Press, 1988), 181.

[19] Evelyn Underhill, *Worship* (London: James Nisbet & Co. 1936), 66.

[20] It is this event and this person that leads us to a full response by acknowledging 'his personal and eternal Spirit—His Absolute Will and love—at work within the world of time.' Ibid., 62.

[21] Johnson, 'Pneumatological Oblation', 317.

[22] Underhill sees this in terms of the three data of religion from von Hügel: 'the absolute Spirit of God, the derived spirit Man, and the relation between His Spirit and our own'. See 'God and Spirit' published in *Theology* in 1930 and included in Dana Greene, *Evelyn Underhill: Modern Guide*, 181.

[23] Johnson, 'Pneumatological Oblation', 316.

our own spirit within ourselves. Our spirit clothes and expresses His; His Spirit first creates and then sustains and stimulates our own.[24]

God's penetration and pervading presence in the world is at the heart of Underhill's vision. But it is beyond the Spirit known diffusely as a pervading force within creation. It includes the creative, animating, unifying, and guiding roles of the Spirit captured in images in Scripture.

The distinctive quality highlighted by Underhill is the Spirit as the expression of *divine fecundity*—its capacity not just to continue life but to *generate new life*.[25] Though the Spirit's action is hidden, we become aware of it through its tendency to continually break into the world particularly in the everyday—in acts of love, in endurance despite difficulties, in the urge to live up to certain standards, in a struggle for a better world. When we transcend ourselves in some way, we respond to the gentle pressure of the divine Spirit.[26]

For Underhill, how does this occur and what are its outcomes? After some general comments on conversion, I will concentrate on two aspects of Underhill's approach to transformation: its structure—in the human response through Adoration, Communion (Adherence) and Cooperation; its content, specifically as reflected in the Fruits of the Spirit.

Conversion

When the creative action of God as Spirit finds personal response, it entails changes in a person's awareness and self-awareness, namely, a conversion. Whatever the form in which the incitement of the hidden God reaches a person, the human response 'follows much the same road' even though its various stages are named in a variety of ways'.[27] It is a shift at the level of Being (not Wanting, Doing, Having, Acting). It is a waking-up, a noticing of spiritual light, a sensitivity to a spiritual atmosphere that reveals our human world in its true reality.

Thus, one's horizon is widened, the landscape is seen differently, personal experience is 'enormously enriched', and responsibilities are enlarged.[28] The mind is enlightened, the heart attracted, power is given to the will to persevere.[29]

---

[24] Underhill, *Modern Guide*, 181.

[25] See *Mysticism*, 428 and 434; my emphasis.

[26] Tastard, *The Spark in the Soul*, 73.

[27] Underhill, *The Spiritual Life,* 49.

[28] Underhill, *The Spiritual Life,* 44.

[29] Ibid., 46.

It is a shift to a greater level of freedom and truth—a broadening of horizon, recognition of what is true and good, a step in self-transcendence and a conscious communion with the Real.[30]

Human Response to the Transcendent

The impulse of the Spirit moves us, then, to receive and surrender—in mind, heart and will.

It is around these operations of human consciousness that Underhill builds her structure of the human response to the Spirit's urgings.

The first stage of her understanding is evident in 1922. Speaking at the general level, she points to three principal and complementary ways of engaging in the spiritual journey, namely, of realizing a relationship with the transcendent realm: first, a sense of awe, of cosmic oneness with the transcendent reality resulting in a sense of deep security and peace; second, awareness of a relationship and union with a Person who brings a 'prevenient and answering love' that prompts surrender and personal response; third, the arousal of energy and creative powers.[31] These three zones of experience overlap and are interfused.

Underhill suggests that this three-fold pattern builds on the structure of human experience as made in God's image. These three moments in awareness of the divine are traces of the Trinity's presence and action.[32] In other words, the object and symbolic expression of each moment is found in a person of the Trinity: in the Father, for the movement towards the transcendent and its ensuing serenity; the Son, for the immanent sense of intimacy and love; the Spirit as the creative response moving outwards.

This brings us to the key elements for Underhill in the structure of the human response to the divine Spirit.

Adoration, Communion (Adherence), Cooperation

In 1922, Underhill goes no further in the first phase outlined above. After 1930, however, her mature thought becomes more specific in adopting a threefold

---

[30] It entails 'on the one hand action, effort, renunciation of the narrow horizon, the personal ambition, the unreal objective; and on the other hand, a deliberate and grateful response to the attraction of the unseen, deepening into a conscious communion which gradually becomes the ruling fact of life'. Underhill, *The Spiritual Life,* 49-50.

[31] Evelyn Underhill, *The Life of the Spirit and the Life of Today* (San Francisco: Harper & Row, 1949), 5-10.

[32] '[I]t seems to me that what we have in the Christian doctrine of the Trinity, is above all the crystallization and mind's interpretation of these three ways in which our simple contact with God is actualized by us'. Ibid., 11.

pattern for the structure of prayer found in the French school of Spirituality especially in Cardinal Bérulle. It revolves around Adoration, Communion (Adherence), and Cooperation.[33]

This choice is probably colored by her experience of practical Christianity and the Social Gospel where she considered the focus was on service to the neglect of awe and prayer. It is worth noting here, however, that beyond these reasons, Underhill offers a rationale for this reading of religious experience, namely, that it has its own internal dynamism. It is marked by the interfusing of intellect, will, and affectivity, thus involving the whole person.

With Bérulle and von Hügel, she sees the first and primary experience of God as wonder or awe that crystallizes in *Adoration*. It is the acknowledgment of who God is as creator and who we are as dependent creatures. Worship and prayer, especially their corporate expression, are the two principal expressions of Adoration. Through sharing in the adoration of Jesus—the perfect adorer, we are enabled to share and experience the inner life of God. It is this attitude of Adoration that draws us, with the Spirit, out of ourselves, to wonder at the Other who is Love. Adoration needs to be sustained by constancy and devotion, a pattern of spiritual discipline.[34]

This awareness permeates further into the affective realm. It moves to *Communion* or *Adherence* where the heart is drawn into union with God in friendship. There is both divine nearness and close dependence on God. While this Reality stoops towards humankind in intimate nearness, it is simultaneously a God of 'awe-inspiring majesty' who 'becomes the ruling fact of existence; continually presenting its standards, and demanding a costly response'.[35]

Consequently, we see ourselves and the world differently. The Kingdom of God's standards are implanted in us. We have insight into the truth of the *Real*, both as a standard that summons us, and the *real* in which there is the gap between God's loving desires for the world and things as they actually are. Since this occurs when we know God's love, our energy and resolve are enhanced. We are drawn inevitably to act from the love we now share.[36] Integral to life animated by

---

[33] In *The Golden Sequence* (1932), *The Spiritual Life* (1937). In the former work, she uses the adaptation found in Jean-Jacques Olier, namely, Adoration/Adherence/Intercession.

[34] Tastard, *The Spark in the Soul*, 76. Tastard suggests that in Adoration we 'focus our intellectual awareness on God'. This is not so much analytical knowledge but the knowing that comes from immediate, non-discursive awareness.

[35] Underhill, *The Spiritual Life*, 48.

[36] Tastard, *The Spark in the Soul*, 76-7.

and guided by the Spirit is a moral imperative and ethical responsibility in the world of relationships.

From communion with (or adherence to) God emerges the transformed self under the momentum of the Spirit to work with God to bring about the Divine Plan in the world. Adoration and Communion flow inexorably to orient and animate the will. The movement away from the self, the ecstatic quality of divine love, experienced in Adoration and Communion, is completed in *Cooperation*—to become a new center of creative life.[37]

In other words, we are called to be both participants in, and agents of, the 'divine fecundity' which is the 'goal of human transcendence'.[38] We wait on the Lord 'for the sake of the world'. Cooperation means that each person open to the Spirit participates in the Body of Christ's call to transform and redeem the world in and through Jesus.[39] This takes two forms: a willed participation in this process through Intercession; action in the world with and for others.

Underhill dismisses the prevalent notion that spirituality and politics have nothing to do with each other. An adequate spiritual life implies that 'certain convictions about God and the world become the moral and spiritual imperatives or our life'.[40] This requires practical involvement in the lives of people who suffer injustice, poverty, hatred, rejection. In her own life, following von Hügel's conviction that spirituality is incarnational ('for the sake of the world'), Underhill committed herself to weekly contact with the poor. This shapes her down-to-earth approach to spiritual direction and her insights into authentic spiritual growth.

From our considerations on the various elements of structure of the transforming process, we move on now to consider the fourth pillar of Underhill's spiritual vision.

---

[37] After noting Bérulle's three-fold relation of the soul with God, Underhill goes on to say that 'adoration is the root, communion the flower, intercessory action the fruit, of that divine-human love which binds in one the total life of prayer'. *The Golden Sequence,* 175.

[38] Underhill, *The Life of the Spirit,* 44 and *Mysticism,* 434. This idea seems to be fed by two sources: human sharing in God's 'absolute repose, absolute fecundity' (Ruysbroeck) and its emergence in expanding and more inclusive love; Bérulle's emphasis on the Spirit as the unique expression of the impulse towards fertility outside the inner life of the triune God. For a contemporary discussion of *ecstasis* and the Holy Spirit see Helen Bergin, 'The Holy Spirit as the "Ecstatic" God', *Pacifica* 17:3 (2004): 268-281.

[39] It entails 'every intervention we make in the world around us to bring it into conformity with the longing, loving intentions of God'. Ibid., 78.

[40] Underhill, *The Spiritual Life,* 66.

Fruits of the Spirit

Underhill outlines the more specific effects of transformation in the gifts and fruits of the Spirit. Her methodology continues to be descriptive and experiential. She does not offer, as does Thomas Aquinas, an extensive correlation of the virtues, the gifts, the beatitudes, and the fruits of the Spirit. While she generally brings a standard approach to the gifts,[41] this is not the case with the fruits.

For Underhill, the divine indwelling is most evident in the Spirit's fruits listed in Gal 5:22. They are not administered or inserted as if a new element, such as a gift or faculty. What is central is the 'receiving'—one receives *God*. As 'new creatures in Christ', we are slowly transformed by the divine pressure to deeper opening of the self through prayer.[42] Charity is given in the 'ground of the soul' (where) 'abiding union with God takes place; and that the divine love then spreads more and more throughout the whole psychic life'.[43]

It follows the *momentum of fecundity*—the Spirit's orientation to reproduce its life in people and action. The fruits of this transformation are modified perceptions and dispositions to respond and act. The sources of resistance to this process are the seven deadly sins, deeply-rooted inclinations to selfishness—highlighted by way of contrast with the fruits (Gal 5: 19-21).

We noted earlier that, for Underhill, the free response to the presence of the Spirit has a ternary pattern: it enlightens the mind, attracts the heart, and strengthens the will.[44] Consequently, we are enabled to move with the ease and suppleness of the truly free (a characteristic of the gifts as sharing in the divine life).[45]

Citing St. John of the Cross, Underhill says that every virtue or quality imprinted by the Spirit on the surrendered soul has three distinguishing marks: Tranquility, Gentleness, and Strength.[46] These qualities emerge from 'deification', or participation in the divine reality bringing membership of a wider family as children of God and being in tune with the harmonizing movement of the Spirit.[47] One's identity and actions are slowly changed. There is a steadiness

---

[41] See *The Golden Sequence*, 78-89.

[42] Underhill, *The Fruits of the Spirit*, (London: Longmans, Green & Co., 1942), 6.

[43] Letters, 199-200.

[44] Underhill, *The Spiritual Life*, 46.

[45] Ibid., 37. See the earlier discussion in chapters four and five of this book.

[46] Ibid., 72.

[47] Ibid., 73.

and depth in the 'soul's abiding temper' since our small action is 'part of the total action of God whose Spirit (…) "Works always in tranquility"'.[48] This pattern becomes visible in our relationships.

As the life of God increasingly possesses us, we more fully and inevitably bring forth its fruits. They are not the result of our deliberate effort as if shaping spiritual plasticine. It is a process of growth stemming from 'the budding point' of Love.[49] From Peace and Joy they stretch out to in love the world. Divine life adapts to the individual in that 'God lets the plant grow at its own pace'.[50] The fruits are indicators of the health of our spiritual life grounded in prayer.[51]

Another Perspective?

Underhill departs from the traditional approach to the fruits construed as ongoing attitudes and affective states. She sees them more in terms of virtues, as dispositions, ways of thinking, speaking, and acting that expand from within, animated by love.[52] They are, in themselves, permanent; promises to be realized in the present rather than in the future.[53] They entail changes in the consciousness of a person (albeit 'soul'). They infiltrate and shape the contours of our awareness of the world and of self-awareness in its reflexive tasks.

In some ways, Underhill subsumes the traditional cardinal virtues into the fruits of the Spirit. For instance, practical wisdom is at work in the experience of fundamental peace disclosing the truth whereby we can adjust to life by being in harmony with God's will, the point where the Spirit guides us as to 'what we want or ought to be at'.[54] Again, for Underhill, temperance brings a realistic appreciation one's identity, one's gifts and one's role in the plan of God. As a spiritual guide, she emphasizes balance in one's life and a realistic appreciation

---

[48] Ibid., 73. The quality of a person's spiritual life is 'not measured by lofty religious notions or in the fervor of feelings. Its criteria are located in the persistent influence of what is tranquil, gentle and strong beneath changes in the surrounding atmosphere, in spite of disappointments, the impact of external events and the variations in religious temperature'. Ibid., 73-74.

[49] This occurs 'at the very centre of our being where the innermost self responds to God'. Underhill, *The Fruits of the Spirit*, 19.

[50] Ibid., 19-21.

[51] They are the 'necessary' fruits of God's Spirit and simultaneously the 'fruits of human nature when it has opened itself to the action of the Eternal Love'. Ibid., 5-6.

[52] They 'are brought forth in us, gradually but inevitably, by the pressure of the Divine love in our souls. They all spring from one root'. Ibid., 6.

[53] Ibid., 17, 12.

[54] Ibid., 15.

of our bodily, psychological, and social needs. Temperance, for her, involves self-care.

Underhill's departure from Aquinas' orderly system enables her to bring a fresh and innovative angle in three respects.[55]

First, the primary context in which she sees the fruits is of the Spirit at work, not in the individual nor in the Church, but as revealing the divine presence and action in *creation*.[56] Christianity's meaning and purpose is the transfiguration of creation so that it is the expression of God's Word and Spirit. This is realized through membership in Christ, but more fundamentally, by being participants in the emergence of the world that will give 'visible expression to the perfection and beauty of God'.[57] For Underhill, the Spirit's fruits in the individual person are part of a wider network of relationships—with God, creation, and other people. Her cosmic and ecclesial approach brings a healthy corrective to any individualistic approach to the fruits of the Spirit.

Second, Underhill sees the list given by Paul (Gal 5) as *progressive* in nature, along the continuum noted earlier of Tranquility, Gentleness and Strength. She suggests that they reflect the 'form and direction' of spiritual growth, one which does not match our expectations. Further, it follows a trajectory of relationships. There is rapport with the transcendent realm, 'a tranquil deep delight in God' (Joy and Peace). In the interpersonal and social domains, there is long-suffering, gentleness, goodness 'in complete acceptance and use of life, of our human relationships and environment'.

Finally, regarding the intrapersonal area, it is self-knowledge, faithfulness, meekness, temperance that bring 'quiet, creaturely acceptance of our own particular limitations and callings'.[58] The influence of the Spirit moves us within creation towards a fuller and deeper embrace of the real within the divine life.

---

[55] Underhill's approach to the fruits bears a modern comparison. Thomas Keating offers a contemporary perspective to the gifts and the fruits. He sees the gifts as helping us to engage with the unconscious—with the undigested emotional material of a lifetime together with the depths of energy and creativity found there. When these are harnessed, they emerge as charity, joy, peace, etc.—the fruits as listed in Gal 5:22-23. Thomas Keating, *Fruits and Gifts of the Spirit* (New York: Lantern Books, 2000), 15.

[56] 'We might call them manifestations of the Mind of God in his Creation; manifestations of his unlimited and generous love, His essential joy, His deep tranquility, the unmarred harmony of His nature, His patient, gentle action, His faithful cherishing care'. *The Fruits of the Spirit*, 6.

[57] Ibid., 6.

[58] Ibid., 8.

This brings us to the third stage of the chapter.

'The Wind Blows Where It Chooses' (Jn 3:8)

Does Underhill's Spirit-based approach have anything to offer today's spiritual seeker who is a) a non-institutional Christian, b) or someone not a Christian, or c) walks conscientiously 'without God' as 'not religious' and even an atheist?

Underhill is convinced of the need for an institutional framework, especially of worship and sacramental life, for a wholesome Christianity.[59] However, she is not inflexible on this matter.

In a letter of 1939, she responds to a believer who receives no nourishment from active participation in worship and sacramental life. She points out that the practice of frequent reception of Holy Communion is a recent development and therefore not essential.[60] She recognizes that a viable spiritual life is possible apart from the sacraments when she notes that:

> God will take care of his own, and will make up in other ways to the really desirous what they can't at present receive through the sacramental channels of the Church.[61]

Underhill is sensitive to the flexibility of the Spirit in dealing with people of good will in their concrete circumstances.

Second, the person whose faith is religious/theistic but not Christian is acknowledged by Underhill in three ways. The spiritual resources of other religious traditions (e.g., Indian, Islamic etc.) are recognized and tapped by her in *Mysticism* and other writings. Second, we have already noted her view that, while responses to the Ultimately Real follow much the same road, God reaches people in many ways.[62] Third, for Underhill, awareness of the creative action of God as

---

[59] Our need for 'humble immersion in the life and worship of the Church'. *Letters*, 261.

[60] '[T]hree times a year was the usual thing for laity, though Mass was always the principal Sunday service. Therefore, it can't be *essential* to the supernatural life'. *Letters*, 276.

[61] *Letters*, 276. Johnson sums it up when he notes that for Underhill 'Even though mysticism was an essential part of the sacraments, the sacraments were not an essential part of mysticism. It was obvious from the non-Christian mystics, the Mystic Way could be traversed without the aid of the sacraments'. *In Spirit and Truth*, 96.

[62] She speaks of the many ways in which the 'incitements of the hidden God' may reach people. *The Spiritual Life*, 49.

Spirit is an 'experimental knowledge' that is 'not on the one hand possessed by all Christians, nor on the other hand is it confined to Christianity'.[63]

Finally, there is the matter of someone whose spiritual quest is 'without God', as an unbeliever, even an atheist. At one stage, Underhill writes about faithful service in the believing disciple at difficult times, 'not to God when we feel Him present, but to God when He seems to be absent'.[64]

On this point, she highlights three lessons from Jesus on faithfulness found in Matthew's Gospel, Ch 25. The Last Judgment offers a lesson that she suggests is 'perhaps the deepest and the most searching'. It is about devoted service to the demands of people 'even although we have no sense of God'. There is 'no glow of religious joy but sheer will and loving compassion. Though he is not visible, the King is there (…) moving disguised among His people at night'.[65]

Up to this stage of the parable, Underhill's concern seems limited to the believer whose sense of the divine presence is darkened as a trial of faith. As she proceeds, the scope of her discussion seems to broaden, in line with the parable itself. She points to 'those who spend their lives serving the unseen Christ in His poor. I expect they are very dear to God'. Such people, in her view, may object 'Oh! I am not a spiritual person at all. I have no experience of God'.[66] Her words now appear to be aimed at those for whom God is not a perceived reality in their lives. Despite this, their constant self-giving and focus beyond themselves is not only part of the Spirit's action ('very dear to God'). It is, Underhill continues, 'a very exacting, complete, penetrating experience of God'.[67]

Underhill is suggesting the silent workings of grace revealed in the 'unselfing', the 'displacing of the ego (that) becomes a giving "place" to others', that is inseparable from union with Christ (even if hidden).[68] It is a love that brings the sure knowledge of those who 'have passed from death to life' (1 Jn 3:14). This persistent self-transcendence in attitude and behavior is a clear sign that God's Reign is present even if it is unrecognized.

---

[63] Ibid., 45.

[64] Underhill, *The Fruits of the Spirit*, 31.

[65] Ibid., 32.

[66] Ibid., 57.

[67] Ibid., 32.

[68] Rowan Williams, *The Wound of Knowledge: Christian Spirituality from the New Testament to St. John of the Cross* (London: Darton, Longman and Todd, 1979), 12.

Evelyn Underhill: Yesterday and Today

I would like to conclude by making some observations on Underhill's work in its own historical context and then in relation to the contemporary world.

Yesterday

In reading Underhill, the spotlight on the Spirit's internal presence in grace seems, at times, to reduce the role of Jesus to that of a moral exemplar. She does not adequately address the relationship of the Spirit and Christ in some form of Ecclesiology. While Christ embodies the Spirit of love, the overall impression is that Christ is more an external model than the one who mediates the Spirit's presence primarily in the Church.

Again, the fruits have their ultimate grounding in the gift of the Spirit as the first fruit of Christ's resurrection, bringing peace and the forgiveness of sins. She refers to peace as a promise in Christ's public ministry and the presence of the fruits in Jesus during his ministry. But the explicit link to the role of the Risen Jesus is not present. Further, the Risen Jesus and the formative role of the Scriptures on identity, perceptions and dispositions are muted in her work.

In the moral realm, notwithstanding Underhill's pacifist stance towards the end of her life, there is a certain passive, conforming angle in her moral vision. The attitude of surrender to the Spirit's movement seems to compromise the need, at times, for creative action and initiative in the face of injustice. This may be a function of her temperament. Her view of sin primarily in terms self-driven resistance, through the capital vices, to God's gift and action, has limits. Only late in life does Underhill come to a sense of the Original Sin, the deep-seated dissonance (even, of destructiveness), in human experience at the roots of selfishness.[69]

For all that, clearly, there is a theology of the Holy Spirit inscribed in Underhill's spirituality. She uses experience rather than a conceptual framework for her theological hermeneutic. Underhill is conscious of the limits and analogical character of theological language. It is only in a qualified theological sense that we can attribute divine actions of the economic Trinity to one person, e.g., the Spirit.[70]

---

[69] It is reflected in her letter to CS Lewis in 1939 responding to his book *The Problem of Pain*. See *Letters,* 302-3. She is also criticized for the lack of a developed Soteriology in her work.

[70] Billy notes concerning the person of the Spirit as the source of the Christian moral life that '[T]he Spirit's claim to the title comes only by way of appropriation due to its present priority of place in the economic plan of redemption as the immanent vivifying and sanctifying force of the new creation' in Dennis J Billy, C.Ss. R., 'The Person of the Holy Spirit as the Source of the Christian Moral Life', *Studia Moralia* 36, 1998: 254-285, at 348.

Perhaps Underhill's position nudges towards, half-echoes that of Pannenberg? For him, the bringing forth of new life and movement in creation and the new creation accompanied by a share in the Spirit's 'own ecstatic self-transcending dynamic' is *properly* the work of the Spirit and not just by way of appropriation.[71]

Overall, the Spirit as the mediating presence of the divine is the dominant and unifying theme of Underhill's transcription of the divine plan ('supernal symphony') unfolding in creation.[72] In listening to its 'elusive music', Underhill is sensitive to the ternary pulse of the Trinitarian life that vibrates gently in the background.[73]

Today

Underhill's vision is embedded in the created world. The knowledge of the transcendent realm disclosed within the visible world shapes the quality and texture of our relationships. It is a spirituality that is *a part of* and not *apart from* our material world. Again, she has certain similarities with Bernard Häring's moral theology with their common starting point of awe, adoration, and worship. Häring, too, subsumes the cardinal virtues into the eschatological virtues (peace, forgiveness, compassion, joy) which tend to overlap with the gifts and fruits of the Spirit.

In Underhill's mature thought, Bérulle's ternary pattern (Adoration, Communion, Cooperation) is the best Christian articulation of the human response to grace (for her 'the transcendent realm'). The universal pattern of awe/ /communion/creative action follows a trajectory of self-transcendence. This characterizes spirituality itself, namely, how grace is encountered universally. It is the human response to God's personal self-communication even if not recognized as grace—a singularly contemporary reality.

Underhill anticipates a contemporary theological anthropology by highlighting the creature/creator relationship. She suggests an organic approach to the Christian life characterized by identification with, and participation in, the divine life than of imitation and conformity to an external ideal. Underhill reminds us that authentic spirituality has an innate momentum towards a moral life. For that reason, 'A Spirituality *for* Moral Responsibility' seems more apt than '*of*' since it expresses the away-from-self momentum of the Spirit's action in a person and in the world so central for Evelyn Underhill's spiritual moral vision. [74]

---

[71] Anne Hunt, *Trinity: Nexus of the Mysteries of Christian Faith*, Foreword by Peter C Phan (Maryknoll, NY: Orbis, 2005), 206 and 212.

[72] Underhill, *The Life of the Spirit*, 11.

[73] The musical image is picked up in Wrigley-Carr's book title, see n. 15 above.

[74] This point is reflected in the title of the original article on which this chapter is based.

Again, recent writing highlights the relationship of spirituality and morality: the first animates, the second embodies and both need each other. Underhill's insistence on a personal God seems grounded in our humanity's prior call to personal moral responsibility. Given this, is it accurate to say that, for Underhill, spirituality provides the underpinnings of the moral life? Perhaps it is the reverse: that her approach suggests that we need a *moral* foundation for an authentic spirituality?

There is, however, a distinctive aspect to Underhill's approach that has resonances for contemporary moral theology. She underlines the fertile, generative, centrifugal power of the Spirit. The Spirit as the divine gift is always expanding in goodness and love. This enables Underhill to underscore two aspects that are currently discussed.

First, in her construal of the Trinitarian pattern of gift/response that reverberates in the intrapersonal realm (knowing, feeling, willing) there is present the same impulse to 'overflow' into the interpersonal realm. For Underhill, the Spirit not only animates the moral sphere but binds it inextricably to the spiritual realm from *within*. The Spirit is the personal gift of God that draws the total, responding person more deeply into the divine life and simultaneously outwards into a more life-giving set of relationships.

Second, in seeing the Spirit as 'the ecstasy of divine generosity' known in the 'splendors of creation', [75] Underhill adumbrates a call today for an experience of the Spirit that goes beyond that of a 'remainder concept', namely as a 'generalized, ubiquitous force in the world'.[76] Del Colle argues that, given the emphasis on experience in contemporary spirituality, we need to articulate a specific presence of God resulting from the *power* of the Spirit. We should move beyond seeing the Spirit as the vague, universal divine presence *intrinsic to* Creation. People give verbal assent to this but, in reality, it has no impact on their lives.

Mercier and de Colle suggest that the power of the Spirit is best viewed as the 'actual experience of God' understood as the *divine bestowal to* Creation (but discerned within it). If one is aware of the pervading, ubiquitous Spirit without a corresponding sense of the Spirit as 'giving gift', then to speak of the wonder of Creation can be 'an assertion without any meaning'.[77] Wonder and awe are

---

[75] Underhill, *The Golden Sequence*, 28.

[76] Ronald A Mercier, 'The Holy Spirit and Ethics: A Personal Gift Making Persons', in James Keating (Ed.), *Moral Theology: New Directions and Fundamental Issues, Festschrift for James P. Hanigan* (New York/Mahwah NJ: Paulist, 2004), 43-65, at 56. Mercier cites Ralph del Colle 'The Holy Spirit: Power, Presence, Person', *Theological Studies* 62 (2001):322-40.

[77] Ibid., 56.

responses to something *given* that Creation reveals to us, a mystery that summons us to reach out beyond ourselves. Mercier sums up this approach, one that is consonant with that of Underhill:

> The Spirit is the donative, intentional (given) reality of God, a personal, experiential gift that awakens the human person not only to the ubiquity of the Spirit's presence but also to the depth and meaning of Creation itself.[78]

Conclusion

This chapter has clarified the four key aspects underpinning Evelyn Underhill's theological development—its nature, goal, scope, and transcendent source. This led us to consider the intersecting themes in her spiritual project: the Spirit's animating presence and centrifugal thrust; the ternary pattern of adoration /communion / cooperation; finally, the resultant fruits of that process. Consideration was then given to Underhill's spirituality in relation to spiritual 'seekers' beyond the institutional Church. This was followed by an evaluation of her work in its original context and in today's world.

Some might suggest that Evelyn Underhill's work has been superseded. Three recent studies on her (noted earlier) from an Australian scholar seem to suggest otherwise.

More specifically, at a time when Church attendance and religious allegiance are plummeting in the western world, Underhill's Pneumatology of the spiritual moral life is timely. The fecundity of the Spirit within the person and in the setting of relationships is crucial in integrating the spiritual and moral dimensions of life.

Again, Underhill reminds us to look not at numbers but at the fruits of God's Spirit evident within and beyond Churches and people of faith. Rather than coming to God through Christ, she described her experience as coming to Christ through God. Evelyn may have something to offer the multitudes in today's world whose encounter with grace is not seen as a religious reality. They seek a hidden God, ignoring, even rejecting, the Christ who moves 'disguised among his people at night'.

Underhill would, no doubt, be reassured by the Catholic liturgy's *Second Eucharist Prayer of Reconciliation* with its more eschatological and social approach to the fruits of the Spirit visible in the world (the subject of the next chapter). We pray in the Spirit who turns people towards peace, who changes

---

[78] Ibid., 56.

hearts, brings enemies into dialogue and those estranged to renewed friendship. This is the Reign of God emerging in our midst.

This offers us as much reason to hope as it did Evelyn Underhill.

The next chapter continues the theme of the moral life and worship with a discussion of moral conversion in the relation to one of the Catholic Church's Eucharistic Prayers of Reconciliation.

9
Moral Conversion and Worship

A priest friend made this observation in a conversation. Parishioners regularly observe that, of all the Eucharistic Prayers in the Roman Catholic liturgy, the one they most like is the Second Eucharistic Prayer for Reconciliation.[1] Such a comment partly motivates this chapter. What is there about this Eucharistic Prayer that is so appealing and why?

I would suggest this appeal has its roots in the first thing people hear in this particular Eucharistic Prayer, namely, the Preface. There seems to be something special, if not unique, about the Preface to EP RII. From this comes a further, and, more general question: if we are moved by the liturgy, does that make us better people? What, then, is the relationship between liturgy and the moral life? [2]

This chapter investigates whether there is a case for saying that the Preface of EP RII approaches a paradigmatic expression of the role of the liturgy in moral transformation. In order to do this, first, there will be an effort to clarify language about conversion, and specifically moral conversion. Second, some key ideas on moral transformation and the liturgy will be outlined. Third, I draw on Bernard Lonergan's models of conversion together with William Spohn's approach to moral transformation as hermeneutical lenses for a reading of the text of the Preface EP R II. Some comments will close the article.

Conversion: Clarifying the Language

When we hear the word 'conversion' perhaps the first reaction for many is the image of a sudden 'turn around' to God—as with St Paul on the road to Damascus. But is this typical? Such 'moments', for instance, may come at the end of a long process, or may take the form of a gradual awareness which comes through reflecting on a change that has been slowly happening. What is true is that such liminal events have a common element—the sense of something 'given', a 'grace' from somewhere or someone else beyond the person.

Conversion has generally been understood mainly as a religious experience. Studies by Walter Conn (and others), building on the work of Bernard Lonergan

---

[1] Henceforth EP RII for easy reference. I am grateful to the two reviewers for their helpful comments.

[2] This chapter is an amended version of Thomas Ryan, 'Moral Conversion, Liturgy and The Preface to Eucharistic Prayer for Reconciliation II,' *Australian Journal of Liturgy*, 13:1, 2012.

SJ, have expanded our understanding of conversion.[3] It is generally agreed that conversion involves, in some way, a personal and social transformation. It is personal in the radical reorientation of the conscious operations of the person (desires, thought processes, choices, actions). It is social in the transformation of society's structures and, more recently, in the human relationship with the natural world. Further, conversion is a developmental reality that needs the sustenance of a community, and for someone of faith, of a worshipping community.[4]

Using the language of Lonergan, Conn defines conversion as 'the radical drive for self-transcendence realized in creative understanding, critical judging, responsible deciding, and generous loving'.[5] This sentence distils Lonergan's scheme of conversion's three forms, namely intellectual ('creative understanding', 'critical judging'); religious ('generous loving'); and moral ('responsible deciding').[6] Our focus will be on *moral* conversion.

Conversion, then, can occur in different ways—in its context, forms, and object. In other words, conversion has different modes of intentionality. Each form of conversion involves a transition from a conventional wisdom or morality to a more responsible, self-critical, adult level of autonomy in some realm of human experience. For Lonergan, these forms of conversion can be understood in a secular framework. They are human realities revolving around the impulse towards self-transcendence that can be expressed in a religious or non-religious context.[7]

---

[3] Walter Conn, *Christian Conversion*. (New Jersey: Paulist, 1986); Donald L Gelpi, *The Conversion Experience* (New York/Mahwah: Paulist, 1998).

[4] See Conn, *Christian Conversion*, 5-32.

[5] Conn, *Christian Conversion*, 1.

[6] In Religious conversion ('generous loving') a person is radically grasped by ultimate concern or love. 'It is a falling in love unconditionally, leading to surrender to the transcendent, and a gracious being-in-wholeness' (R N Fragomeni, 'Conversion', In Downey, M, ed. *The New Dictionary of Catholic Spirituality*, (Collegeville, MN: The Liturgical Press. 1993), 230-235, at 234. Faith in a self-revealing God differentiates this form of conversion. Christian conversion for Lonergan is the phenomenon of God's love being poured into our hearts through the Holy Spirit given in Christ. It is possible for a person to experience this without naming or 'thematizing the phenomenon in Christian categories' (Fragomeni, 'Conversion', 234). Intellectual conversion ('realized in creative understanding, critical judging') is concerned with the clarification of perception and meaning so that one actively and critically appropriates the truth about reality. It entails the need 'to advance beyond ideologies, prejudices, and oversights that blind one to the truth' (Gelpi, *The Conversion Experience*, 34).

[7] Gelpi, *The Conversion Experience*, 24 and Fragomeni, 'Conversion', 234 seq. Drawing on the work of Jung, Gelpi argues that Lonergan's model of conversion should be modified to include 'affective' or 'psychic' conversion. Here, a person takes responsibility for their emotional development along lines that are psychologically sound. Affective conversion, then, involves identifying and rejecting biased archetypes, scenarios or paradigms that distort

Two Forms of Moral Conversion

In *moral* conversion there is a move from satisfying the self or being influenced by bias in oneself or the culture, to the pursuit of true value, of the truly good as providing the criteria for moral decisions. Gelpi distinguishes two forms in this process. *Personal moral* conversion 'evaluates interpersonal relationships in the light of individual rights and duties'. *Socio-political* conversion 'evaluates the justice or injustice of social institutions in the light of the common good'.[8]

What precisely makes *personal* moral conversion different from other forms of conversion? Essentially, it engages a particular dimension of human experience, namely, that of 'prudential deliberation'. By calling on norms that are 'proper to ethical thinking', one judges and makes choices 'in the light of the absolute and ultimate claims that individual rights and duties make upon the human conscience'.[9] Gelpi gives an example from his own life. He decided he would not allow himself to be influenced by racial prejudice or bigotry in his personal dealings with African-American people.

Socio-political conversion also deals with making wise and prudent judgments but differs in its scope and criteria. As Gelpi notes, it goes beyond the interpersonal realm to the larger, impersonal, social institutions in which we live, namely, government, Church, economy, culture. Second, the measure of moral discernment and judgment goes beyond personal rights and duties to that benchmark of the common good which 'seeks to create a society in which every member can with reasonable access share in and contribute to its benefits'.[10] Again Gelpi cites his own personal experience whereby he reached a point where he made a public commitment to struggle for justice—against racism, poverty, and social violence, for women's rights and defense of the environment.

Liturgy: Moral Formation in Reconciliation

This brings us to the formative role of the Mass (celebration of the Eucharist) in the expansion and sensitizing of ethical consciousness, namely, in facilitating moral conversion. Naturally, the sacrament of reconciliation is a privileged

---

one's emotional responses and affective life. The 'raising of consciousness' concerning, for instance, racism or sexism, is an effort to reconfigure one's perception and to restructure one's emotions. See William Spohn, SJ, 'Notes on Moral Theology, 1990: Passions and Principles,' *Theological Studies,* 52: 1 (1991): 69-87, at 80.

[8] Gelpi, *The Conversion Experience,* 28-32.

[9] Ibid., 31.

[10] Ibid., 31.

moment by which the saving mercy is God is present in the individual and the Church's life. But, by entering regularly into the mystery of the Eucharist ('the sacrament of reconciliation par excellence'[11]), we progressively are freed from being slaves to sin, from fear of death, and over time, 'put on the mind of Christ' (1 Cor 2:16).

The Mass begins with the Penitential Rite in which we acknowledge the need for the mercy and healing action of God in that 'in our sins we go before God'.[12] It is important here to acknowledge the danger of denial, of 'forgetting' our reality. 'I confess' said together is an act of naming and claiming sin in our lives, in what divides us within and with others. Further, while this is done as a community, sin's formative influence in our various relationships and in social structures has its roots in the individual person. Finally, the penitential rite opens the community in prayer to allow God's action to bring to conscious awareness those unconscious influences that shape our attitudes and actions.[13]

In the Liturgy of the Word that follows, the acknowledgment of our reality moves to being open to the awakening of conscience 'eager to be formed in truth'.[14] Important here are two things. Scripture as God's 'word' is not just statements or stories that are read and heard. It is the *person* of the Word who is present and communicating. Second, the Hebrew understanding of 'word' was much more than an expression in writing or in speech. It has a dynamic function. It is active, bringing about what it conveys. It is, then, as Pope Benedict points out, not just informative but *performative*.[15] Something or someone is changed. The first Creation account is clearly an instance of this. "Let there be light"; and there was light' (Gen 1:3). Creation is the result of the divine *Word*—in its very utterance. Liturgy itself, then, is performative action.

Consistently present in the liturgy and the Eucharist is Christ's role as the 'integrative power of reconciliation'—of the world to the Father and of his gift of himself to us as the bread of life to become one with Him and to share with us 'his

---

[11] Joyce Ann Zimmerman, 'EP RII: The Mystagogical Implications', in Edward Foley et al, eds. *A Commentary on the Order of Mass and* **The Roman Missal** (Collegeville, MN: Liturgical Press, 2011), 503-508, at 503.

[12] Dennis J Billy, C.Ss. R., and James Keating, *The Way of Mystery: Eucharist and Moral Living* (New York: Mahwah: Paulist, 2006), 63.

[13] Billy and Keating, 63.

[14] Billy and Keating, 71.

[15] 'In our language we would say: the Christian message was not only "informative" but "performative". That means: the Gospel is not merely a communication of things that can be known—it is one that makes things happen and is life-changing' *Spe Salvi,* (Strathfield: NSW, St. Pauls, 2007), 2

power and capacity to become good and holy'.[16] God in Christ is reconciling the world to Himself and we called to share in that task—as ambassadors for Christ (2 Cor 5:20).

We must also remember that this transforming action of Jesus' Spirit is precisely the work of the 'same power that raised Jesus from the dead'.[17] Abbot Columba Marmion notes that the Eucharist as the bread of life 'places in our bodies the germ of the resurrection'.[18] Marmion, in his writings, continues the tradition of French spirituality from Cardinal Pierre de Bérulle and Jean-Jacques Olier in its emphasis on our call to conform ourselves to Jesus especially in his states (*états*). This word denotes the interior dispositions, inclinations and attitudes through which Jesus lived his earthly life and brought to his passion, death, resurrection, and ascension. These dispositions and 'states' endure and are available to us today so that we 'live his life and walk his ways'.[19]

Moral Imagination: Perception, Disposition, Identity

Having considered conversion and the role of the liturgy in moral formation, can we get a more detailed picture of how we are transformed as ambassadors for Christ?

William Spohn sees the story of Jesus as paradigmatic in shaping the Christian imagination, namely, through moral perception, disposition, and identity. Jesus' story 'enables us to recognize *which* features of experience are significant, guides *how* we act, and forms *who* we are in a community of faith'.[20]

Moral *perception* (the lenses through which we see, interpret, and evaluate the world and people) is shaped by images, metaphors and stories that captures Jesus' way of seeing the world and others—not as competitors or strangers but as sisters

---

[16] Billy and Keating, 73.

[17] Billy and Keating, 77.

[18] Billy and Keating, 77.

[19] Lowell M Glendon, SS, 'French School of Spirituality', in Michael Downey, ed. *The New Dictionary of Catholic Spirituality* (Collegeville MN: The Liturgical Press, 1993), 420- 422, at 421.

[20] Drawing on William Wimsatt, Spohn argues that Jesus, in his person, embodies the 'concrete universal of Christian ethics' in that, similar to a work of art or literature, which 'presents an object which in a mysterious and special way is both highly general and highly particular'. William C Spohn, *Go and Do Likewise: Jesus and Ethics,* (New York, NY: The Continuum International Publishing Group Inc. 1999; reprinted in 2007), 2; italics in original. See William Wimsatt, *The Verbal Icon: Studies in the Meaning of Poetry* (Kensington, KY; University of Kentucky Press, 1954), cited Spohn, *Go and Do Likewise,* 189, n. 4.

or brothers. Similarly, we are shaped in *dispositions*—attitudes and patterns of emotional responsiveness that crystallize in convictions, values, in character so that we act in certain ways. Perceptions and dispositions are encapsulated in *identity*—the deliberate and morally conscious sense of what we are and want to become.[21] Sharing in Jesus' story cannot be separated from sharing the life of an actual body of his disciples, a common life sustained by the Eucharist, by forgiveness and solidarity with the poor.

The Role of Worship?

Central to correcting perceptions, forming dispositions and identity is coming together in worship. Prayer in all its forms sharpens our way of seeing the world. Further, as Don Saliers points out, prayer, particularly in its communal forms, 'both shapes and expresses persons in fundamental emotions...providing us with emotional capacities whereby the world may be perceived as God's'.[22]

For instance, in the Liturgy of the Word, to hear the 'hard sayings' of the Gospel (e.g., the workers in the vineyard) can act as 'shock tactics' that disturb moral blindness or apathy, namely, a call to radical conversion. Ongoing conversion is perhaps expressed more in the Gospel narratives of Jesus' ministry. Such considerations may be very relevant in parish community's life. Does the unity of my local parish community take precedence over disagreements about liturgical changes, or increasing presence of diverse ethnic groups and cultures in the local area and parish—the face of the 'other', or disagreement over political, social, or ecclesial issues?

Spohn makes the point that, from the New Testament witness, whenever the early Christian communities gathered for worship, 'their divisions came to the surface'. He suggests that members of Paul's community at Corinth, for instance, were called to share the Eucharistic table 'precisely because to bring out their divisions'.[23] Then and now, Spohn wonders whether the coming together in

---

[21] Spohn, *Go and Do Likewise*, 2. In an unpublished paper, Therese M Lysaught, discussing the relationship between liturgy and ethics, suggests four approaches amongst scholars on 'what is affected' by liturgy—cognitive faculties, vision, affections, and community. There are two general perspectives on 'how' this happens—through divine agency and through liturgy as drama. Lysaught suggests the need to address the role of the body as it engages in ritual as another 'what' and 'how' in the moral dimension of liturgical formation. While there is some overlap in the discussion that follows in this present chapter, to cover all areas is, realistically, beyond the scope of our discussion. See 'Inritualed Bodies: Ritual Studies and Liturgical Ethics', *Society of Christian Ethics,* 1998. I am grateful to Dr. Lysaught of Marquette University for her permission to cite her paper.

[22] Don E Saliers, *The Soul in Paraphrase: Prayer and the Religions Affections* (New York: Seabury, 1980), 36.

[23] Spohn, *Go and Do Likewise,* 166.

Eucharistic worship, as a sacrament that 'effects what it signifies', confirms division rather than commemorates Jesus and receiving his life.

Spohn argues that this can be as much a reality today as in the early Church. The acknowledgement of the 'scandal of division' and the need for reconciliation is, he suggests, 'entirely appropriate'. It anchors us in the reality of our need for the reconciling power of Jesus in our midst. It urges us to recognize our need for the grace of forgiveness and solidarity 'which are necessary constituents of the practice of the Eucharist'. [24] Being ambassadors of God's reconciling work is as much within the Church community as it is to the society and world around us.

This leads us into considering the Preface of EP RII.

Moral Conversion and Eucharist Prayer for Reconciliation II

Our discussion moves to its specific focus, approached according to four aspects of the Preface of EP RII, namely, theme, tone, *tempo* and, more extensively, of template.

EP RII Latin Version	EP RII English Version ICEL 2010 Translation
Deus Pater Omnipotens	O God, almighty Father,
pro omnibus, quae in hoc mundo operaris 10	for all you do in this world
per Dominum nostrum Jesus Christum	through our Lord Jesus Christ
Cum enim genus humanum	For though the human race
dissensione atque discordia divisum	is divided by dissension and discord
experiendo tamen cognovimus te animos flectere	yet we know that by testing us
ut sint ad reconciliationem parati 15	you change our hearts
	to prepare them for reconciliation.
Per Spiritum namque tuum permoves hominum corda	Even more, by your Spirit, you
ut inimici iterum in colloquia veniant	move human hearts that enemies
adversarii manus conjungant	may speak to each other again,
populi sibi obviam quaerant venire	adversaries join hands, and
	peoples seek to meet together.

---

[24] Spohn, *Go and Do Likewise*, 166.

Tua operante virtute fit etiam, Domine,	20	By the working of your power
ut odium vincatur amore, ultio cedat indulgentiae,		it comes about, O Lord, that hatred
discordia in mutuam dilectionem convertatur.		is overcome by love, revenge gives way to
		forgiveness, and discord is changed to
		mutual respect.[25]

Theme

Susan K Roll provides helpful background here. This EPII came from the work of a study group of the German Liturgical Commission and approved by the German conference of Bishops. While its composition was prompted by the Holy Year of 1975 and focused on personal reconciliation (in the sacrament of penance), its broader context was of a Europe divided by the Iron Curtain with little hope of reconciliation.[26]

From the Preface, the text of EP RII builds on a reflection, in thanksgiving and hope, on 'the signs of the times' present in the world, one made in the light of the mystery of reconciliation.[27] Its specific *theme* is the various realms of human relationship where the forces of division (hatred, revenge and discord) are engaged by the power of the Spirit of God.[28] This is significant, and even, as Roll notes, 'remarkable', in that the emphasis right from start of this EP is on the 'living and efficacious work of God in our world here and now', namely, 'even in a secular world where God is often experienced as absent'. Roll continues by noting that the strength of EP R II is its 'global' scope in that:

> God's gracious mercy is poured out in secular matters as well as religious, on private relationships as well as world crises, and on persons without regard for their individual characteristics or circumstances. God works in the present no less than in the past.[29]

---

[25] These renditions are taken from Edward Foley et al, eds. *A Commentary*, 442-3.

[26] Susan K Roll, 'EP RII Theology of the Latin Text and Rite', in Edward Foley et al, eds., *A Commentary on the Order of Mass and **The Roman Missal*** (Collegeville, MN: Liturgical Press, 2011), 493-499, at 493-4.

[27] Richard E McCarron, 'EP RI and II: History of the Latin Text and Rite', in Edward Foley et al, eds. *A Commentary*, 453-463, at 457.

[28] Zimmerman suggests that by starting with the open acknowledgement of sin in terms of grave violations of both human and divine 'rights', EP RII might function as a sort of 'truth and reconciliation commission' for the worshipping community that opens the way to reconciliation. See Joyce Ann Zimmerman, 'EP RII: The Mystagogical Implications' Edward Foley et al, eds. *A Commentary*, 503-508, at 503.

[29] Roll, 'EP RII Theology of the Latin Text and Rite', 493-4.

The Church is seen within this global context. The community of faith, at the local or international level, is not apart from, and immune to, the division, dissension, and discord of the world. The community gathered around the Eucharistic table needs the healing gift of the Spirit to take away 'everything that estranges us from one another'. The Church pleads to God, the Holy Father, that it be a 'sign of unity and an instrument' of God's 'peace among all people'.[30]

McCarron reminds us that this is not a Eucharistic Prayer 'about reconciliation'. As a 'theme' it is drawn into the same dynamic of other Eucharistic Prayers, namely, of 'memorial thanksgiving and intercession'. It is a compression of past, present, and future. In EP RII (with its counterpart EP RI), reconciliation and conversion act as 'particular lenses to narrate and remember the whole economy of salvation, which culminates in the paschal mystery of Christ'.[31]

Tone and Tempo

This Preface, then, has its specific theme and focus. But, as with a poem or a piece of literature, one can investigate its peculiar *tone* and affective structure. It has its own 'voice' which is carried by the images, language, and sentence structure that give the Prayer its own cadence and rhythm, revealing and creating an affective state in the participants. Allied to this, particularly in language that is meant to be publicly proclaimed, arises the question of *tempo* in that process.

EP RII is marked by tripartite rhythms, alliteration and images that act as rhetorical devices which, in their very performance, tend to create a sense of peace. The contrast between enemies /dialogue, adversaries/join hands, people/meet together with the triple binaries of hatred/love, revenge/forgiveness and discord/mutual respect are so phrased that there is an interfusion of form and content.

As Roll notes, 'the text embodies what it states' and the repetition of these tripartite rhythms brings 'a certain resolution of tension and a coming to rest'.[32] To convey this tone and highlight contrasting images, its contrapuntal structure and the musicality of the 'triplets', the overall 'pace' of the Preface is meant to be, not that of ebb and flow (as in EP RI), but something perhaps closer to *legato*. With a constant forward movement, the 'dissonance' of counterpoint, as in music, must come to a final resolution in consonance. So too, the structure of EP RII is

---

[30] McCarron, 'EP RI and II: History of...', 463.

[31] McCarron, 'EP RI and II: History of...', 457.

[32] Roll, 'EP RII Theology of the Latin Text and Rite', 493.

such that the effect on the hearer resembles the end of a piece of music in which an harmonic cadence brings a sense of resolution and repose.

These rhetorical strategies are aimed at deepening the conviction that frames the Eucharistic Prayer itself, namely, that reconciliation and peace are beyond human capacities. They are gifts. God through the Spirit alone can bring these about through the conversion of mind and heart. In this Preface is found the unity of form and content, the interplay of tone and tempo, the resolution of opposites and the coming to rest as in a piece of music. All these appear to combine to evoke a sense of hope, peace, and renewed confidence in the listener. These may well explain the appeal of EP RII.[33]

We now move on to examining more specific aspects of reconciliation in relation to conversion. Can we gain more insight from probing the text and the 'intentionality' of the Preface itself? Does it offer some form of *template* for the relationship between liturgy and ethics?

Preface of EP RII as Template: Theological Anthropology and Spohn's Model

We have noted that the Preface of EP RII presents the principal theme as a move from the vertical to the horizontal—the Spirit's action in the world. It is true that the Preface begins by acknowledging the role of the Trinity in the salvific process: all that the Father is doing in the world through Jesus Christ and through the transforming and unifying power of the Spirit. But the spotlight is on God's gift of the Spirit to the human family and the call to be open to the Spirit's presence to change hearts, to restore and strengthen various relationships in our world.

Anthropology of the Person in Relationship

Underpinning this, and expressed later in the anamnesis of EP RII, is the Biblical notion of *sedaqah* (as justice or upright relations) whose embodiment and fulfilment is in Jesus as reconciling the world to himself through the gift of his

---

[33] One could ask if this is still the case with the new translation or whether it has changed people's perceptions. In comparing the new 'literal' translation with its earlier 'dynamic equivalent', one cannot but notice, at times, the difference and wonder: which is better when measured by rhetorical and stylistic standards? At times, the old EP R II version has a 'flow' that is more satisfying to the ear. The phrasing of the antitheses is rhythmically and musically more balanced. It is worth reading the two versions aloud. For example, which has a cadence that is more persuasive: 'we know that by testing us you change our hearts to prepare them for reconciliation' (new) compared with 'we know it is you who turn our minds to thoughts of peace' (old)? Or consider the verbal images of 'hatred overcome by love' (new) with 'hatred is quenched by mercy' (old). 'Overcome' seems univalent – connoting power; 'quenched' is polyvalent – to slake the thirst (of desire) and to quell the fire (of passion).

Spirit, restoring people to right relationships and giving the foundation to social responsibility.[34] The peace of an ordered society is the fruit of justice. Jesus as the reconciling action of God heals the deepest sources of evil and sin as disharmony and division in relationships—personal, social and in creation. Without upright relations there is no justice. Without justice, there is no peace. *Sedaqah* connotes *shalom*—the harmony resulting when relationships with God, with the community, with self and with creation are properly ordered. Jesus in his person is the embodiment and realization of God's peace.[35]

As noted above, sin and evil in this Preface are couched in the language of fractured relationships and division. The specific focus of the divine action is the human race 'divided by dissension and discord'. This acknowledgment of the reality of human existence through the 'signs of the times' is an inductive approach. This sets the stage for the predominantly pneumatological nature of the Preface.

On that basis, the remainder of the Preface readily lends itself to a hermeneutic drawn from Spohn's approach to the moral imagination. It was noted above that the story of Jesus is paradigmatic in forming the Christian moral imagination (perception, disposition, identity). The application of Spohn's schema suggests that EP RII, particularly in the Preface, goes some way in offering an integrated framework for the *process* of moral transformation in the liturgy.

Identity and Modes of Conversion

Foundational is the sense of *identity*. This hub of the Spirit's transforming action suggests the elements of a theological anthropology. First, the trajectory of 'division' has three stages in Paragraph 3 (L. 16-19)—extreme ('enemies'), moderate ('adversaries') and mild ('people') as it moves towards 'human unity', namely, Gelpi's *socio-political conversion*. The call for 'enemies to speak to each other again' implies, at the very least, an attitude of basic tolerance needed for mutual co-existence and needed also for the other two stages.[36]

This 'call' is consonant with the approach to the human person, found in Pope St Paul VI and Pope St John Paul II: that dialogue is integral to the nature, exercise, and realization of personhood.[37] Seen in this light, the 'call', noted

---

[34] Daniel G Groody, *Globalization, Spirituality, and Justice* (Maryknoll, NY: Orbis Books, 2007), 28.

[35] 'Peace' in Carroll Stuhlmueller, ed. *The Collegeville Pastoral Dictionary of Biblical Theology* (Collegeville, MN: Liturgical Press, 1996), 709-714, at 709 and 713.

[36] 'Translated in the older version as 'enemies begin to speak to one another'.

[37] In *Ecclesiam Suam,* Pope St Paul VI talks of the four circles of dialogue within a broader setting of the *colloquium salutis* (the colloquium, dialogue, conversation of salvation). Later, John St Paul II says that 'dialogue is an indispensable step along the path toward human self-

above, points beyond a basic 'strategic' attitude for survival. Dialogue, understood as a conversation, means that we come to the truth and to deeper understanding of truth and goodness through listening and learning from others, especially those who are different, who are 'other'.

Second, the theological anthropology's underlying *identity* is captured in the model of friendship and *shalom* as an underlying goal. This refers initially to 'enemies' (*inimici,* namely, those who are 'not friends') talking to each other again. Roll notes that the Latin suggests 'a richer range of occasions for conflict resolution' than is captured in the translation 'enemies may [can] speak to each other again'. She suggests the cessation of military conflict brings parties to the negotiating table and, in industrial disputes, to the 'bargaining table'.

Again, she points out that the Latin rendered as 'adversaries may join hands' does not catch the more concrete image of two persons who use a hand shake either as a greeting or as a 'pledge of honesty' or as a 'binding ratification of mutual commitment and promise'.[38]

Finally, when 'people seek to meet together', it is somewhat general. Roll notes that this rendition could capture the sense of 'diplomatic relations'. It also makes clear that 'this prayer emerges from the hard practicalities of the world'.[39] While the moral life is a call to sharing in friendship with God and with others, there is an acknowledgement, in the phrasing and dynamic of the prayer, of the art of the possible. Sharing in God's friendship and *shalom* is a gift while being a gradual process which has several stages in its realization.

The third aspect of the human person's *identity* is reflected in focus of the Preface concerning the Spirit's action in Paragraph 2 (L.12-15) and Paragraph 3 (L.16), to 'change our hearts' and 'move human hearts', namely, towards Gelpi's *personal conversion.* While the word 'heart' is used to translate both words, etymologically, the Latin words 'animus' and 'cor' can both refer to the rational capacities of the person and embrace the cognitive and the affective. Given the Spirit's transforming action within a theological anthropology of relationship (dialogue, friendship, shalom/reconciliation), these renditions of the Latin as 'heart' are best viewed as standing for the whole person, hence, by way of synecdoche.

Seen in that light, the two words are convergent with the Biblical anthropology. In Hebrew and Christian Scriptures, the 'heart' is a symbol of the whole person,

---

realization, the self-realization both of each individual and of every human community', *Ut Unum Sint,* 28.

[38] Roll, 'EP RII Theology of the Latin Text and Rite', 495.

[39] Roll, 'EP RII Theology of the Latin Text and Rite', 495.

as noted in earlier chapters of this book. Scripture does not use modern psychological terms, with thinking or knowledge in the intellect and love and decision in the will. *Heart* embraces all that. As a symbol for the 'inside' of a person 'it embraces feelings, memories, ideas, plans, decisions'.[40] In the global and concrete anthropology of the Bible, the heart is the principle of morality, the center of one's freedom, of decisive choices and the place where one enters to be in dialogue with oneself and where one opens oneself or closes oneself to God.[41] Finally, Jesus sums up in himself and his teaching the Hebrew understanding of the '*heart*'.

Virtues: Perceptions and Dispositions

From a setting that is external and global, the Preface then shifts to considering the interior and attitudinal aspects of personhood, namely, to the language of the virtues. The Preface points to the specific points of transformation (*personal conversion*) that enhance this understanding of the human person, namely, the *perceptions* and *dispositions* that guide and animate actions in the realm of interpersonal, social, and global relationships.

Earlier, we find the foundation for actions leading to dialogue, friendship and peace and the transforming of a humanity 'divided by dissension and discord'. 'We know' that it is through 'testing us' that the change of 'hearts' preparing for reconciliation is brought into effect by the Father through the Spirit of Jesus.[42]

The wording is revealing here. 'Experiendo' can signify a form of trial, a purifying or refining of sensitivity or consciousness, in, for instance, an event that brings suffering. This can be one aspect of the broader sense of 'learning *by* experience' or rather 'learning *as* experience', namely, the experiential knowledge that can accompany, even mediate, practical reason. It is a deepening appreciation of what is truly good which has been appropriated as personally significant.

But a further layer of meaning of 'experiendo' is characteristic of the action of the Holy Spirit. As discussed in earlier sections of this book, following on his medieval predecessors, Aquinas speaks of 'quasi-experimental knowledge' to

---

[40] Léon-Dufour, X, 'Heart' in *Dictionary of Biblical Theology*, (Geoffrey Chapman, London, 1988), 228.

[41] Ibid., 228.

[42] '...experiendo tamen cognovimus te animos flectere...' Chupungco considers the new ICEL 2010 translation here is 'flawed' because 'experiendo' is a gerund whose implied subject is 'cognovimus (nos) and not 'flectere.' On that understanding it should read 'we have known by experience that you change hearts.' See Anscar J Chupungco, 'EP RII: The ICEL2010 Translation', in Edward Foley et al, eds. *A Commentary*, 501-502, at 501. The reading suggested here incorporates this criticism.

describe the kind of knowing that is associated with an affective experience of love and is properly called wisdom—the gift whereby the Spirit refines our 'instinct' for true value.[43] It is a knowing (appreciative *perception*) that comes through loving (affective *disposition*). The Spirit cultivates our divine 'taste' to make the corresponding prudential or wise judgments.[44]

What are the specific expressions of this 'change of hearts' in EP RII? We have noted their 'fruits' at the level of social and international divisions and their various forms (Paragraphs 2 & 3). The underlying sources for these outcomes must necessarily be found at the level of personal conversion (as in Paragraph 4, L. 20-22). These sources are couched in the language of the virtues and vices, specifically those habitual *perceptions* and *dispositions* that shape and direct our affective lives and deeper convictions. They are the responsive aspects of the relationship in which we form and express our *identity*.

Love, Respect and Forgiveness

The goal of the working of the Spirit's 'power', then, is that 'hatred is overcome by love, revenge gives way to forgiveness, and discord is changed to mutual respect'. 'Forgiveness' translates 'indulgentiae'. This is richer in its suggestiveness than 'misericordiae'. Beyond merciful treatment of others, it suggests also tenderness, giving way to others in thoughtfulness and, particularly, in making 'room' for the other, for those who are different.

Roll makes a helpful point when she notes that the translation of 'mutuam dilectionem' as 'mutual respect' may miss the mark for its accuracy since *dilectio* is normally rendered as 'love'. But she points out that it does 'strike a necessary note to support the theological credibility of this strophe'. Her explanation merits full quotation:

> All three of these events hinge on the full mutual respect of the parties involved. Love without respect could lead to condescension. Forgiveness without respect has too often marked the counsel given to abused wives and children: the victim was to forgive the perpetrator and not ask for mutual respect.[45]

A further aspect merits consideration, namely, the grammar and sentence structure. In Paragraphs 2-4 (L. 11-22) in the Latin version, the principal verbs, while couched in the indicative mood in English, are in the subjunctive mood in the Latin original. They are governed by 'ut' which determines whether they are final or consecutive clauses. Paragraph 2 ('to prepare [hearts] for reconciliation')

---

[43] See *Summa Theologiae* 1.64.1.

[44] See discussion above in Gelpi at nn. 6-8.

[45] Roll, 'EP RII Theology of the Latin Text and Rite', 496.

appears to be a final clause in that it is ordered to future outcomes. Alternatively, Paragraphs 3 and 4 appear as consecutive clauses that indicate observable outcomes (past and present) emerging from the action of the Spirit, namely, the various forms of reconciliation specifically mentioned concerning enemies, adversaries, hatred, revenge etc. ('the signs of the times').

This linguistic device does two things.

First, it expresses the Eucharist as the 'setting where the habits and practices of peace ought to be learned'.[46] Second, it captures the temporal dynamic of the Spirit's action and the Paschal Mystery. The text, then, embraces the three dimensions of time. It offers evidence of the Spirit's past and present action in the world and as an activity with a trajectory towards the future.

Forms of reconciliation and peace exist as observable historical realities yet are drawn forward by hope to fuller realizations. All these dimensions are totally reliant on the Spirit's action. In other words, it is a *process*. Division/dissension/ discord are progressively overcome and love/forgiveness/mutual respect gradually displace and transform hatred/ revenge/and discord.

Observations

In a variation of the adage *lex orandi lex credendi,* Don Saliers adds the phrase *lex bene operandi,* namely, 'the order of prayer is the order of believing is the order of doing well'.[47] Our investigation has been tantamount to probing that added phrase in a specific context. In terms of its central *theme*, while acknowledging the centrality of the individual, the Preface sees the person as essentially *relational.*

Again, the Eucharistic Prayer is unique in having, as its starting point, the action of the Spirit of Christ in the *world*, as in movements for justice and peace. It is anchored primarily in the reality of our world—its politics, economics, cultures, and their associated structures. This converges with Pope St John Paul II's approach to the presence of the Holy Spirit outside the visible body of the Church.[48]

In the process, we uncovered some of the liturgy's riches as a source of moral transformation. The chapter explored the theological underpinnings and specific

---

[46] 'Peace' in Carroll Stuhlmueller, ed. *The Collegeville Pastoral Dictionary*, 714.

[47] Don Saliers, 'Liturgy and Ethics', *The Journal of Religious Ethics* 7:2 (Fall 1979): 139-171, at 139.

[48] See his *Redemptor Hominis*, par. 6; *Dominum et Vivificantem*, par. 53.

aspects of the person that are affected by moral conversion. The reading offered of the Preface of EP RII distils some, but not all, key elements of that process and, in that sense, goes some distance in offering a *template* for the process of moral transformation enacted through the Liturgy. It includes its source (the Spirit), model/vision (Jesus and his story), subject (the person in identity, perceptions, and dispositions), outcomes (virtues and attitudes guiding judgments and actions), context (the realm of relationships from personal through communal to global) and its goal (realization God's reign in justice, love, and peace).[49]

This Eucharistic Prayer's appeal may reflect the increasing sense of interdependence that is associated with globalization (and of global 'friendship' in the thinking of Pope Francis). Further, implied in this is the global embrace of the Eucharist. Perhaps the attraction and popularity of the third rite of Reconciliation has similar roots. There is a surge of faith that is more communal in expressing responsibility for sin and evil and of the need for healing and forgiveness. We are all in it together. The Preface of EP RII is a persistent antidote to any culture of contentment and of excessive individualism.

Again, this Eucharistic Prayer is a wholesome reminder of the critical role of the Holy Spirit in arousing and forming the hearts of the faithful. Moral formation in worship is not so much something we do but is grounded in what Christ has done and continues to do through his Spirit. Moreover, the formative and guiding work of the Spirit is of a community of faith whose election is *for the world*. Lay people are not 'objects' in the liturgy—listeners to homilies, recipients of the sacraments. They are 'subjects', called to active participation in the Church's worship for the sake of 'authentic engagement with the in-breaking of God's reign in the "liturgy of the world"'.[50]

Further, the *tone* of EP RII is set at the very start and is strengthened by the *tempo*. These are captured in the harmonic cadences embedded in the structure and language of the Preface. Combined with theme and template, what is more apparent is the care and balance in its design—theologically, ethically, liturgically, and rhetorically. How it touches people clearly, but not exclusively, depends on human factors. It looks to central characters in the liturgy as a 'drama', particularly, musicians, readers in the Liturgy of the Word and, overall, the gathering 'sense' of the Celebrant of the Eucharist in pastoral sensitivity and rhetorical skills.

---

[49] In the light of Lysaught's review of liturgy and ethics, 'goes some distance' covers four of her 'what is changed' categories, namely, cognitive faculties, vision, affections, community and one of 'how this occurs'— divine agency. The aspect of liturgy as drama and the associated role of the body and ritual are not addressed in this present discussion. See n. 21 above.

[50] Mary Collins and Edward Foley, 'Mystagogy' in Edward Foley et al, eds. *A Commentary*, 73-102, at 98-9. The authors are drawing on Karl Rahner's distinction between the 'liturgy of the church' and the 'liturgy of the world'.

Conclusion

This chapter opened by clarifying the notion of conversion and gave specific attention to moral conversion and its two modes, namely, personal, and social/political. On that basis, we examined the dynamics of the Eucharistic liturgy in relation to moral formation with specific reference to our perceptions, dispositions, and identity. From there, we approached Eucharistic Prayer for Reconciliation II in terms of its theme, tone, *tempo* and, importantly, as a template of the human person in responsive relationships.

Overall, EP RII is designed to reassure the worshipping community that the Spirit of God is at work. Ultimately, it is as a gift of the Spirit that true reconciliation and peace come—for us and for our world. God's *shalom* gives hope to humanity. Perhaps hearing this Preface resonates with the divine words received by Julian of Norwich: 'All shall be well, and all shall be well, and all manner of thing shall be well'.

From these considerations on virtue and worship, we move to the final chapter of the book—a retrospective of the field of theological ethics in the Catholic tradition.

RETROSPECTIVE

10
The Changing Landscape of Catholic Theological Ethics

This final chapter will attempt to do two things: first, present an overview of developments in Christian ethics since the second Vatican Council in relation to understanding the nature and process of the moral life; second, highlight significant changes to the landscape of Christian ethics as a theological discipline in the past twenty years or so.

So, to the first part of our discussion.

Christian ethics as a Way of Living

Consider this experience.

I normally begin a course in Christian ethics by asking the students to say the first image or word that comes to mind when they hear the words 'morality' or 'ethics'. It is intriguing how often the response is 'rules' or 'solving moral dilemmas'.

Perhaps the first phrase indicates a view of the moral life that is deeply-embedded for cultural or religious reasons. The second response is more understandable, given the nature of public life. Church leaders are called to respond to legal and moral questions concerning, for example, beginning and end of life, IVF, same-sex marriage, genetic engineering, economic justice, asylum seekers etc.

When morality is seen as a particular approach to solving moral problems or as a set of rules, we are reminded that any perspective is limited. Making judgments about difficult ethical matters is important; further, that rules encapsulate the demands of reality. But our capacity to make wise judgments and to appreciate the values beneath rules rests on a more basic role of Christian ethics, namely, to clarify what it means to lead a good life, what that requires and to help people to do so.[1]

---

[1] These days, the term 'Christian ethics' is used interchangeably with 'theological ethics' and 'moral theology '(more common in the Roman Catholic tradition).

There have been many advances in this area in the past two decades. This chapter aims to highlight the more significant developments, with specific reference to the Catholic tradition.[2]

Where do We Begin—a Love Story

The students' responses noted above could be seen as the residue of the common approach to Christian ethics in the Catholic tradition until the Second Vatican Council and the 1960s. Within the discipline of Christian ethics itself, its specialist practitioners moved beyond the law-based approach to the Christian moral life to one centered more on the call-response of discipleship, namely, following the way of Jesus. This sort of transition does not happen overnight—for ordinary people as much as for specialist theologians. For instance, the North American Jesuit moral theologian, James Keenan, writes in 2004:

> I teach an introductory course on moral theology, and during my fifteen years teaching it. I only recently learned to begin my course on the topic of love. Not only did I not begin my course on love, I never even taught a class on it.

He goes on to say 'I always started with freedom', namely, the basic freedom in grace 'to realize the call of God'.[3]

Here we have, nearly forty years after Vatican II, a leading Christian ethicist suddenly realizing that when we ask 'Where do I begin?' about Christian ethics, the answer is that it is a love story. It does not start with *us* in, for instance, the experience of conscience or of our freedom. It starts with *God*—the God who only wants to love, to share the divine life with us and all creation.

But there is more. To be able to respond to the gift of God's love, we need the wherewithal that comes from God. God alone can give us the 'yes' to say 'yes' to his call to love. In other words, the gift of *faith* enables us to respond in love to God's invitation to love and to share a life. This gift—that we name as 'grace'—involves faith that seeks greater understanding. It shapes us at the level of head, heart, and hands. Our identity, perceptions and dispositions are slowly transformed.

To appreciate the significance of this change of focus about the moral life, it may help to stand back and look at the context behind the shift.

---

[2] This chapter combines and expands two earlier articles: 'Christian Ethics: Moral Dilemmas or Something More?', *Compass: A Review of Topical Theology* 46:1, Autumn 2012: 33-37 and 'Christian Ethics Today: Is the Ground Shifting?', *Compass: A Review of Topical Theology* 48:1, Autumn 2014: 14-19.

[3] James F Keenan. SJ, *Moral Wisdom; Lessons and Texts from the Catholic Tradition* (Maryland: Rowman & Littlefield Publishers Inc., 2004), 14.

Where Have We Come From?

Generally, it is not unfair to suggest that an attitude associated with the more legal approach to the moral life over hundreds of years was summed up in one sentence: 'If I don't sin, God will love me'. Beneath this lies, what Patrick O'Sullivan refers to, as an 'operational' image of God.[4] It is the one that, at the heart-level, guides a person's expectations of God. Here, God, as a judge, demands that I will gain God's love if I measure up to what God requires. God's love is something I earn. If I don't sin, then, God will love me. If I do sin, God won't love me.

Another way of expressing this view of the Christian moral life is in the phrase 'You can't be too careful'. Such an approach implies four outcomes. The spotlight is on 'don't get sick'. The moral life is basically about pathology rather than healthy living. Second, it is often driven by fear, namely, of avoiding potholes on the road of life, even if it is the way of Jesus. Third, actions come before character and attitudes. *What I do* is more important than *who I am*. Finally, this approach is individualistic. It tends to put the emphasis on *me* and only secondarily on God, even less on relationships with others and in society.

More Recently?

What has emerged with greater emphasis in the past fifty years? We should start with 'God *loves us*—no conditions'. Here, the underlying operational image of God is that of a God of unconditional love. It is embodied in the parable of the loving father and the two sons. It is a move from saying 'God loves me because I am good' to 'I am good because God loves me'. All God asks is that we let ourselves be loved—to receive that gift. In receiving that gift, I am enabled to say 'Yes'. Perhaps being saved is less from sin than from our fear of being loved?

If God loves me no matter what, then four things follow in how we view Christian moral living and its tasks. Everything begins with God *loves* us. I am called to share in the divine life and, through that, to work together with God. Second, this shapes my identity, my attitudes and is reflected in my actions. Most importantly, it is not about avoiding sin but growing in loving responsiveness and *responsibility* in my various relationships—with God, others, the world, creation, and oneself. Finally, the emphasis has shifted from 'me' to 'us'.

Understood thus, the Christian moral life has a spiritual foundation. Spirituality and morality need each other. Spirituality grounds and animates the moral life. Morality ensures that spirituality has 'skin on'—that it is embodied in our everyday relationships.[5] It is important to recall that the emphasis here is on

---

[4] Patrick O'Sullivan SJ, *'Sure Beats Selling Cardigans': Fostering Our Relationship with God* (Richmond, Victoria: Aurora Books, 1995), 5-7.

[5] Richard Gula, 'Morality and Spirituality' in James Keating, ed. *Moral Theology: New Directions and Fundamental Issues* (NY/Mahwah, NJ: Paulist, 2004), 162-177.

God's action. As discussed in earlier chapters, right from the start, with the gifts of Spirit given at Baptism, God's transforming action is at work. Living a moral life is more God's work than ours.

When I sin—fail in my relationships, hurt others, when am not my best self—God still loves me. Does guilt have a role? Yes, of course it does. A sense of guilt (and shame) tells me that something is amiss within my various relationships and that has repercussions in my relationship with God.

So, how does that influence how I understand 'being saved'? It might well be from fear of being loved. But I need to be saved in my *person* with all its aspects. We are not exempt from the scriptural reminder that the just person falls 'seven times a day' (Prov 24:16). Being 'saved' manifests our need for God to heal us from destructive or divisive tendencies that are often beyond our conscious awareness. Most importantly, we are saved *from* something because we are saved *for* something—a shared life with God.

Edward Vacek SJ captures the Christian spiritual/moral life in four phrases:

God loves us
We love God
We and God form a Community
We and God cooperate. [6]

Our discussion, captured in Vacek's compact summary, distils a range of ingredients. What are some of its more significant elements? This can be approached in two stages: the first will focus on the discipline of Christian ethics as its addresses the shape and content of Christian discipleship; the second stage will highlight some developments within Christian ethics precisely as specific field of theological enquiry.

Living the Christian Moral Life

The Second Vatican Council called on Christian ethics (moral theology) to ground itself in the Scriptures with its focus on Jesus Christ. Hence, the 'call-response in love' model of the moral life. After the Council, advances in Scripture studies uncovered some of the difficulties for Christian ethics concerning Scripture as a source of moral insight and of moral norms.

Centrality of the Person

While this change in focus is central, the emphasis on the human person is, arguably, the most important element in the renewed understanding of Christian ethics since that time. A commonly cited reflection of this shift in theological anthropology is from the official 1965 commentary on *Gaudium et Spes* No. 51

---

[6] Edward Collins Vacek, SJ, *Love: Human and Divine: The Heart of Christian Ethics* (Washington, DC: Georgetown University Press, 1994), xv.

concerning the criterion of morality, namely, 'human activity must be judged in so far as it refers to the human person integrally and adequately considered'.[7]

What is the significance of this quote?

It marks a transition from seeing human existence in terms of nature (what we have in common with each other and, especially, as corporeal beings) to what is unique about the human rational animal, namely, personhood. It is characterized by embodiment, certainly. It is through our bodies that the unique quality of each person is expressed, namely, the capacity for rationality, relationship and creativity combined with the call to grow in the divine image through collaboration with divine providence. Many of the recent advances in Christian ethics in the Catholic tradition in the past fifty years have been built on this foundation. But there is another aspect to this.

Personhood, Relationship, and the Trinity

Discussion amongst Catholic theological ethicists for two or more decades after Vatican II was predominantly in terms of autonomy and personal conscience, whether in itself or in relation to the Church. From the mid-nineties there has been a marked swing to a more relational and communitarian view of the person. 'Relationship' is not an added extra, argues Joseph Ratzinger in 1990 (a view continued in his encyclicals as Pope Benedict XVI).[8] Starting from the Trinitarian Word as a person constituted from and in relationship, to be-in-relation is constitutive of the human person. Seen in that light, rationality is less dominant in this view of personhood. It is important, clearly, but is understood more as rationality 'for the sake of', 'at the service of' relationship.

Allied to this are recent advances concerning Trinitarian theology together with their impact both on Christian ethics and on understanding the moral life. There is a deepened appreciation that God's self-gift in grace entails a share in the life and relationships of the persons of the Trinity. As 'participants of the divine nature' (2 Pet 1:4), we are called to be increasingly transformed in our rational operations at the cognitive, affective, and volitional levels. We are enabled by divine action to know, judge, love and will in harmony with the persons of the Trinity.

Further, this dynamic activity is at the service of the relationships that constitute the 'event' of the Trinity's life—the incessant giving and receiving of love, the affirming of the truth and goodness of each person (Father, Word, Spirit)

---

[7] Cited in R McCormick, SJ, *Notes on Moral Theology 1981 through 1984* (Lanham, MD: University Press of America, 1984), 49.

[8] See Joseph Ratzinger, 'Retrieving the Tradition: Concerning the notion of person in theology,' *Communio* 17 (Fall, 1990): 440-454 and his later call for a 'deeper critical evaluation of the category of relation' in *Caritas in Veritate* (Strathfield, NSW: St. Pauls, 2009), par. 53.

that generates infinite joy and overwhelming happiness.[9] It spills over into the service of the various relational dimensions of human existence—with others, society, the natural world, and oneself.

In so far as 'we and God form a community' (as Vacek reminds us), we are slowly transformed in the process. As part of the community of faith in the Church, we have the guidance of its leaders, its teaching and, in particular, the presence and action of the Holy Spirit. Together with the liturgy and the Scriptures, who we are (our identity), how we see and interpret the world (perceptions) and our attitudes (dispositions to respond to what is truly good) are slowly shaped such that we 'put on the mind of Christ'.

Virtues and Emotions

This approach above, suggested by the late William Spohn (discussed elsewhere in this book) parallels the language of the virtues, as developed, for instance, by James Keenan.[10] For Keenan, the virtues are not so much good habits that perfect the self. They are more those readily responsive dispositions to be increasingly sensitive to what fosters growth in the various relationships that make up our lives.

Further, there is an enhanced appreciation of the role of emotions and human affectivity in moral living. Our emotions are meant to be our friends not our enemies. Without them, as Charles Taylor points out, 'we become incapable of understanding any moral argument at all'.[11] They are integral to what it means to be rational. Without them, we cannot grow in the virtues. Emotions are an integral part of the virtues and are meant to exist within the purposes of rationality, namely, to be at the service of relationships. Being affected and being responsive manifest the realization of the divine image in the world.

The gradual transformation of identity, perceptions and dispositions provides the bridge between Vacek's sharing in the divine 'community' and how 'we and God cooperate'. The focal point of all this is that of 'transformed judgment'—to evaluate, judge and choose with the mind and heart of God through identification

---

[9] See Anne Hunt, 'Trinity, Grace and the Moral Life' in her *Trinity: Nexus of Mysteries of the Christian Faith* (Maryknoll, NY: Orbis, 2005), 165-182.

[10] William C Spohn, *Go and Do Likewise; Jesus and Ethics* (New York, NY: The Continuum International Publishing Group Inc., 1999), (reprinted in 2007). Daniel Harrington and James F Keenan. *Jesus and Virtue Ethics; Building Bridges between New Testament Studies and Moral Theology* (Lanham, MD: Rowman & Littlefield Publishers, Inc., 2005).

[11] Charles Taylor, *Sources of the Self: The Making of the Modern Identity* (Cambridge University Press, 1996), 73. This aspect has been elaborated in chapter seven of this book, particularly, with regard to the recent work of Darcia Narvaez.

with Jesus and guided by his Spirit.[12] This converges with Pope St John Paul II's comment that the Church:

> puts herself always and only at the *service of conscience* ...helping it not to swerve from the truth about the good of man [sic]...to attain the truth with certainty and to abide in it.[13]

This brings us to the second phase of this discussion.

Christian ethics as a Domain of Theological Enquiry.

From what we have said above, Christian ethics as an academic practice is clearly more interdisciplinary as in, for instance, closer links with spirituality and systematic theology. There is a pressing need to explore other areas concerning personhood that have implications for theological anthropology as the underpinning of Christian ethics. Integral, here, is the role of the human sciences—psychology, anthropology, and sociology. Again, with questions emerging in bioethics, genetics, neuroscience and the world of virtual reality, there is a consequent need for Christian ethicists to be *au courant* with the latest advances in scientific research that bear on moral issues arising in these fields.

In surveying the landscape, it is evident that the practitioners of Christian ethics are today characteristically lay people and, increasingly, women theologians.[14] Moral issues are seen less from a clerical perspective and more from that of secular and married life. Again, Christian ethics is becoming increasingly international in character, inclusive in scope and culturally pluralistic. For instance, the North American journal *Theological Studies* is, in many ways, a mirror of the changing face of Christian ethics mainly, but not exclusively, in the English-speaking Catholic world. Between 1998 and 2011 in its annual 'Notes on Moral Theology' in its March issue, it devoted separate treatments to moral theology in Western Europe, East Asia, Africa, Latin America, beyond Western Bioethics and the search for a global ethic.

Since then, between 2018 and 2022, for instance, more attention has been given in the journal to issues around immigration ethics, racial injustice, domestic violence, prisons and punishment, the grace of conflict and, most recently, the crisis and tragedy around Covid 19. There is a clear pattern, then, in which the

---

[12] See L Gregory Jones, *Transformed Judgment: Towards a Trinitarian Account of the Moral Life* (Eugene, OR: Wipf and Stock, 2008), 1-19.

[13] *Veritatis Splendor* (Homebush, NSW: St. Pauls) 64; my emphasis.

[14] For example, Jean Porter, Lisa Sowle Cahill, Margaret Farley, Cathleen Caveney, Linda Hogan, Kristin E Heyer, Julia Fleming etc. plus an increasing number of women from Europe, Latin America, Africa, and Asia.

March issue of the journal is sensitive to current moral questions, e.g., leadership in political life and in the Church; movements such as Black Lives Matter.[15]

On the other side of the ledger, the 'shrinking' global world using virtual means of communication has provided the platform for the emergence of new forms of interaction between theologians. Representative here is an initiative of younger scholars in North America, namely, the *Journal of Moral Theology*.[16] From its first issue in 2012, the journal not only offers a platform sharing research and ideas in the field of moral and social concerns. It is freely available online; it takes advantage of social media platforms (i.e., Twitter) to comment on emerging issues and stimulate interchange, articles and books with greater immediacy than was possible before. This is an initiative that is helping to breathe new life into the field of Catholic ethics as a discipline, keeping it anchored in the wider world of social and global life.

Overall, Christian ethics, as a discipline, tends to be more at the service of the world than a purely 'in house' concern with its own language and debates. Nevertheless, the past two decades have seen Catholic ethicists engaged in historical studies leading to greater self-understanding and self-evaluation of the tradition of moral theology.[17]

Self-Understanding of The Moral Theologian

For instance, in an article along these lines, Keenan and Black offer an insightful discussion on the manualist tradition.[18] It can be facile to dismiss this tradition as legalistic and sin-oriented. One of the advantages of the manualist heritage was its respect for the place of differing theological opinions on a particular issue. There could be arguments for a particular theological position that made it a 'probable' opinion and, hence, could be followed as a guide to a judgment of conscience.

---

[15] See Linda Hogan, 'Moral Leadership: A Challenge and a Celebration', *Theological Studies* 82:1 (2021): 138-155; James F Keenan, 'The Color Line, Race, and Caste: Structures of Domination and the Ethics of Recognition', *Theological Studies* 82:1 (2021): 69-94. A valuable recent study is also found in Maureen H O'Connell, *Undoing the Knots: Five Generations of American Catholic Anti-Blackness* (USA: Beacon Press, 2022).

[16] Journal of Moral Theology | Catholic Moral Theology (on line)

[17] See James F Keenan, *A History of Catholic Moral Theology in the Twentieth Century: From Confessing Sins to Liberating Consciences* (New York: Continuum, 2010); Charles Curran, *The Origins of Moral Theology in the United States* (Washington DC: Georgetown University Press, 1997); John Gallagher, *Time Past, Time Future: A History of Catholic Moral Theology* (New York: Paulist, 1990).

[18] Peter Black and James Keenan, 'The Evolving Self-Understanding of the Moral Theologian: 1900-2000', *Studia Moralia* 39 (2001): 291-327, at 303-7.

Until the mid-twentieth century, as Keenan and Black note, when moral questions were sent to Rome, curial offices or episcopal conferences, the general response was to direct the petitioners to the judgments of 'approved' manualists. This recognized the role of probable opinions in the Catholic theological tradition, the role of the local church and the standing of theologians in relation to the teaching tradition of the Church. In the recent half century or more, a more centralized approach emerged—from a range of reasons and influences, one of which is speed of communication. Decisions are often than not given from Rome. This prompted the question: had we lost something from the Manualist tradition in the process?

Since these concerns were raised by Keenan and Black, a major influence for change appeared on the landscape, in the person of Pope Francis. In his document *The Joy of Love* (Amoris Laetitia, 2016)), in the treatment of marriage and, specifically, of those in 'irregular' situations, a pastoral perspective is presented that has its roots in the Catholic moral tradition. Francis places greater focus how God meets each individual person with the 'gaze' of mercy and love. [19]

In complex, even, messy situations in life, divine grace can be at work. It is the Church's task to help and to nourish, to reach out in mercy and love. Importantly, Pope Francis acknowledges there is no one, clear-cut answer and that there may be variations of valid pastoral approaches depending on cultural differences and local needs. In other words, a return to a focus on, and confidence, in the local Church.

Let's widen the lens of this discussion and return to a point noted earlier. In the first two decades of this third millennium, Christian ethics, in becoming more clearly global, offers a different and expanding context as a discipline. To explore this, we can make some representative soundings under five headings: moral consciousness as international and global; global discourse on suffering and solidarity; Catholic social teaching and moral theology; theological ethics in a) a synodal Church and b) a post-pandemic world, leading to some concluding comments.

Moral Consciousness as International and Global

At the outset, it should be noted that cross-cultural theological discourse was the aim of the international journals *Concilium* and *Communio* since their inception over fifty years ago. Again, as suggested earlier, between 1998 and 2007 *Theological Studies'* 'Notes on Moral Theology' reveals an emerging sense of

---

[19] Much has been written on this matter but two representative and recent examples are: Antonio Auterio, 'Resistances to *Amoris Laetitia:* A Critical Approach', *Journal of Moral Theology* 11:2 (2022): 1-14; Emily Reimer-Barry, '*Amoris Laetitia* at Five', *Theological Studies* 83:1 (2022):109-132.

pluralism in moral theology which is inclusive in its scope and its participants, a trend which continues.

Our discussion is best guided by what is, probably, a most significant development within moral theology, namely, the establishment from 2006 of *Catholic Theological Ethics in the World Church* and its three international conferences in Padua (2006), Trento (2010) and Sarajevo (2018).[20] Padua's Mission Statement captured their aims, though, as will be noted later, Trento had a more specific context. The Statement's key points indicated a) need for an international exchange of ideas amongst Catholic theological ethicists; b) need to interconnect within a world church: and c) the opportunity for cross-cultural dialogue from and beyond local cultures motivated by mercy and care.[21] To be truly international, the organizers ensured the presence of scholars from the developing world by underwriting their expenses. The focus of the later conference at Sarajevo was on identifying global challenges, particularly, climate and political crises.

Each conference was shaped by its overarching purpose. Our focus here is on the first two gatherings. 'At Padua we gathered to meet and listen to one another', observes one participant.[22] In 2006 'cross-cultural' and 'global' are the key words. Foundation papers responded to 'How can theological ethicists respond to the world's needs?' Speakers from each of the five continents (Africa, Asia, Europe, Latin America, and North America) addressed the same three questions: what are our moral challenges; how are we responding; and what hope do we have for the future? These were followed by papers under the rubric of 'applied ethics'— ranging from globalization, justice, and the environment, to questions about gender, HIV/AIDS, bioethics and justice, sexuality and marriage and method in moral theology.

In 2010, rather than a gathering for listening and interchange, there was a 'need for a defining context'. Hence, the choice of Trent—for many reasons, but perhaps the most important was that 'theological ethics was defined by the Council of Trent: we became a specific discipline within theology'. It was fitting that Trento, given its historical and ecclesial significance, was the location where theological ethicists could 'share fundamental insights and claims, to reflectively and

---

[20] See Home | Catholic Theological Ethics in the World Church (catholicethics.com. An initiative from James F Keenan, SJ, (with others), the website contains information on the plenary papers from the three conferences (and later local gatherings).

[21] James F Keenan, ed. *Catholic Theological Ethics in the World Church: The Plenary Papers from the First Cross-cultural Conference on Catholic Theological Ethics* (New York: Continuum, 2007), 3 (henceforth *CTEWC*).

[22] James F Keenan, 'Notes on Moral Theology: What Happened at Trento 2010', *Theological Studies* 72:1 (2011): 131-149 at 139.

respectfully consider the needs of today within the context of a world church and its evolving and constantly emerging traditions'.[23]

Again, this second conference, rather than build on the five continents, attempted (and successfully so) to 'target seven populations': more representation from theologians from some European national groups and moral specialists (such as the Redemptorists); participation of the hierarchy and some formal, institutional recognition of the Conference; scholars engaged in inter-religious dialogue; women theologians together with financial assistance for women scholars on the African continent for further graduate studies; 'new' or young scholars and financial assistance for them to attend; senior theological ethicists; finally, the support of a local committee at Trento and its Archbishop.

The opening theme for Trento was 'Ethics and Religious Dialogue in a globalized world (Catholic, Protestant and Muslim perspectives).' It then moved in three stages: the past— evaluation of the Council of Trent, interaction of history and theological ethics and the 'unheard' and 'missing' voices in that history; the present—moral reasoning, political ethics, and health issues; the future—which considered identity, reciprocity, and familial relations, pressing global social challenges and theological ethics in the future.

What was achieved in these gatherings in 2006 and 2010? They were clearly about a *theological* approach to ethics. The international 'conversation' continued through the publication of plenary papers and selected presentations in applied ethics. For the participants, a frequent comment after Padua was 'We shared the same vocation'.[24] This was experienced as a strong intellectual and affective solidarity of participants and a renewed sense of their contribution to the Church. It was both 'inter-national' and 'inter-cultural'. It brought a solidarity that reached across generations, gender, and cultures. With good will and respect in place, there was a freedom to challenge and question each other. Finally, the process generated the need for other groups and structures to continue the dialogue in local conferences and associations.

An important development emerged from the first two conferences; to appreciate the need for dialogue from and beyond local culture and that the world church should not be dominated by a norther paradigm. This resulted in locally based conferences, for instance, the Bangalore Conference for the region of Asia in 2015 as a preparation for Sarajevo (2018).[25]

---

[23] Keenan, 'Notes on Moral Theology: What Happened at Trento 2010', 139-140.

[24] Keenan, *CTEWC*, 5.

[25] Yiu Sing Lucas Chan, James F Keenan, Shaji George Kochuthara, eds. *Doing Asian Theological Ethics in a Cross-Cultural and an Interreligious Context* (Bengaluru, India: Dharmaram Publications, 2016).

To return to a point made earlier. A key area of development in moral theology in the past two decades has been virtue ethics. The virtues provided a needed conceptual 'bridge' and common moral vocabulary between differing historical and cultural contexts —relevant for cross-cultural and global dialogue today.

Other religious and cultural traditions have virtues that function in ways similar to the cardinal virtues. Across all cultures there seems to be a call to treat all people fairly and impartially, to be faithful to one's commitments and promises and to care of ourselves. These are guided by practical wisdom (prudence) that adjudicates between their claims. Again, it must be noted that the more ethicists use the virtues, the more they work beyond local contexts.[26] Finally, compassion and solidarity are needed virtuous dispositions for 'receiving' the texts and experiences from within any tradition (whether one's own or others') and 'for developing the moral perception to understand them'.[27]

As the Trento conference closed, the young African women scholars summed it up for James Keenan: 'Jim, we are so surprised that we actually belong to something so big, so dedicated, and so dynamic'. Keenan then concludes 'At Trento we discovered our catholic vocation'.[28] That vocation, he explains, is a call to read the signs of the times 'as they actually are'. That involves the search for the truth, 'and in part that means naming what is lacking, not yet seen understood or articulated. It also means being *aware of those not heard, rejected, oppressed, or abandoned*'.[29]

This brings us to our next shift in the landscape of Christian ethics.

Suffering, Solidarity and Global Discourse [30]

With some exceptions, for all the advances made by European moral theologians in the twentieth century, their concerns were predominantly conceptual and concerned with 'in-house' issues arising from their theological community and amongst their peers. *Suffering* and poverty were only addressed in general terms and from a distance.

Three main strands form the historical backdrop to an increasing response to suffering: the Holocaust, liberation movements in the developing world and the various forms of struggle for human rights at the global level. In that context, we

---

[26] Keenan, *A History*, 217.

[27] Keenan, *A History*, 77.

[28] Keenan, 'Notes on Moral Theology: What Happened at Trento 2010', 149.

[29] Keenan, 'Notes on Moral Theology: What Happened at Trento 2010', 148-9; my emphasis.

[30] Adapted from the heading for chapter nine of Keenan, *A History*, 197.

are reminded of René Girard's comment that the emerging concern for victims in history is 'the secular face of Christian love' and of Anthony Kelly's added comments that this unprecedented 'stirring of conscience' is the transforming effects of one particular 'risen' victim—Jesus Christ.[31]

Theologically, one can detect initial changes in perspective in the final third of the twentieth century. European theologians such as Metz, Schillebeeckx and Moltmann together with liberation theologians from Latin America (e.g., Sobrino and Boff) found common cause on the tasks of theology. They saw suffering (and its 'dangerous memory') as the appropriate starting point for praxis—the interaction of faith with lived experience.

During this period, an increasing sensitivity to the poor and marginalized appears amongst a handful of European theological ethicists (e.g., Enda McDonagh, Kevin Kelly, Enrico Chiavacci etc.) and this further developed in the next generation of moralists, especially, in the USA, by women scholars. In the new millennium, when combined with theological work outside Europe, especially in Africa, Asia and Latin America, the overall effect today is summed up by Keenan: '…the call to respond to human suffering shapes contemporary theological ethics'.[32] In the USA, Lisa Sowle Cahill is typical of women ethicists (and others) who offer responses that are specific and concrete, based on a theological approach that is both personalist and relational but also formative of communities of concern and solidarity.[33]

Representative of this call is Australia's Robert Gascoigne's discussion of suffering as a source for moral reasoning. He observes that 'although it is suffering that most confounds our search for ethical intelligibility, it is likewise suffering that is the most profound source of insight and conversion'.[34] Human experience is a contested source for Christian ethics. But when, as here with suffering, it provides an occasion for self-transcendence in terms of moral response to what is truly good, truly just, it is both authentic and normative.

We have noted above some of the many current studies in Christian ethics that probe suffering in its various forms (injustice, alienation, oppression, poverty,

---

[31] René Girard, *I See Satan Fall Like Lightening* (Maryknoll, NY: Orbis, 2001), 161 and Anthony J Kelly, C.Ss. R, 'The Resurrection and Moral Theology: Does It Make Any Difference?', *The Australian Ejournal of Theology*, Issue 10, Pentecost 2007: 5.

[32] Keenan, *A History,* 198.

[33] Keenan, *A History,* 213.

[34] Robert Gascoigne, 'Suffering and Theological Ethics: Intimidation and Hope', *CTEWC,* 163-6, at 163.

HIV/AIDS).[35] It may help to glance back to 1975 for Dorothy Soelle's *Suffering*—a landmark study of the dynamics of how to engage with suffering.

In the first step, one is mute, dumbfounded with the evil as experienced. At this stage, it is just about survival. In the second phase, one makes explicit and conscious the horror, the pain of what has been experienced (whether from human agency or nature, whether personal or social). It is named and claimed in two ways. 'We can feel the suffering in solidarity with others and give voice to our anguish'.[36] We can tap resources from Scripture of crying out from the depths, such as with Jesus on the cross. Then, it is through lamentation that we are enabled to acknowledge suffering and loss.

We are also empowered for the third phase, namely to act—to 'aim' in a constructive manner what we have experienced. Justice demands that these sources of suffering and evil can be alleviated or eradicated as part of the ongoing redemptive work of Christ. At times, such suffering can be transforming through deepening and expanding our consciousness of what is true and good at the personal or communal level.[37]

Going beyond Soelle, complementing suffering is the call to *solidarity*. Interdependence is a reality in human society. Pope St John Paul II argues that this is the grounding of solidarity as a moral virtue, attainable for everyone. It is not a feeling of vague compassion or shallow distress at the sufferings of others. It is a 'firm persevering determination to commit oneself to the common good, since we are all really responsible for all'.[38] Together with the theologians mentioned above, there is a call to human solidarity amidst suffering. God enters into and shares in all human suffering. In a special way, those 'who suffer injustice remain indelibly etched in God's memory and ought to be inscribed in human consciousness'.[39]

---

[35] Keenan in his various 'Notes' and chapter nine of his *History* gives detailed evidence supporting this and for our next section on social justice from papers, authors, institutes and journals from Europe, Asia, and Africa.

[36] Richard Sparks CSP, 'Suffering' in Michael Downey, ed. *The New Dictionary of Catholic Spirituality* (Collegeville, MN: Liturgical Press, 1993), 950-3, at 952. See D Soelle, *Suffering* (Philadelphia: Fortress, 1975).

[37] Sparks CSP, 'Suffering', 952-3.

[38] John Paul II, *Sollicitudo Rei Socialis*, 38.

[39] Sparks, 'Suffering.' 953. With the announcement of a Royal Commission into sexual abuse in Australia, in the light of what is said here, what should be a theological response from the Catholic community? Suggestions along these lines were noted in chapter three of this book. Perhaps, on this matter, Dorothy Soelle has something important to offer us about solidarity in suffering.

In surveying moral theology in the past decade, what stands out is the increasing concern for suffering, solidarity, and the precarious nature of human existence. These realities have been highlighted most especially by the global pandemic since 2020. Again, there is an associated deepening sense, for many reasons, of social sin and structural evils in which the sexual abuse 'crisis' is a major factor. The overarching perspective of Christian ethics is not autonomous ethics but the Reign of God revealed in Jesus Christ.

Overall, amongst Christian ethicists, we have seen a growing awareness of those who are 'not heard', those 'rejected or abandoned'. This leads to our third consideration: Catholic social teaching on justice as an indispensable constituent of contemporary moral theology.

Catholic Social Teaching and Moral Theology

From what we have seen, with the international and local theological ethics conferences, the associated literature, and the increasing attention to suffering and solidarity, what stands out is the frequency of a concern for social justice. We can only take a few examples.

At Padua, the social justice emphasis clearly resulted from the three questions guiding the plenary papers from the five continents. For instance, the challenge of world poverty; from Africa, issues concerning identity, instability and democracy, horrendous suffering and theology needing to be located with 'the wretched of the earth', 'anthropological poverty'—what affects the deepest recesses of the personality in terms of self-belief and initiative; from India, Christian ethics in relation to cultural complexity and social inequality.

At Trento, while the focus was different, we still find, for instance, Bryan Massingale exploring the absence, if not erasure, in the U.S Catholic ethical reflection, of 'Black Experience' and, hence, of the bodies of those who experienced survival amongst oppression. Again, we find papers under headings such as 'Justice and Equity in the Health Care world' and 'Pressing Social and Global challenges' concerning Economics, Sustainability and Citizenship.

As we have seen, Keenan's extensive surveys show that the social justice direction is also evident in theological journals internationally, representative of which is *Theological Studies* in the English-speaking world. Earlier in the twenty-first century we find discussions on a global ethic and on the overlap between natural law and human rights and their implications for marginal individuals and groups'.[40] The same theme is found in the March issue of the 'Notes' in 2008-

---

[40] Jean Porter, 'The Search for a Global Ethic', *Theological Studies* 62 (2001): 105-122. Lisa Sowle Cahill, 'Towards Global Ethics', *Theological Studies* 63 (2002): 324-44. There is also an excellent discussion in Anthony J Kelly, C.Ss. R, 'The Global Significance of Natural Law:

2010, with commentaries on the two volumes of the Padua conference (e.g., in a discussion on identity crises in a globalized world).[41] In a broader ecclesial context, we find in the 2010 'Notes' essays on *Caritas in Veritate* from Maura Ryan, Lisa Sowle Cahill, Phillip Gabriel Renzes and Drew Christiansen.

Overall, what has been emerging in the past decade or so is a moral theology 'from below'. It is a critical ethical reflection on real problems that face real people, communities and nations and their structural roots. Issues of injustice, poverty, health, human rights, political and social life are the staples of life experience for inhabitants of Africa, Asia, and Latin America. They are increasingly the concern for the global community in the light of the 2007 GFC and its impact on economic and social life.[42]

Participative Bioethics (a phrase from Lisa Sowle Cahill) underlines the practical, embodied, and communal nature of ethical life and responsibility. She sees bioethics in the context of social justice. This mirrors a more explicit presence of bioethics within Catholic social thought and of both areas seen within the broader sphere of theological ethics.

But there are other signs of ethical involvement on the ground level. Maureen O'Connell, in her innovative work on muralism, explores the connections between theological aesthetics and ethics.[43] In 2007, *Time* magazine ran a short feature on Philadelphia's Mural Arts Project (MAP). In the space of twenty years, it changed the city's visual landscape. By bringing together artists, inner-city neighborhood associations, and charitable trusts, MAP helped to transform the city's neighborhood wastelands. Jane Golden, MAP's executive director says 'Art saves lives. Murals can play a catalytic role in healing the wounds of the city'.[44]

Which brings us to a closing comment to encapsulate our discussion above.

James Keenan observed that Benedict XVI's encyclical *Caritas in Veritate* (2009), as a development in Catholic Social Teaching, offers resources from

---

Opportunities, Quandaries and Directions,' *The Australian EJournal of Theology*, Issue 12, July, 2008.

[41] Keenan, James F, 'Notes on Moral Theology: Crises and other developments', *Theological Studies* 69.1 (March 2008): 125-144.

[42] From an Australian source, see Neil J Ormerod and Shane Clifton, *Globalisation and the Mission of the Church* (London and New York: T & T Clark, 2009).

[43] O'Connell, Maureen H, 'Painting hope: the murals of innr-city Philadelphia', *Commonweal* 135.1 (2008): 19-21. See also her *If These Walls Could Talk: Community Muralism and the Beauty of Justice* (The Liturgical Press, 2012).

[44] O'Connell, 'Painting Hope', 19.

Scripture and the Church's tradition to make judgments, guided by practical wisdom, to respond to specific practical challenges facing the world today. Its focus is on justice centered on, and animated by, *love*— now better appreciated as at the heart of the Christian moral life.

It is not unreasonable to conclude, as does Keenan, that, as both a mirror and a catalyst of theological ethics becoming more integrated with Church Social Teaching, *Caritas in Veritate*, in many ways, exemplified 'the developments in theological ethics over the past 70 years'.[45] These words were written in 2010.

Three years later (13th. March, 2013) marked a turning point. With Pope Francis and, his pontificate, we find a surge of change, which brings us to our fourth consideration.

Theological Ethics in a Synodal Church

Any survey of the changing landscape in Catholic moral theology in the twenty-first century must acknowledge the influence of Pope Francis (briefly noted in the earlier discussion of the self-understanding of the moral theologian).

In Francis' various writings and statements, and perhaps, best encapsulated in *Amoris Laetitia* (The Joy of Love, 2016), there is a persistent emphasis on how precious the individual is in God's eyes; on how the face of mercy comes to meet each person in the complexities of life; on the mysterious ways in which divine grace can be actively present in a person's life.

In all this, Francis suggests a working axiom: time is 'greater than space', which points to a priority for 'initiating processes' rather than 'possessing spaces'. In terms of evangelization this 'calls for attention to the bigger picture, openness to suitable processes and concern for the long run'.[46] He concludes his discussion with the gospel metaphor of the wheat and the weeds (Mt 13: 24-30).

The influence of Pope Francis has helped to foster enhanced appreciation of, and appeal to, the inductive dimension of moral theology, of human experience as a source of moral insights, and how moral norms are the outcome of judgment and evaluation. In other words, the moral sphere is one of practical reason—where certitude is not absolute but 'moral', namely, the best that we can do in the circumstances (seen earlier in chapters one and two).

To return to a concern raised earlier—the understanding of the human person. As noted in chapter nine, the twentieth century Church finds Pope St Paul VI

---

[45] Keenan, *A History*, 242.

[46] *Evangelii Gaudium* (The Joy of the Gospel), (Strathfield, NSW: St Pauls, 2014), par 223.

speaking of the three circles of dialogue, and how the human person is essentially a dialogical being—ideas developed by his successors, Pope St John Paul II, and Pope Francis. As we have seen, we grow as persons, made in the image of God, through relationships with others, especially in dialogue and a shared search for truth and goodness.

This brings us to 'synodality' and its importance for Pope Francis. This term is meant to capture the call (if not right) of *all* members of the Church to contribute to the life of the Church and its decisions. It means walking together with a common goal; a constant attitude of listening; the effort to understand the perspectives of others.

From our discussion in this chapter, such a pattern has been emerging in the field of theological ethics as a discipline, and, importantly, in the community of the Church in its ongoing search for, and living of, the true and the good in following the way of Jesus.

But there is a fifth and final issue, involving a global threat, that requires our attention.

Theological Ethics in a Post-Pandemic World

Consider one author on this matter:

> No other single crisis since the Second World War has left so many people in so many nations traumatized, overwhelmed by grief, and stunned by the cultural and economic consequences of the disease.[47]

These words highlight a reality that is an inescapable part of the context in which this chapter (and the others in this book) were collected and revised. The rise of COVID-19 and the ensuing pandemic has accelerated use of words such as: 'solidarity'; 'vulnerability'; 'precarity' and 'keep safe'. With a sense of emerging chaos, the insights of cultural anthropology (such as the work cited above) are increasingly relevant.

Again, such developments remind us that the approach argued by virtue ethicist Alasdair MacIntyre is timely; that we humans need virtues of acknowledged dependence in the search for a common good with of a community.[48] This is the language of conscience and of 'virtues at work'.

---

[47] See Gerald A Arbuckle, *The Pandemic and the People of God: Cultural Impacts and Pastoral Responses* (Maryknoll, NY: Orbis Books, 2021), xv.

[48] Alasdair MacIntyre, *Dependent Rational Animals: Why Human Beings Need the Virtues* (Chicago & La Salle, IL: Carus Publishing, 1999).

Further, such social changes are consistent with perspectives found in authors such as Judith Butler. For her, vulnerability and precariousness are intrinsic to the human condition. They are also conditions that are shared, as in experiences of suffering, grief, and loss.[49] Her thought is complemented by other studies that build on the intersection of virtue theory and the thought of Emmanuel Levinas (such as from Daniel J Fleming).[50]

Finally, within the Catholic tradition, James Keenan finds common cause with MacIntyre, Butler and Fleming in his recent lecture series 'Preparing for the Moral Life' where he addresses the question: 'what type of Catholic Theological Ethics do we need to develop as the 21st century unfolds?'[51] Keenan argues that grief, vulnerability, and recognition are the buildings blocks of conscience and that personhood is essentially social. The person as the image of the vulnerable Trinitarian God bears fruit in discipleship with Jesus, collective responsibility, and the practice of the virtues by proclaiming and working for the Reign of God.

Conclusion

This final chapter has offered a survey of major developments in Christian ethics in the Catholic tradition since the second Vatican Council. The first area of focus was the greater emphasis on the moral life as centered on the human person, relationships, love, and the role of virtue and the emotions. The discussion then turned to the second aspect, namely, Catholic theological ethics as a discipline over the past two decades.

Are we seeing the beginnings of a seismic shift in Christian ethics? It may not be 'seismic' but the ground has somehow moved and the landscape is not quite the same. While the person, conscience, Scripture, spirituality, and the virtues are still clearly visible, one's gaze is caught by the insistent presence of vulnerability, social injustice, and inequality. There is a deepening sense of evil and sin as social and structural, factors needing to be viewed through the lens of Christian faith and the Reign of God.

Further, there seems to be emerging, perhaps instinctively, a stronger sense of a praxis methodology, or alternatively, on a 'theological reflection' approach to Christian ethics. Allied to this is an enhanced (and more confident?) appreciation

---

[49] See Judith Butler, *Precarious Life: The Powers of Mourning and Violence* (Verso Books, 2004); also, Kate Ward, 'Virtue and Human Fragility', *Theological Studies* 81:1 (2020): 150-168.

[50] As noted in chapter three, Daniel J Fleming, *Attentiveness to Vulnerability: A Dialogue Between Emmanuel Levinas, Jean Porter, and the Virtue of Solidarity* (Eugene, OR: Wipf and Stock, 2019).

[51] The D'Arcy Lectures 2022 | campion-hall (ox.ac.uk)

of the place of experience in moral reasoning that guides action. This is particularly the case with the normative potential of suffering, especially of grief and of precarity. But it is also evident in how the descriptive aspect of experience relates to what is normative. As noted earlier, Pope John St Paul II argues that interdependence is a reality in human society and that, as a source of ethical insight, it grounds solidarity as a moral virtue.

The clearer presence of social questions in Christian ethics is consistent with global changes bringing a new local awareness of social, economic, and political issues in people's lives elsewhere. With global discourse (cultural, gender, national), the moral horizons of those living in the developed world are being broadened by closer interchange with the developing world. Perhaps there is occurring, in Bernard Lonergan's words, a differentiation of consciousness.[52]

In our post-pandemic world, with crises surrounding the future of our planet and of humanity, when mutual need and interdependence are becoming more pressing and real, it is timely to recall Keenan's observation earlier concerning *Caritas in Veritate*—with its focus on justice permeated by *love*.[53] His comment returns us to our earlier discussion about a model of theological ethics, as summed up by Edward Vacek:

God loves us
We love God
We and God form a Community
We and God cooperate.

These words, resonating with the thought of Pope Francis, are pointers to the future. Care of the earth is 'a way of sharing with God and our neighbours on a global scale.'[54] Five years later, responding to the pandemic crisis of COVID-19, Francis appeals to what makes 'true universal openness possible', namely, 'a love capable of transcending borders is the basis of what in every city and country can be called "social friendship"'.[55]

Such language brings us full circle and marks a fitting point on which to close this book.

---

[52] This phrase is distinctive in relation to the various phases of history in the work of Eric Vogelin, for instance, *The New Science of Politics* (Chicago: University of Chicago Press, 1960).

[53] See above n. 45.

[54] *Laudato Si'* (2015), par. 9.

[55] *Fratelli Tutti* (2020), par. 99.

Index

A

Absolute, 148, 150
Adoration, 149, 151, 152, 153, 154, 161
Affection, 29, 117, 207
Affections, 170
Affective, 28, 99, 118, 166
Amoris Laetitia, 114, 127, 192, 200
Analogy, 72
Anamnesis, 207
Anthropology, 22, 43, 174
Aquinas, 7, 11, 13, 19, 20, 21, 22, 26, 27, 28, 29, 30, 31, 32, 33, 36, 37, 43, 44, 45, 46, 49, 53, 55, 56, 76, 77, 78, 79, 80, 81, 82, 83, 84, 85, 86, 87, 88, 89, 90, 91, 92, 93, 98, 99, 102, 104, 107, 112, 116, 117, 126, 128, 155, 157, 177
Arbuckle, 9, 61, 64, 65, 67, 201, 207
Attention, 77, 86, 89, 103, 105, 111
Attitude, 207
Attitudes, 207
Aulén, 96, 100, 101, 103, 105, 123, 207
Autism, 207
Awareness, 7, 13, 18, 22, 25, 26, 28, 119

B

Beauty, 99, 110, 114, 199
Bible, 20, 35, 60, 61, 62, 63, 66, 67, 72, 98, 131, 132, 134, 137, 177
Brown, 34, 35, 132, 134, 136, 139, 140, 207
Buber, 117, 118, 119, 123, 207
Byrne, 63, 70, 131, 132, 133, 134, 135, 138, 140, 207

C

Caritas in Veritate, 64, 188, 199, 200, 203
Catholic, 7, 9, 11, 13, 15, 18, 19, 20, 21, 27, 35, 36, 37, 40, 44, 47, 49, 50, 51, 52, 54, 55, 57, 58, 59, 65, 66, 68, 71, 76, 80, 86, 108, 114, 119, 123, 125, 126, 130, 132, 146, 147, 163, 164, 165, 166, 169, 181, 184, 185, 188, 190, 191, 192, 193, 194, 197, 198, 199, 200, 202
Choice, 120
Choices, 207
Christ, 11, 13, 20, 23, 31, 38, 42, 47, 49, 67, 76, 77, 78, 79, 80, 81, 82, 83, 84, 86, 87, 91, 92, 93, 96, 103, 109, 110, 112, 124, 125, 127, 128, 132, 148, 149, 150, 154, 155, 157, 159, 160, 163, 166, 168, 169, 171, 173, 174, 179, 180, 187, 189, 196, 197, 198, 207

Christian, 9, 11, 15, 18, 20, 24, 25, 28, 31, 35, 36, 37, 42, 43, 52, 59, 60, 62, 64, 69, 72, 76, 80, 81, 88, 92, 95, 98, 100, 102, 109, 116, 119, 123, 125, 127, 130, 131, 132, 143, 147, 148, 150, 152, 158, 159, 160, 161, 166, 168, 169, 170, 175, 176, 184, 185, 186, 187, 188, 189, 190, 191, 192, 195, 196, 198, 200, 202, 203, 207
Church, 7, 11, 13, 15, 18, 20, 21, 22, 34, 35, 36, 37, 38, 40, 42, 47, 48, 49, 50, 51, 52, 53, 54, 55, 56, 57, 58, 59, 60, 62, 63, 65, 66, 67, 68, 69, 70, 71, 72, 73, 74, 76, 81, 83, 92, 112, 114, 119, 124, 125, 127, 129, 130, 131, 146, 157, 158, 160, 163, 164, 167, 168, 171, 173, 179, 180, 184, 188, 189, 190, 191, 192, 193, 194, 199, 200, 201
Cognition, 28, 29, 117
Collaboration, 26
Communion, 107, 135, 149, 151, 152, 153, 154, 158, 161
Connaturality, 28, 29, 30, 33, 117, 126, 128
Conscience, 7, 11, 13, 14, 18, 20, 21, 24, 25, 26, 34, 36, 37, 38, 40, 58, 76, 119, 120, 123, 130, 132, 136, 137
Conversion, 7, 15, 151, 165, 166, 167, 171, 175
Cooperation, 149, 151, 152, 153, 154, 161
Covenantal Ethics, 58, 59, 62, 63, 64, 65, 66
Creation, 23, 78, 157, 162, 163, 168
Cross, 68, 96, 98, 120, 125, 128, 155, 159, 193, 194
Culture, 7, 13, 51, 58, 61, 66, 121

D

Dark, 103
Darkness, 86, 89, 109
Desire, 207
Development, 7, 14, 52, 53, 114, 121, 122, 126
Dignitatis Humanae, 21, 40, 41, 42, 47, 51, 53
Dignity, 21, 22, 24, 40, 42, 43, 44, 49
Dilemma, 131
Discernment, 207
Discipleship, 207
Disgrace, 7, 13, 58, 65
Disposition, 169
Dispositions, 177, 207
Divine image, 207
Divine law, 53, 207
Division, 179
Doctrine, 52, 69
Duty, 207

E

Emotions, 31, 189
Ethics, 7, 9, 15, 25, 28, 32, 36, 40, 59, 64, 65, 68, 76, 78, 86, 87, 89, 91, 92, 114, 116, 118, 119, 120, 121, 162, 169, 170, 179, 184, 185, 187, 189, 191, 193, 194, 196, 198, 200, 201, 202
Eucharist, 60, 72, 83, 92, 147, 163, 167, 168, 169, 170, 171, 179, 180
Evangelii Gaudium, 120, 127, 200
Evil, 70, 207
Exemplar, 76, 77, 78, 86, 87, 92

F

Faith, 20, 22, 59, 69, 84, 88, 89, 91, 92, 112, 161, 166, 189
Fear, 139
Fleming, 9, 14, 59, 71, 114, 119, 120, 122, 190, 202
Forgiveness, 178
Formation, 13, 14, 20, 119, 120, 147, 167
Francis, 15, 40, 48, 69, 114, 120, 126, 127, 128, 129, 130, 132, 134, 135, 138, 141, 142, 143, 180, 192, 200, 201, 203
Freedom, 7, 13, 21, 40, 41, 47, 51, 53, 70
Friendship, 80, 81, 83
Fruits, 146, 151, 155, 156, 157, 159, 207

G

Gaita, 14, 114, 115, 116, 117, 119, 120, 121, 122, 123, 124, 129
Gaudium et Spes, 18, 19, 20, 21, 22, 23, 24, 25, 34, 35, 36, 37, 38, 45, 46, 48, 125, 137, 187
Gelpi, 166, 167, 175, 176, 178
Genesis, 60, 135
Gift, 60, 67, 86, 90, 91, 149, 162
Good, 12, 23, 64, 65, 73, 103, 130, 148
Gospel, 7, 14, 24, 38, 63, 70, 86, 106, 107, 112, 120, 125, 130, 131, 132, 133, 135, 138, 139, 140, 141, 142, 153, 159, 168, 170, 200
Grace, 7, 14, 114, 123, 126, 147, 189

H

Hammarskjöld, 7, 14, 93, 95, 96, 97, 98, 99, 100, 101, 102, 103, 104, 106, 107, 108, 109, 110, 111, 112, 113, 122, 123
Hatred, 207
Healing, 66, 69, 73
Heart, 21, 29, 34, 35, 117, 118, 130, 177, 187
Holiness, 124, 125
Holy Spirit, 11, 14, 24, 53, 62, 76, 77, 78, 79, 83, 86, 87, 88, 91, 93, 95, 97, 105, 106, 108, 111, 113, 114, 116, 123, 124, 125, 129, 132, 133, 154, 160, 162, 166, 177, 179, 180, 189

Humanity, 115, 116

I

Identity, 61, 67, 169, 175, 189
Image, 19
Imagination, 28, 98, 169
Inclusive, 61, 136
Integrity, 7, 14, 99, 130, 141
Intersubjectivity, 116, 117, 119

J

Jesus, 7, 11, 13, 23, 28, 38, 47, 49, 54, 59, 60, 63, 64, 65, 67, 70, 71, 76, 77, 78, 79, 81, 82, 83, 84, 85, 86, 91, 93, 96, 100, 108, 121, 128, 129, 130, 131, 132, 133, 134, 135, 136, 137, 138, 140, 141, 142, 143, 153, 154, 159, 160, 169, 170, 171, 174, 175, 177, 180, 185, 186, 187, 189, 190, 196, 197, 198, 201, 202, 207
John of, 53, 96, 125, 128, 155, 159
Joint Attention, 105
Joseph, 7, 14, 19, 22, 26, 34, 35, 36, 40, 48, 66, 76, 129, 130, 131, 132, 133, 134, 135, 136, 137, 138, 139, 140, 141, 142, 143, 188
Journal of Moral Theology, 76, 132, 191, 192
Judgment, 120, 132, 159, 190
Justice, 50, 51, 58, 66, 73, 115, 147, 175, 197, 198, 199

K

Kasper, 50
Keenan, 5, 68, 71, 120, 185, 189, 191, 192, 193, 194, 195, 196, 197, 198, 199, 200, 202, 203, 208
Kelly, 28, 84, 87, 88, 91, 92, 98, 112, 116, 196, 198
Knowledge, 7, 14, 34, 54, 95, 99, 125, 159

L

Laudato Si', 203
Law, 21, 27, 28, 31, 32, 33, 34, 55, 60, 63, 69, 77, 79, 80, 81, 85, 86, 93, 116, 131, 133, 134, 135, 136, 138, 198
Leadership, 66, 68, 191
Learn, 68, 136
Levinas, 59, 118, 119, 202
Lewis, 20, 22, 23, 31, 160
Light, 25, 104, 106, 107
Liturgy, 7, 9, 14, 146, 165, 167, 168, 170, 179, 180
Lonergan, 23, 52, 165, 166, 203
Love, 28, 30, 81, 83, 92, 96, 97, 99, 106, 111, 115, 116, 127, 150, 153, 156, 178, 185, 187, 192, 200
Loving knowledge, 208

M

MacIntyre, 51, 201, 202
Maritain, 32, 33
Markings, 7, 14, 93, 95, 96, 97, 98, 99, 100, 101, 102, 103, 104, 105, 106, 107, 108, 109, 110, 111, 112, 113, 123
Mary, 11, 58, 129, 130, 132, 133, 134, 135, 136, 137, 138, 139, 141, 142, 180
Mass, 158, 167, 168, 172
Matthew, 7, 11, 14, 27, 40, 63, 86, 128, 130, 131, 132, 133, 134, 135, 136, 137, 138, 139, 140, 141, 159
McGinn, 43, 44, 45
Melina, 80, 81, 83, 84, 92
Mercy, 130, 132
Modern, 76, 150, 151, 189
Moral, 7, 11, 13, 14, 15, 18, 20, 21, 22, 23, 24, 25, 26, 28, 31, 33, 36, 37, 58, 59, 61, 62, 76, 80, 85, 114, 116, 119, 120, 121, 123, 126, 130, 131, 132, 146, 149, 160, 161, 162, 165, 167, 168, 169, 171, 180, 185, 186, 187, 188, 189, 190, 191, 192, 193, 194, 195, 196, 198, 199, 202
Moral awareness, 208
Moral conversion, 208
Moral theology, 208
Murray, 40, 41, 42, 44, 47, 48, 51, 52, 53, 54, 55, 56, 57
Mystery, 100, 168, 179
Mysticism, 96, 99, 101, 109, 146, 147, 148, 150, 151, 154, 158

N

Narvaez, 36, 121, 122, 126, 189
Natural law, 208
Neurobiology, 121, 122

O

Obligation, 208
Orsy, 40, 42, 43, 44, 49

P

Padua, 193, 194, 198, 199
Pandemic, 201
Participation, 19, 25, 26, 27, 28
Paschal, 60, 179
Pastoral, 60, 61, 69, 127, 175, 179, 201
Peace, 50, 156, 157, 175, 179
Pedagogy, 7, 14, 114, 123, 126
Perception, 115, 169
Person, 21, 22, 48, 63, 85, 86, 105, 152, 160, 162, 174, 187
Pinsent, 81, 86, 87, 88, 89, 90, 91
Practical reason, 19, 208

Prayer, 15, 20, 35, 149, 163, 165, 170, 171, 173, 174, 179, 180, 181
Prudence, 208

R

Rational, 120, 201
Ratzinger, 22, 24, 26, 27, 30, 31, 33, 34, 35, 142, 188
Reason, 20, 29, 30, 31, 52, 55, 58, 85
Recognition, 25, 64, 67, 191
Reconciliation, 15, 163, 164, 165, 167, 171, 180, 181
Relationship, 22, 60, 174, 186, 188
Religious freedom, 46, 55
Respect, 89, 178
Response, 54, 152
Revelation, 23, 59, 84, 112, 142
Righteous, 132
Righteousness, 131, 132
Rights, 37, 46, 47, 50, 51, 52
Rome, 192
Royal Commission, 58, 59, 65, 68, 71, 197

S

Sacrament, 147
Saint, 28, 138, 143
Saliers, 170, 179
Sarajevo, 193, 194
Second person, 208
Self-transcendence, 208
Senses, 97, 98
Sexual Abuse, 58, 65, 66, 67, 69
Shame, 58
Shanley, 76, 78, 86, 87, 92
Sin, 7, 13, 58, 104, 160
Social, 9, 40, 50, 61, 64, 65, 120, 147, 153, 198, 199, 200, 208
Social Teaching, 198, 199, 200
Soelle, 68, 197
Solidarity, 9, 40, 59, 195, 202
Spirit, 14, 38, 50, 53, 76, 79, 83, 86, 87, 88, 91, 92, 97, 105, 108, 109, 110, 111, 112, 114, 125, 140, 146, 147, 148, 149, 150, 151, 152, 153, 154, 155, 156, 157, 158, 159, 160, 161, 162, 163, 169, 171, 172, 173, 174, 175, 176, 177, 178, 179, 180, 181, 187, 188, 190
Spiritual, 97, 98, 147, 148, 149, 151, 152, 153, 154, 155, 158
Spiritual senses, 208
Spirituality, 7, 9, 14, 43, 49, 95, 99, 101, 108, 124, 125, 146, 147, 153, 159, 161, 166, 169, 175, 186, 197
Spohn, 64, 114, 121, 165, 167, 169, 170, 171, 174, 175, 189
Stump, 86, 89, 90, 91
Subversion, 65

Suffering, 64, 68, 86, 195, 196, 197
Summa Theologica, 43, 77

T

Tallon, 13, 29, 31, 37, 117, 118, 119, 121, 128
Taste, 91, 111
Temperance, 157
Temple, 13, 66, 72, 73
Theological, 7, 13, 15, 18, 23, 27, 28, 29, 40, 47, 50, 65, 68, 70, 71, 72, 81, 95, 101, 114, 120, 124, 162, 167, 174, 184, 190, 191, 192, 193, 194, 196, 198, 199, 200, 201, 202
Theological anthropology, 208
Theological ethics, 208
Theological Studies, 23, 27, 28, 40, 47, 65, 71, 124, 162, 167, 190, 191, 192, 193, 198, 199, 202, 208
Thornhill, 50, 62
Tone, 173
Torah, 50, 60, 62, 63, 131, 132, 135, 136, 138
Transcendentals, 208
Trento, 193, 194, 195, 198
Trinity, 38, 43, 44, 45, 46, 77, 92, 152, 160, 161, 174, 188, 189
Truth, 20, 25, 26, 34, 66, 73, 99, 109, 110, 115, 147, 158

U

Underhill, 7, 14, 144, 146, 147, 148, 149, 150, 151, 152, 153, 154, 155, 156, 157, 158, 159, 160, 161, 162, 163, 164

Union, 96

V

Vacek, 187, 189, 203
Vatican Council, 13, 15, 40, 45, 57, 124, 137, 184, 185, 187, 202
Veritatis Splendor, 18, 19, 20, 21, 23, 24, 25, 26, 27, 28, 29, 30, 31, 34, 35, 36, 37, 38, 48, 80, 127, 190
Victims, 67
Virtue, 13, 36, 59, 76, 80, 81, 101, 113, 129, 189, 202
Virtue ethics, 208
Virtue of, 59, 202
Virtues, 32, 80, 81, 84, 87, 177, 189, 201, 208
von Hügel, 147, 150, 153, 154

W

Wainwright, 133, 136
Will, 150
Williams, 103, 125, 148, 159
Wind, 106, 158
Wisdom, 7, 13, 14, 27, 28, 30, 33, 77, 82, 85, 86, 90, 91, 92, 93, 95, 99, 101, 102, 103, 105, 112, 121, 130, 185
Witness, 7, 14, 114, 116
Worship, 7, 13, 14, 15, 147, 150, 153, 165, 170
Wynn, 115, 116, 123

www.ingramcontent.com/pod-product-compliance
Lightning Source LLC
Chambersburg PA
CBHW052116300426
44116CB00010B/1678